HOLIDAY LAW IN IRELAND

To Al,

Many th[anks for]
all you've done
for me over the
years,

Love
Jonathan

About the Author

Jonathan Buttimore graduated with a BCL degree and a First Class Masters Degree in European Law from University College Dublin in 1992, where he was also a Tutor in commercial, company and European law. He has been a practising Barrister since 1994, and works mainly in the chancery, commercial and European law areas with experience as both counsel and arbitrator in package holiday cases. He is an Associate of the Chartered Institute of Arbitrators and has undertaken post-graduate courses in the law and practice of both domestic and international arbitration. He has also written numerous articles on various aspects of law and practice in legal journals, including on European law, addressed several legal conferences and was one of the Irish Rapporteurs for the FIDE European Law Conference in 1996. He has lectured in commercial and insolvency law at the Honourable Society of King's Inns since 1995.

Holiday Law in Ireland

JONATHAN BUTTIMORE

BCL, LLM (Eur. Law) (NUI) ACI Arb.
Dip. Art. Law, Dip. Int. Comm Arb of King's Inns,
Barrister-at-law

BLACKHALL
Publishing

This book was typeset by
Gough Typesetting Services for
BLACKHALL PUBLISHING
26 Eustace Street
Dublin 2
Ireland
e-mail: blackhall@tinet.ie

ISBN: 1 901657 24 8   pbk
1 901657 04 3   hbk

A catalogue record for this book
is available from the British Library.

Printed in Ireland
by e print.

Table of Contents

Preface

The package holiday industry has grown rapidly in recent decades with the advent of more widely available air travel at increasingly lower cost, so it is now common for most people to holiday abroad at least once a year. This growth has seen even more rapid progress in recent years with ever increasing competition on air fairs and the price and range of package holidays, fuelled by the ever louder roar of the Celtic Tiger. It is against this background that the EU first took action in the form of the Directive 90/314 on Package Holidays, Package Travel and Package Tours in order to ensure equally effective protection of the consumer in all Member States of the EU. Such uniform protection among Member States is vitally important in this area due to the inherently multinational nature of package holidays taken by citizens of one Member State in another Member State. This protection was subsequently granted to the Irish consumer in 1995 by the Package Holidays and Travel Trade Act.

The importance of this protection for the consumer is obvious, as well as the economic importance of the package travel business itself. Thus, now we have a statutory regime which covers the licensing of tour operators and travel agents, since the Transport (Tour Operators and Travel Agents) Act 1982 and the rights and obligations of both the consumer, travel agents and tour operators in the 1995 Act. This area has, to date in this jurisdiction, been largely an unexplored area. Therefore, I have tried to bring together, in one volume, all the relevant issues of law both under the Acts and in those related areas of the common law. It is hoped that this will assist practitioners and all professionals in this area to have a more easily accessible and ready understanding of the many potential issues involved.

I am very grateful to Mr Justice McCracken for his very insightful and complimentary foreword, and for allowing to impose upon his time during the long vacation.

I would like to acknowledge the ever-courteous assistance of all the library staff of the Law Library, without whose ever-ready advice and knowledge no barrister can subsist, also my former Masters, Paul Coffey BL, John Trainor SC and John McBratney SC for the benefit of whose wide knowledge, encouragement and advice I am eternally grateful. The staff at Blackhall Publishing, particularly Gerard O'Connor and Claire Rourke, deserve my sincere thanks for allowing me the opportunity to produce this book and for their skill and enthusiasm in ensuring that publication was completed in time.

Finally, words cannot express my gratitude to my new bride Michele, who has foreborne with infinite tolerance and grace the trials of authorship in the first months of married life and to whom this book, as with my life, is dedicated.

I have attempted to state the law as of 1 September 1998. All errors or omissions or infelicities of style are the sole responsibility of the author.

Jonathan Buttimore
January 1999

Foreword

The last 30 years have seen a holiday revolution. It is now as easy to get to the Canary Islands as the Aran Islands, and the cost of a holiday in each destination is comparable. This has primarily been brought about by the huge increase in air travel, which in real money terms is getting progressively cheaper. This revolution has in turn spawned a whole new industry, namely the provision of package tours. No longer does your travel agent make all your travel arrangements, the travel agent is now largely a retailer of someone else's product, that is the package holiday.

As with many revolutions, the consequences are largely beneficial and foreign travel has become available to the public in general at a comparatively low cost. But while the benefits are obvious, so too are the problems. If a holiday goes wrong, it can go horrendously wrong, leaving the unfortunate holidaymaker staying in appalling conditions in a foreign country, often not knowing the language and seemingly having little or no recourse against the real wrongdoer, which may be the anonymous owners of a hotel or apartment block in a strange country with different laws from ours.

Probably one of the greatest advantages of membership of the European Union is that it provides an organisation, which can harmonise laws in all its Member States, particularly where consumer affairs are concerned. On 13 June 1990 a Council Directive was adopted which had two basic purposes. One was to allow more freedom of trade by encouraging holidaymakers to be able to purchase package holidays from organisers in other Member States. The other, which is far more important to the consumer, was to ensure that the consumer would have a remedy in his own country against identifiable persons or businesses, which would be amenable to the laws of that country. Although the Directive provides that Member States should bring into force the measures necessary to comply with it by 31 December 1992, in fact it was not until 1995 that the Oireachtas passed the Package Holidays and Travel Trade Act.

This belated action was very welcome. It introduced a whole new concept of liability, very much to the benefit of the consumer. However, like all new concepts, it also brought in complicated and detailed procedures, together with the problem that frequently occurs with such legislation, namely that it can be very difficult to adapt the legal language of the statute to the everyday problems of the consumer.

This book is a comprehensive guide to the individual's rights on the one

Holiday Law in Ireland

hand and to the liability of travel agents and tour operators on the other. It will be a great practical assistance to practitioners and to those in the trade, particularly those who are wrestling with these new concepts for the first time. It explains the rights and obligations in a practical way, and also relates them to the pre-existing common law position and provides a very useful guide to the nature of damages, which may be recoverable. It also deals in detail with other international conventions and their continuing impact on holiday travel, a point, which might well be forgotten in the euphoria of the consumer protection provided by the Act. All in all, this book will provide a invaluable aid to those in the travel trade and in the legal profession, and it is to be hoped that it will find its way onto all their shelves as a practical reference book which no doubt will be consulted frequently.

Brian McCracken
The High Court

October 1998

Table of Cases

Table of Statutes

Package Holiday and Travel Trade Act 1995—*contd*

TABLE OF STATUTORY INSTRUMENTS AND REGULATIONS

UK LEGISLATION

EUROPEAN LEGISLATION

INTERNATIONAL CONVENTIONS

Warsaw Convention on International Carriage by Air

Introduction

The aim of this book is to examine the effect the Package Holiday and Travel Trade Act 1995[1] will have on the legal rights of the holidaymaker under common law and statute. Particular reference will be given to compensation for personal injury sustained while on a package[2] holiday or tour as a result of the breach of contract of the package holiday organiser[3] or provider.[4] Focus will also be put as to how this Act facilitates an Irish consumer suing a foreign package organiser or provider in this jurisdiction under the Brussels Convention of the Recognition and Enforcement of Judgments 1968.

The Act aims to implement Directive 90/314 on Package Holiday, Package Travel and Package Tours[5] the purpose of which was to harmonise aspects of national provisions relating to package travel in the EC with a view to improving protection for consumers and eliminating distortions of competition in the tourism market between the various Member States.[6] The importance of the Directive, in the context of the Act, is reinforced by the fact that a word or expression in the Directive should have the same meaning as in the Act, and that the Act should be interpreted to give effect to the Directive, considering the provisions of the Directive, including its preamble.[7] The purpose and

---

1. The Act was passed by both Houses of the Oireachtas on 7 July 1995 and was commenced pursuant to s. 1(3) on 1 October 1995 by S.I. No. 235 of 1995, though s. 5 was commenced on 1 September 1995. See, for the full text, Appendix 2 and the Commencement Order at Appendix 3.
2. As defined in s. 2 as including a pre-arranged combination of transport, accommodation and other services accounting for a significant proportion of the package, when it extends over 24 hours or includes overnight accommodation, all for sale at an inclusive price.
3. As defined in s. 3(1) as persons otherwise than those who occasionally organises and sells packages directly or by a retailer to a consumer.
4. As defined by s. 2 who can be either the organiser or retailer.
5. OJ L159/90 21/6/90 p. 59. For the UK position see Nelson-Jones & Stewart, *A Practical Guide to Package Holiday Law and Contracts* (3rd edn, 1993); Bowen, *The Implementation of the European Directive on Package Travel* (1994); Grant & Mason, *Holiday Law* (1995). Also see generally Zunarelli, "Package Travel Contracts: Remarks on the EC Legislation" in *Fordham Int. Law Journal* (1994) Vol. 17 No. 3, p. 489; Storm, "Consumer Protection and 1990 Package Holiday Directive: A Scandinavian Viewpoint" in *Consumer Law Journal* (1993) Vol. 11 No. 3, p. 33.
6. See the Act's explanatory memorandum – General: Article 1 and the preamble to Directive 90/314.
7. Sections 2(6) and 2(7) of the 1995 Act.

importance of the Directive was emphasised by Advocate General Darmons in his opinion in *Hacker v. Euro-Relais*,[8] when he said:

> If the holidaymaker were to benefit from protective legislation it would be in order to put him back on equal terms with the business rather than to safeguard his right to accommodation or to stay in the property for instance. The adoption by the Council of Directive on Package Travel, Package Holidays and Package Tours is significant in this regard.[9]

The significance of the introduction of the Act was emphasised by the Minister for State Emmet Stagg,[10] in opening the Bill, when he commented:

> The Directive makes a significant contribution to the protection of consumers and the completion of the internal market by laying down common rules in a common framework for holiday packages in all Member States.[11]

He also commented that:

> On the provisions relating to the Regulation of Travel Contracts a consumer buying a package holiday is in the vulnerable position of paying in full in advance for a product almost entirely on the basis of description of a product contained in a holiday brochure. Intending purchasers of pre-arranged packages will now be able to place great reliance on descriptions in the brochure. Package organisers would not be able to make exaggerated claims about holidays as they will have to be able to stand over any advance descriptions given in brochures. In addition, the brochure must also contain general information about passport and visa requirements which apply to the purchase of the package and health formalities required for the journey and stay.[12]

COUNCIL DIRECTIVE OF 13 JUNE 1990 ON PACKAGE TRAVEL, PACKAGE HOLIDAYS AND PACKAGE TOURS

The purpose of this Directive is to approximate the laws, regulations and administrative provisions of the Member States relating to packages sold, or

---

8. C–280/90; [1992] E.C.R. 1111.
9. C–280/90; [1992] E.C.R. 1111 para. 29. Where a type of package travel contract was held not to be within Article 16(1) of the Brussels Convention concerning the jurisdiction for a dispute arising out of a tenancy agreement, as the contract included much more than the mere letting of holiday accommodation.
10. 451 *Dáil Debates* Col. 314 *et. seq.*
11. 451 *Dáil Debates* Col. 315.
12. 451 *Dáil Debates* Col. 316.

offered for sale, in the territory of the Community.[13] This is quite a short Directive, with the ten Articles enacting the basic principles which the Member States should incorporate into their national laws. It was mandated to be implemented by 31 December 1992, but was not implemented in this jurisdiction until some three years later.[14] The basic rationale of the Directive is set out in its preamble, which indicates the areas of concern at which the Directive was aimed. These include the completion of the internal market, of which the tourist market is an essential part, which is evidenced by the fact that the tourist industry is worth many millions in Europe annually. It was commented by Minister Stagg in this regard that:

> I understand that the home holiday business generated approximately £400,000,000 last year as of March 1995. It is important that the national economy makes a significant contribution to year-end tourism. In recent years the trend has been one of steady increase in holidays outside Ireland. It also generates substantial employment. Tourism made 20,000 jobs in the Irish economy in 1994. I hope the protection accorded to consumers by the legislation will encourage people to stay in Ireland for their holidays, generating additional business and assisting in job creation. Outbound tourism is also a major business. It is estimated that in the region of 350,000 people will take holidays abroad in 1995. For those customers a package holiday is a once a year experience, for which they have gone to considerable personal expense they are entitled to a safe and enjoyable holiday which runs as smoothly as possible.[15]

In order to achieve these aims, the Directive recognised that the laws of the Member States in the area were redolent of disparities and markedly different national practices. This in turn gives rise to obstacles to the freedom to provide the services in tourist areas and distortions of competition among the providers in different Member States. These difficulties and obstacles are intended to be eliminated by the common rules introduced by the Directive to achieve a common market for tourist services in all Member States, allowing consumers to purchase package holidays under comparable conditions.

The preamble draws attention to the fact that the community interest for consumer protection in the tourist sector has been long standing, stemming back to 1981 when a study was proposed into the tourist industry, with the proposed harmonisation of tourist packages outlined in a Council Resolution in 1986.[16] There was always a basic economic imperative for these proposals

---

13. See Article 1 of the Directive.
14. See Article 9 of the Directive.
15. 451 *Dáil Debates* Col. 324.
16. OJ C188 7/3/1986, p. 28.

as it recognised the increasingly important role of tourist and the tourist packages as part of the Member State economies and that the package was a fundamental part of tourism. These common rules would stimulate that growth of
the industry benefiting both European consumers and non-EC consumers at-
tracted by the protections of common rules. Indeed, until the Directive was
adopted in 1990 there were varying rules in all Member States, as some had
no specific legislation, some had such legislation and some had adopted the
1970 Convention on International Travel Contracts (CCV)[17] and the OECD
Recommendations on Package Holidays by Air in 1979 to deal with the international position.[18]

The other consequence of the lack of common rules at this stage was that
consumers from other Member States were discouraged from buying packages in another Member State – with particular regard to the special nature of
the services involved and the expending of substantial amounts of money in
advance for the supply of services in a Member State other than their own.
These difficulties necessitated the various provisions in the Directive for the
protection of the consumer, from strict liability of the tour organisers and
operators to detailed provisions on consumer information and the bonding of
organisers in case of insolvency, all of which are outlined in principle in the
preamble. The important last qualification in the preamble is the provision
that Member States should be allowed to adopt or retain more stringent provisions relating to package travel for the purpose of consumer protection.

The most significant aspect of the 1995 Act is the imposition, in sections
20(1) and 20(2)[19] of direct liability on the holiday organiser for the non-performance and improper performance of the holiday contract, irrespective of
whether such obligations are to be performed by the organiser, the retailer or
other suppliers of services. The major concern voiced with regard to the Bill
was the increase in insurance costs which, it was suggested, may rise to more
than 40 or 50 per cent, a figure supported by the history in other countries.
This was outlined by Deputy Brennan when he stated:

> I welcome the general thrust of the Bill but I stand over information
> that the Directive's effect has been to rocket insurance costs for small
> travel agents when introduced in Britain, Holland and Germany. It is
> likely to be the same here in the coming years as people engage in

---

17. See Chapter 2 below, p. 23.
18. See the explanatory memorandum to the draft Directive, Com 88/41 Final, and Storm,
    "Consumer protection and the 1990 Package Holiday Directive – a Scandinavian View"
    in *Consumer Law Journal* (1993) Vol. 11 No. 3, p. 33.
19. See for the difficulties of proving negligence on the part of the tour organiser at com-
    mon law in *Kavanagh v. Falcon Leisure Group (Overseas) Ltd* as noted by Skeffington
    in "Liability of Tour Operators for Injury Abroad" [1995] I.L.T. 211 and Chapter 5
    below, p. 69.

litigation. It will result in a great amount of litigation in the travel industry. It will increase insurance costs.[20]

The prospects for increased litigation were pointed out by Deputy Brennan when he said:

> In Germany, there is similar legislation and consumers have resorted to litigation against tour operators in cases where they have been rained out or have fallen off a camel in Tunisia and suffered injury as a result. Incredibly, a case was brought because a holidaymaker suffered psychological stress to the atmosphere prevailing in a holiday city. It gives me no joy to say that this Bill is a recipe for litigation. Wait until the lawyers get their hands on it. Under its provisions one can sue for defamation while on holiday, taking a case against a local travel agent. There is no limit on the Bill when one has suffered defamation. I do not think it is the Minister's intention to put the culture of litigation in place but this is what happened in Germany and a number of other countries.[21]

These concerns, regarding the insurance increases and the consequent price rise of package holidays being sold, were rejected by the Minister saying:

> I would like to stress that any increase in the prices of package holidays would be minimal as a result of these measures as some extra insurance by owners may be necessary to cover the actions of foreign suppliers for the services, there should not be any need for large increases in liability insurance because there will be little change in the levels of liability already carried under the Sale of Goods and Supply of Services Act. There may be a small increase in holiday prices in the first year but, as the travel trade industry is a highly competitive business, I anticipate that the usual market forces will bring prices down again very quickly. Indeed, the added benefits in security which the consumer will enjoy will more than compensate for any small increase in prices in the short term. The new legislation will enhance even further the already high quality of the Irish travel trade industries. It will provide a framework which will give a better quality of service and improve the protection of the consumer while at the same time can be keeping to a minimum the potential costs for the package organiser.[22]

Thus, it supplements the Brussels Convention on the Recognition and

---

20. 451 *Dáil Debates* Col. 840.
21. 451 *Dáil Debates* Col. 320.
22. 451 *Dáil Debates* Col. 321.

Enforcement of Judgements 1968 in a substantive manner and equates contractual liability with tortious liability for personal injury and death.

THE DIRECT EFFECT OF DIRECTIVE 90/314

The issue arises, as with all Directives, as to whether the Directive is directly effective when a Member State fails to implement it on time. The test is based on Article 189 of the EEC Treaty, whereby for the Directive to be directly effective it must impose duties of non-action, be sufficiently precise and unconditional so as to exclude any discretion of Member States.[23] Previously there has been speculation as to the direct effectiveness of the various provision of the Directive, particularly as to the liability of organisers for the non-performance of their duties.[24] The position has now been resolved in principle with the case of *Dillenkofer v. Germany*[25] which held that Articles 7 and 9 of the Directive are directly effective, as to the bonding arrangement for an organiser's insolvency, which were held not to be correctly or adequately incorporated in German law. The result prescribed by Article 7 of Directive 90/ 314 on Package Travel, Package Holidays and Package Tours, which provides that the organiser and/or retailer party to the contract is to provide sufficient evidence of security for the refund of money paid over by the consumer and for his repatriation, entails the grant to package travellers of rights guaranteeing a refund of money paid over and their repatriation in the event of the organiser's insolvency; the content of these rights is sufficiently identifiable.[26] It follows that, in order to comply with Article 9 of Directive 90/314 on Package Travel, Package Holidays and Package Tours, which provides that the Member States are to bring into force the measures necessary to comply with the Directive before 31 December 1992, the Member States should have adopted, within the period prescribed, all the measures necessary to ensure that, as from 1 January 1993, individuals would have effective protection against the risk of the insolvency of the organiser.[27] Thus, it shows that although the Directive may have been implemented on time, it can still be challenged for not adequately reflecting the provisions of the Directive, and any loss arising from such failure must be compensated for by the Member State as in the inadequate protection for a consumer on the insolvency of a tour organiser, as per *Francovich v. Italy (No. 1)*[28] and *Francovich v. Italy (No.*

---

23. See *Van Gend en Loos v. Nederlandse Adminstaties der Belalstingogne* C–26/62, [1963] E.C.R. 1.
24. See for example, Zunarelli, "Package Travel Contracts: Remarks on the EC Legislation" in *Fordham Int. Law Journal* (1994) Vol. 17 No. 3, pp. 508–510.
25. C–178/94; [1996] 10 E.C.R. I–4845.
26. [1996] 10 E.C.R. I–4845 at para. 50.
27. *Ibid.* at para. 55.
28. C–6 and 9/90; [1991] E.C.R. 5357.
29. C–479/93; [1995] E.C.R. 3845.

2).[29] This was applied in *Dillenkofer* where it was held that failure to take any measure to transpose a Directive in order to achieve the result it prescribes within the period laid down for that purpose, constitutes per se a serious breach of Community law and consequently gives rise to a right of reparation for individuals suffering injury if the result prescribed by the Directive entails the grant to individuals of rights whose content is identifiable and a causal link exists between the breach of the State's obligation and the loss of damage suffered.[30]

CONCLUSION

The 1995 Act is a major contribution to the safety and legal protection of the consumer while on a package holiday, especially when abroad. This is due both to the obligations on the retailer and organiser to provide accurate information in brochure and in pre-departure details (to prevent consumers being misled and consequently disappointed), and with the right to compensation for personal injury suffered due to non-performance or improper performance of the contract by the organiser, provider or even by third-party supplier of services, rendering truly comprehensive protection for the holidaymaker.

The twin pillars of consumer information and the direct liability of the package organiser, which are supported by significant implied terms and criminal liability for offences under the Act, result in a strong framework of protection for holidaymakers, both prior to and after departure. In all areas of interpretation open in the Act, one must always remember the Directive which it is implementing, and the very consumer-oriented purpose behind it.[31] This is expressly supported by the obligation on the courts to interpret the Act in a manner which will give effect to the Directive.[32] This is especially important in construing the defences of the organiser to liability, and hopefully it will be the judicial foundation to enforce fully the Act for the true benefit of the consumer, and ensure that the consumer's right to compensation directly from the organiser is not undermined by an excessively wide interpretation of the defences in section 20.

The provisions of the Directive, as implemented by the Act, are not exhaustive in seeking to regulate all aspects of the tourist industry or the applicable common law, but they do introduce entirely new statutory consumer protections, in terms of both civil and criminal liability. Therefore, there still remain areas, which are solely governed by the common law, as with the rules regarding the quantification of damages, remoteness and the general law of contract. Thus, the common law has been supplemented by the introduction of these new rules, but it still co-exists as one of the twin prongs of the overall regulation of the tourist industry.

---

30. [1996] 10 E.C.R. I–4845 at para. 29.
31. See paras 10, 15 and 22 of the preamble to the Directive and s. 2(7) of the Act.
32. Section 2(7) of the Act.

CHAPTER ONE

Package Holidays and Travel Trade Act 1995

The 1995 Act was preceded, with regard to the regulation of tour operators and the travel industry, by the Transport (Tour Operators and Travel Agents) Act 1982.[1] The 1982 Act had two primary objectives. Firstly, there was the licensing of tour operators to carry on a business and secondly, there was the provision of, what was termed, the Travellers' Protection Fund as an original form of bonding for losses and liabilities of tour operators by virtue of insolvency in order to protect consumers while abroad.

LICENSING UNDER THE TRANSPORT (TOUR OPERATORS AND TRAVEL AGENTS) ACT 1982

The licensing of tour operators was dealt with in Part 2 of the 1982 Act, where, in section 4, it is required that a person shall not carry on business as a tour operator or hold himself out, by advertisement or otherwise, as carrying on such business unless he is the holder of a licence under this Act and authorised to carry on such business. This also applied to a travel agent by virtue of section 5. Licences were granted by the Minister for Transport by virtue of section 6 where the main requirements to be satisfied for the grant of a licence were set out in section 6(3) which required that the Minister must be satisfied that:

> (a) the financial, business and organisational resources of such person in any financial arrangements made or to be made by him are adequate for discharging his actual and potential obligations in respect of the activities (if any) in which he is engaged or which he proposes to engage if the licence is granted, or

> (b) having regard to the past activities of such person of any person employed by him or, if such person is a body corporate, having regard to the past activities of any directors, shareholder, officer or servant of

---

1. See Appendix 1.

the body corporate, such person is a fit and proper person to carry on business as a tour operator or travel agent, as the case may be.

Therefore, the two basic requirements are, firstly, that the financial standing of the travel agent or tour operator is necessary and sufficient for the discharge of the actual undertaking of carrying on business as a tour operator or travel agent. Secondly, that the past history of the person or body corporate is such as to make him, or it, a fit and proper person to carry on the business of a tour operator or travel agent.

It can, therefore, be seen that the discretion in the granting of licences is quite broad and those two general requirements are naturally broad in their scope and allow a wide basis for refusing a licence in any particular case, but would still be subject to the general principles of judicial review as being a fair and reasonable use of a discretionary power.[2] However, it seems to have been the case since 1982, that rarely has a licence been not granted to a travel agent or tour operator, and rarely has an issue arisen as to the refusal of same.

After the grant of the licence, the Minister retains the power to revoke or vary and determine conditions of the licence, by virtue of, section 8. A licence can be revoked if the holder of a licence is in breach of or fails, neglects or refuses to comply with, any term or condition of the licence. Further, if the licensee's financial standing is no longer sufficient or adequate for discharging his actual potential obligations or that, having regard to manner of carrying on the business, the Minister considers that the licensor is no longer a fit and proper person to carry on such business, the licence can be rescinded. There is an appeals procedure for any proposed revocation of the licence whereby the Minister must give seven days notice to the licensor by virtue of section 9 and there is a Statutory Appeal to the High Court within seven days for any revocation or variation of the licence. Appeal from the High Court is limited, insofar as there can only be an appeal to the Supreme Court with leave of the High Court on the specified question of law.[3]

This is naturally contrary to the usual practice of being able, by virtue of Article 34 of the Constitution, to appeal all decisions of the High Court to the Supreme Court as a matter of right. However, this right to appeal is further limited by virtue of section 9(5) whereby an appeal shall not apply in any case where the Minister refuses to grant a licence to an applicant where that applicant does not comply with section 13 of the Act, regarding the required bonding arrangements in case of insolvency. Further, with regard to the bonding requirement,[4] section 10 allows the Minister further grounds for revoking a licence where, owing to the failure or inability of a tour operator or a travel

---

2. See Hogan & Morgan, *Administrative Law in Ireland* (3rd edn, 1998) Chapter 12, p. 617 *et seq.*
3. See s. 9(4).
4. See Chapter 9, pp. 112-116 below.

agent to meet his financial or contractual obligations, any payment is or fails to be made pursuant to the bond or from the fund to a customer, the Minister shall forthwith revoke any licence granted under the Act.

The 1982 Act has been amended in certain provisions by virtue of Part 4 of the 1995 Act in sections 26 to 34. The primary amendments relate firstly to the definitions contained in section 2 of the 1982 Act which have been amended to relate more closely to the present position and the relationship to the definitions under the 1995 Act.

Firstly, 'carrier' is defined as a person (other than a package provider where the package includes transport commencing in the State to destinations outside the State and Northern Ireland) whose principal business is the provision of transport by land, sea or air on vessels, aircraft or other modes of transport owned and operated by such a person. Hence, it is limited purely to the carriage of people and not to any of the greater functions that a package provider may provide in terms of additional accommodation or tourist elements. Further, the definitions all now relate to the definition of 'overseas' as being not only outside the State, but also outside Northern Ireland.

An 'overseas travel contract' is now defined as a contract for the carriage of a party to the contract (with or without any other person) by air, sea or land transport commencing in the State to a place outside the State or Northern Ireland, where the provision of the carriage is the sole subject matter of the contract or is associated with provision thereunder of any accommodation, facility or service. It further states that 'overseas' is outside Northern Ireland and a point of departure within Northern Ireland is permissible under the Act and allows carriers to sell such holidays in this jurisdiction and Northern Ireland. The point of departure in Northern Ireland is deemed, in effect, to be part of the State for these purposes and so allows carriers to depart from Northern Ireland and only by doing so, would it be an overseas travel contract, provided they have the necessary licence from the Department of Transport, Energy and Communications in this jurisdiction.

A 'tour operator' is then defined as a person (other than a carrier) who arranges, for the purposes of selling or offering for sale to any person, accommodations or travel by air, sea or land transport commencing in the State to destinations outside the State or Northern Ireland or who holds himself out, by advertising or otherwise, as a person who may make available such accommodation, either solely or in association with other accommodation facilities or other services. This point is finally reiterated by the fact that the definition of 'travel agent' is again amended in similar terms to mean a person (other than a carrier) who as an agent sells or offers to sell to, or purchases or offers to purchase on behalf of any person, accommodation on air, sea or land transport commencing in the State to destinations outside the State or Northern Ireland who holds himself out by advertising or otherwise as one who may make available such accommodation, either solely or in association with other accommodation facilities or services.

Another significant amendment is by virtue of section 29 of the 1995 Act, which that amends section 8 of the 1982 Act with regard to the grounds for revocation of a licence by the Minister. These grounds now relate firstly to the resources of the tour operator of the licence being inadequate, and then to him not being a fit and proper person to carry on such business either having regard to the past activities of the holder of the licence or the manner which the holder of the licence now presently carries on the business.

The other amendment of note is contained in section 34 of the 1995 Act, which includes a new section under the 1982 Act that allows the High Court on the application of the Minister to make Orders requiring persons engaging or proposing to engage in any practices, business or activities as are, or are likely to be, contrary to the obligations imposed on them by the provision of the Act of 1982 to discontinue or refrain from such practices, business or activities. This effectively allows the High Court to make Orders preventing actual or prospective breaches by licence holders with regard to the terms of their licence or bonding arrangements thereby entered into. Further, it would also cover any other person who purported to carry on business as either a tour operator or travel agent, without the necessary licence by virtue of the Act, so thereby Orders could be granted by the courts on the application of the Minister to prevent such breaches of the Act.

THE PACKAGE HOLIDAY AND TRAVEL TRADE ACT 1995: DEFINITIONS

Consumer

The primary definitions in the Act which determine the scope of its application are to be found in sections 2 and 3. The first definition which is of primary importance is that of a 'consumer' which is defined in section 2(1) as follows:

(a) In relation to a contract, it means the person who takes or agrees to take the package ('the principal contractor');

(b) In any other case, it means, as the context requires:
  (i) the principal contractor;
  (ii) any person on whose behalf the principal contractor agrees to purchase a package ('another beneficiary');
  or
  (iii) any person to whom the principal contractor or another beneficiary transfers the package ('the transferee').

It is important to note that with this definition (as with all the definitions in the Act) that under section 2(6) except where the contrary intention appears, the meaning to be attached to a word or expression used in this Act is to have the same meaning as that found in the Directive. This is further supported by the fact that under section 2(7) the interpretation of the Act is to be purposive *vis-à-vis* the Directive, and that the words in the preamble to the Directive are to be considered by a court for interpretative purposes. Therefore, as with all Acts implementing EU Directives, any doubt as to interpretation should firstly be seen in the context of the Act and then checked to see if that is consistent with the intent and phraseology in the Directive combined by the rationale and purpose of the Directive as exemplified in the preamble.[5]

In essence the word 'consumer' derives from the Directive, as the primary rationale of the Directive was seen to be as a consumer protection measure. The first part of the definition relates to the 'principal contractor', namely the person who actually negotiates or books the package in the first place and who has the right to be regarded as a consumer for the purpose of the contract, including for any contractual cause of action deriving under the Act. Usually this would be normal as the person booking the contract would inevitably be one of the people partaking in the holiday, but that may not always be the case, for example, parents booking a holiday camp for children or when it is booked on behalf of another party by means of a credit card booking.

In any other context, apart from the contract, the consumer is either the principal contractor or a person on whose behalf the principal contractor has actually agreed to purchase the package, 'another beneficiary' for example, a founder member of the family with whom he is going on the said package, which again would be the normal course. This person is deemed under the section to be another beneficiary under the Act for the purpose of being a consumer under the Act. The final element in the scope of the definition of 'consumer' is that of the transferee, namely a person to whom the package is transferred from either the principal contractor or from another beneficiary, i.e. a member of the family or group on whose behalf the contract was initially purchased. The concept of a beneficiary derives from section 16, which determines when a booking can be transferred from one person to another.

The scope under the Act of the meaning of 'consumer' does seem to be wide, as not only does it include the obvious principal contractor, but also a beneficiary or transferee of the package. This is particularly important in the context of a beneficiary (i.e. a family member or member of the group on whose behalf the booking was made), as otherwise these people would normally only have a remedy in tort, as they would be outside at common law the normal doctrine of privity of contract, being mere third parties to the contract between the principal contractor and the package holiday provider. The only way that such a third-party beneficiary could maintain an action in contract, apart from the Act, would be if there was an agency between the principal contractor and the said beneficiary.[6]

---

5. See the Introduction, p.1 *et seq.*
6. See generally the cases of *Woodar Investment Development Ltd v. Wimpey Construction* [1980] 1 All E.R. 571 and *Saville and Isaac v. ILG Travel* [1989] I.C.L 390, but see

In *Woodar v. Wimpey*[7] the majority of the Court of Appeal followed (with express reluctance in the case of Goff L.J.) its previous decision in *Jackson v. Horizon Holidays Ltd.*[8] Lord Wilberforce stated that he was not prepared to dissent from the actual decision in that case and was of the view that:

> It may be supported either as a broad decision on the measure of damages (per James L.J.) or possibly as an example of a type of contract, examples of which are persons contracting for family holidays, ordering meals in restaurants for a party, hiring a taxi for a group, calling for special treatment. As I suggested in *New Zealand Shipping Company Ltd v. A M Satterthwaite & Company Ltd* [1975] A.C. 154 at 167, there are many situations of daily life which do not fit neatly into conceptual analysis, but which require some flexibility in the law of contract. Jackson's case may well be one.[9]

He further expressly disagreed[10] with the fiduciary basis for recovery on behalf of non-contracting parties on which Lord Denning M.R.[11] based his decision in that case. Lord Keith was also careful to circumscribe the prospect of recovery for non-contracting parties in damages saying:

> *Jackson v. Horizon Holidays Ltd.* That case is capable of being regarded as rightly decided on a reasonable view of the measure of damages due to the plaintiff as the original contracting party, and not as laying down any rule of law regarding the recovery of damages for the benefit of third parties. There may be a certain class of cases where third parties stand to gain indirectly by virtue of a contract, and where their deprivation of that gain can properly be regarded as no more than a

---

contra the leading English case of *Jackson v. Horizon Holidays Ltd* [1975] 1 All E.R. 92.

7. [1980] 1 All E.R. 571.
8. [1975] 1 All E.R. 92 and see Chapter 7, p. 93 *et seq.* below.
9. [1980] 1 All E.R. 571 at 576. For a more detailed analysis of *Jackson v. Horizon Holidays*, see Chapter 7, p. 93 *et seq.* below.
10. As did Lord Wilberforce at 576, which was echoed by Lord Russell at 585.
11. Reliance was there placed by Lord Denning M.R., not for the first time, on an extract taken from the judgment of Lush L.J. in *Lloyd's v Harper* Vol. 16 Ch. D. 290 at 321. That case was plainly a case in which a trustee or agent was enforcing the rights of a beneficiary or principal, there being a fiduciary relationship. Consequently, Lord Denning M.R. in *Jackson v. Horizon Holidays Ltd* at 95–96, said:
   The case comes within the principle stated by Lush L.J. in *Lloyd's v Harper* (Vol. 16 Ch. D. 290 at 321): "... I consider it to be an established rule of law that where a contract is made with A for the benefit of B, A can sue on the contract for the benefit of B and recover all that B could have recovered if the contract had been made with B himself." [Lord Denning continued:] It has been suggested that Lush L.J. was thinking of a contract in which A was trustee for B. But I do not think so. He was a common lawyer speaking of the common law.

consequence of the loss suffered by one of the contracting parties. In that situation there may be no question of the third parties having any claim to damages in their own right, but yet it may be proper to take into account, in assessing the damages recoverable by the contracting party, an element in respect of expense incurred by him in replacing by other means benefits of which the third parties have been deprived or in mitigating the consequences of that deprivation. The decision in *Jackson v. Horizon Holidays Ltd* is not, however, in my opinion, capable of being supported on the basis of the true ratio decided in *Lloyd's v. Harper*,[12] which rested entirely on the principles of agency.[13]

Lord Wilberforce then stated the consensus view of *Jackson v. Horizon Holidays Ltd*:[14]

Nor do I think that on this point the Court of Appeal was correct in thinking it was constrained by *Jackson v. Horizon Holidays Ltd* to award substantial damages. I do not criticise the outcome of that case: the plaintiff had bought and paid for a high-class family holiday, he did not get it, and therefore he was entitled to substantial damages for the failure to supply him with one. It is to be observed that the order of the Court of Appeal as drawn up did not suggest that any part of the damages awarded to him were 'for the use and benefit of' any member of his family. It was a special case quite different from the instant case...[15]

In *Jackson v. Horizon Holidays Ltd*, Lord Denning M.R. stated the following, based essentially on a fiduciary basis, and not the more generally accepted basis of agency:

We have had an interesting discussion as to the legal position when one person makes a contract for the benefit of a party. In this case it was a husband making a contract for the benefit of himself, his wife and children. Other cases readily come to mind. A host makes a contract with a restaurant for a dinner for himself and his friends. The vicar makes a contract for a coach trip for the choir. In all these cases there is only one person who makes the contract. It is the husband, the host or the vicar, as the case may be. Sometimes he pays the whole price himself. Occasionally he may get a contribution from the others. But in any case it is he who makes the contract. It would be a fiction to say that the contract was made by all the family, or all the guests, or all the choir, and that he

---

12. Vol. 16 Ch. D. 290 at 321.
13. [1980] 1 All E.R. 571 at 588.
14. [1975] 1 All E.R. 92.
15. [1980] 1 All E.R. 571 at 577.

was only an agent for them. Take this very case. It would be absurd to say that the twins of three years old were parties to the contract or that the father was making the contract on their behalf as if they were principals. It would equally be a mistake to say that in any of these instances there was a trust. The transaction bears no resemblance to a trust. There was no trust fund and no trust property. No, the real truth is that in each instance, the father, the host or the vicar, was making a contract himself for the benefit of the whole party. In short, a contract by one for the benefit of third persons.[16]

He thereby concluded that:

It is the only way in which a just result can be achieved. Take the instance I have put. The guests ought to recover from the restaurant their wasted fares. The choir ought to recover the cost of hiring the taxis home. There is no one to recover for them except the one who made the contract for their benefit. He should be able to recover the expense to which they have been put, and pay it over to them. Once recovered, it will be money had and received to their use. (They might even, if desired, be joined as plaintiffs.) If he can recover for the expense, he should also be able to recover for the discomfort, vexation and upset which the whole party have suffered by reason of the breach of contract, recompensing them accordingly out of what he recovers.[17]

However, as already discussed, this view of Lord Denning was expressly disapproved by the House of Lords in *Woodar v. Wimpey*,[18] with the accepted basis for the recovery of non-contracting parties in such cases being that of agency, as suggested by James L.J. in the following terms:

According to the form which he completed, which was the form of Horizon Holidays Ltd, he booked what was a family holiday. The wording of that form might in certain circumstances give rise to a contract in which the person signing the form is acting as his own principal and as agent for others. In the circumstances of this case, as indicated by Lord Denning M.R., it would be wholly unrealistic to regard this contract as other than one made by Mr Jackson for a family holiday.[19]

There is also a possibility in Irish law[20] that under section 8 of the Married

16. [1975] 1 All E.R. 92 at 94.
17. [1975] 1 All E.R. 92 at 95.
18. [1980] 1 All E.R. 571, see p. 13 above.
19. [1975] 1 All E.R. 92 at 96.
20. As suggested by Clark, *Irish Current Law Statutes Annotated* [*I.C.L.S.A.*] (1995) p. 1704 and in *Contract Law in Ireland* (3rd edn, 1992) pp. 390-391.

Women's Status Act 1957, family members can sue in their own name, even if the contract has been concluded by one family member only. However, this would still leave the problem of whether friends or other members of the family could benefit from section 8 of the 1957 Act or under some other common law exception to the privity rule, particularly in the light of the strict approach taken in *Woodar v. Wimpey*.[21]

It is important to note that this broad definition of 'consumer' is not limited to merely a private individual buying a package for his own private purposes. It includes 'any person who takes or agrees to take the package', so it can, in principle and viewed on this basis alone, cover a businessman buying a package for a business trip or for any other purpose, which could then be covered by the Directive, although the stated legislative intent was different.[22] In contrast, this goes against the definition of a 'consumer' given in the Sale of Goods and Supply of Services Act 1980, where it is defined[23] as a "person buying not in the course of a business of a product of a type ordinarily supplied for private use or consumption" therefore it can be argued to have a wider view of a consumer in the package holiday context, than in more traditional related legislation.

Package

The next significant definition is that of 'package' which is defined in section 2(1) as:

> a combination of at least two of the following components pre-arranged by the organiser when sold or offered for sale at an inclusive price and when the service covers a period of more than 24 hours, or includes overnight accommodation:
>
> (a) transport;
> (b) accommodation;
> (c) other tourist services, not ancillary to transport or accommodation, accounting for a significant proportion of the package.

This definition is supported by section 2(2) which provides that the submission of separate accounts for different components of the package shall not cause the arrangements to be other than a package for the purpose of this Act.

Since the Directive was primarily aimed at protecting tourists and consumers and not business or commercial travellers, the Act only applies if two of the following three required components are present:

---

21. See generally, Clark, *Contract Law in Ireland* (3rd edn, 1992) pp. 383-394, for the exceptions of agency, equitable trust and covenants running with land.
22. See 453 *Dáil Debates* Col. 317.
23. Section 3(1) of the 1980 Act.

(a) pre-arranged packages, namely those arranged prior to their being sold or offered for sale;

(b) packages which last for longer than 24 hours; or

(c) include overnight accommodation.

Therefore, it doesn't include business or short hop travellers flying to and from a particular destination within the same day. However, as already indicated,[24] due to the broad definition of a consumer, business travellers would be consumers within the meaning of the Act, but often their travel arrangements by their nature, may not come within the definition of a package.

It is true to say that the definition of package in the Act is the one definition which ultimately and conclusively determines the scope of the application of the Act and its protections. It is always possible that the scope of the Act may be drawn too widely, where it would not really be appropriate or sensible to include lesser forms of packages (although within the strict terms of the definition) within the provisions of the Act. In particular, it may not be appropriate to impose the obligations of contractual liability and other obligations to the consumer which the Act imposes on package holiday providers. For example, in the Dáil Debates there were fears that ordinary bed and breakfast accommodation may be caught by the Act. Clearly, on the face of the definition, that would not be the case as there is no transport or other element in that type of accommodation. It was importantly pointed out by the Minister of State that:

> I again assure the House that business travel will not be covered under the terms of the Bill, and that the Regulations being drawn up by the Director of Consumer Affairs[25] will ensure that bed and breakfast accommodation will not be met by the provisions of the Bill except where packages are offered, which is the case in only a small minority of bed and breakfasts. I am quite satisfied that also the price of holidays will not be adversely affected by the terms of the Bill. This is an important Bill from the point of view of consumer protection.[26]

However, it is possible that lesser forms of package holiday (such as specialist sporting or activity tours and packages) as opposed to the usual and most common form of commercially offered package holiday, will be caught by the Act. These would be included in the Act, if they contained not simply the

---

24. See above, p. 11 *et seq.*
25. An information booklet entitled "Travel and the Consumer: Package Travel" has been produced by the Director of Consumer Affairs, setting out the basic rights under the 1995 Act.
26. 453 *Dáil Debates* Col. 836.

availability of facilities within a locality (such as a golf course, shooting, fishing etc.), but also went further by providing that the accommodation component is linked to the said fishing, shooting or golfing rights or involvement in the workings of a farm.[27] This was emphasised by Senator Howard stating that:

> The other aspect of that question which I wish to raise relates to agri-tourism. The reduced potential in agriculture and farming in this country has led to the development of what is known as agri-tourism, which invariably offers some sort of activity in addition to accommodation, such as fishing. I am not sure to what extent golf forms agri-tourism, but perhaps if accommodation is offered in conjunction with a local golf course, it does. Also walking, cycling, boating and open-farm holidays. I am concerned that this provision might inhibit the development of agri-tourism which is important in many areas of the country.[28]

This goes further with the possibility that a travel package which does not necessarily include accommodation, but may give a traveller a right to a ticket to a sporting or other event, such as all-in trips to football or rugby matches or cultural festivals, while leaving the traveller to find the accommodation locally, would also be included.

Business conferences in principle may also be included where they include overnight accommodation, as often is the case and either transport, which would be the case if the group were going on behalf of a company, or the provision of significant other tourist services, which would include organised excursions, tours, dinners etc. The problem of including business conferences in this definition is whether there is organised travel or the provision of tourist services, which may not be the case with a large number of conferences. However, as it may not include a delegate himself, it could include an accompanying person or spouse who availed of the significant tourist services arranged by the conference organisers. However, although such conferences can be within the definition of a package, they are effectively excluded from the scope of the Act by virtue of the Package Holidays and Travel Trade Act 1995 (Occasional Organisers) Regulations 1995.[29] It can be seen that the definition of a package on its face, is wider than the most common forms of package holiday. Therefore both consumers and providers of such packages, or any types of package including transport or accommodation or another element, should be well aware of the possible application of the Act and its obligations on them. So both consumers and practitioners should not consider the Act as applying to only the usual package holidays to the Costa del Sol.

---

27. See Clark, *I.C.L.S.A.* (1995) p. 1705.
28. 143 *Seanad Debates*, Col. 1644.
29. S.I. No. 271 of 1995. See Appendix 7 and p. 21 below.

With regard to the limited inclusion, or as some see it the exclusion of business travellers,[30] this is achieved by the requirement for the package to be pre-arranged prior to conclusion of the contract, although it has been said that the use of the words 'sold or offered for sale' could be said to limit this purpose. This is because a business traveller could be covered by the Act, if a package was being sold in a pre-arranged nature, but not otherwise. It was commented by the Minister for State, Mr Stagg, during the Dáil Debates[31] that if a business traveller asked a travel agent to book a flight and an overnight stay in a hotel of the travel agent's choice, the traveller would not be protected by the Act, unless an all-in offer had been made prior to the conclusion of the contract. Thus it was the booking, which rendered it not pre-arranged, despite the fact that it had the required two separate components of the individual's choice of two components making up a package.

He commented with regard to the scope of the Bill that:

> *Ad hoc* arrangements made by travel agents specifically for individual customers requirements do not come within the scope of the proposed legislation. For example, if somebody, say a business person, walks into a travel agency and asks the agent for a flight to London, to book a particular hotel, this does not constitute a package. If however the travel agent advertises a weekend in London, which includes flight and accommodation, this would be pre-arranged and would constitute a package. The Directive is not as exact as it might have been in clarifying what precisely constitutes a package. However, the number of possible bookings narrows this region. It would be completely impossible for any legislation, no matter how detailed, to cover all the possible combinations.[32]

The concern about the inclusion of business travel was echoed by Deputy Brennan when he said:

> Many newspapers carry advertisements for airline companies which offer the flight, hotel accommodation, a car and other frills that can be packaged. That would seem to make an ordinary trip to London on business for two days a package holiday. That is unreasonable. We not interfere with business travel because businesses are well able to look after their own interests in regard to their business travel arrangements. They do not require the protection of legislation such as this which is designed, primarily, for the ordinary traveller.[33]

---

30. See Clark, *I.C.L.S.A.* (1995) p.1705.
31. 451 *Dáil Debates*, Col. 317.
32. 453 *Dáil Debates*, Col. 317.
33. 453 *Dáil Debates*, Col. 837.

It was also indicated that during the Dáil Debates by the Minister for State that the Director for Consumer Affairs had suggested that his office would draw up guidelines in conjunction with the travel industry on what constitutes a package, and an information booklet entitled 'Travel and the Consumer: Package Travel' has been produced by the Director of Consumer Affairs, setting out the basic rights under the 1995 Act.

The other issue relating to the definition of a package is the fact that it is not limited either in Article 2 of the Directive or in the Act to international packages, as it also includes purely domestic and national packages. The rationale for this is obvious, since it is necessary that the consumer should have equally strong protection both when travelling within his own Member State and when travelling on a package to another Member State. This is reflected by the preamble to the Directive, which recognises the difficulties involved in having different national rules for package holidays between the Member States, with differing national and international package rules.

It is also important to note that from the three elements required for the package, one element can be excluded. For example, the element of transport may be excluded, such as when you hire a cottage and a service such as skiing, shooting or fishing. Since this includes overnight accommodation and significant proportion of tourist services, it would be within the scope of the Act. The important point which follows from this and the nature of the definition of a package in general, is the fact that the application of the Act is much wider than would at first seem to be the case from the normal understanding of a package holiday, prior to the implementation of the Act. Therefore when the element of transportation is missing, it can still be a package within the Act, which is a point which should not be lost on practitioners and consumers alike.

The other limitation within the definition of a package is that of the 24-hour duration, which has the effect that it excludes a mini package (for example, a day trip by coach or a day trip to a sporting or cultural event by train or coach). Naturally, this Directive is a minimal Directive by virtue of Article 8, as the Member States are permitted to adopt more stringent measures for the protection of the consumer. Therefore, Member States are still free to extend the scope of the application to such packages, but this has not been done in the 1995 Act, but could be in future legislation, although it could be questioned whether such as extension would be either necessary or appropriate.

Tour Organiser

The definition of the final party to the package holiday contract is that of the tour organiser, who is defined in section 3(1) as "a person who, otherwise than occasionally, organises packages and sells or offers them for sale to a consumer, whether directly or through a retailer".

The organiser of a package holiday is, in essence, the tour operator who is therefore primarily responsible for ensuring that all the obligations arising under the contract – both expressly and by virtue of the Act – are performed as he would usually also be the 'package provider' as defined in section 2(1). The Act in general ensures that the tour operator rather than the retailer is responsible to the consumer for any breach of duty that occurs. This is supported by the fact of the strict liability of the tour operator for any breach of duty by subcontractors (such as airlines, hotels etc.), which is dealt with in section 20 of the Act.[34] This is further supported by the fact that the tour operator/organiser is a professional entity, expert in dealing with the organisation and supervision of such travel packages and so the imposition of such apparently harsh liabilities is justified. However, this would not be the case for a person who only occasionally organises such packages. Therefore, it is not only the ordinary commercial and corporate tour operators who would be covered, but also any person who organises such packages, as long as it is not done occasionally, in the ordinary course of business and not merely an occasional event, with such organisers being covered prima facie by the Act. This would include private associations and clubs and non-profit making bodies which organise such packages, and could be seen as an unduly harsh imposition of obligations and liability on such non-professional package organisers.

The limitations which exclude occasional package organisers have been clarified and ameliorated by means of the Package Holidays and Travel Trade Act 1995 (Occasional Organisers) Regulations[35] which provided that certain categories of exempt groups will be considered to be occasional organisers and hence will be excluded from the scope of the Act. The main classes of exemptions include:

(a) a professional, medical, scientific, cultural or trade association or society which organises a package, either directly or through an organising committee established for that purpose, during a conference, convention, meeting or seminar held in pursuance of aims and objective of any such body;

(b) a firm which organises a package for its employees;

(c) community, social, sporting or voluntary organisation which organises a package as part of the general objectives of that organisation, including a club or association operating within a firm;

(d) a school or educational institution which organises a package for its teachers and students;

(e) a religious or denominational group which organises a package involving a pilgrimage for members of that group;

---

34. See Chapter 5 below.
35. S.I. No. 271 of 1995. See Appendix 5.

(f) a package organised by a charitable or benevolent institution in pursuance of its objectives.

Therefore, it can be seen that it was recognised that such exemptions should be given to these classes of packages, otherwise the ambit of the Act would be too broad and would impose too many burdensome obligations on such groups who would not have the resources, knowledge, experience or expertise to comply fully with the provisions of the Act. Therefore it should not include such occasional packages as those as part of a conference, an employee outing, a community or sporting outing, a school outing, a pilgrimage or a charitable outing.

These Regulations may ameliorate the problem with the application of the Act to business conferences as indicated earlier.[36] These exemptions are all perfectly reasonable and necessary to avoid the over broad application of the rigours of compliance with the Act, and in particular the contractual strict liability of section 20. The only qualification which the Regulations put on these exemptions is the fact that they will not apply, if the package provider requires a licence under the Transport (Tour Operators and Travel Agents) Act 1982[37] or one that has been covered by arrangements which have been entered into for the purpose of the 1982 Act, namely bonding requirements. All these indicate that such licensed package providers/tour operators under the 1982 Act are carrying on more than an occasional business, so should be subject to the rigours of the 1995 Act and are sufficiently protected in case of insolvency by the Travellers' Protection Fund.[38]

Package Provider

The other parties to the contract which are defined in section 2(1), are firstly that of the 'package provider' which means:

(a) in circumstances other than those described at paragraph (b), the organiser, or where the retailer is also a party to the contract, both the organiser and the retailer, or

(b) in the case of a package sold or offered for sale by an organiser established outside the State through a retailer established within the State (and where the transport component of the package commences outside the State) the retailer.

Therefore, the package provider for the purpose of the Act is, in the first instance, either the tour organiser (i.e. the travel company or tour operator

36. See above p. 18.
37. See ss. 4 to 12 of the 1982 Act.
38. See s. 18 of the 1982 Act.

who actually organises the package) or, where the retailer, namely the travel agent, is also a party to the actual contract, then it includes both the organiser and the retailer. This definition is significant particularly in terms of the liabilities and duties imposed on package providers being both the tour organiser and the travel agent and determines the range of liability under the Act.

This is the basic destination for the purpose of national packages sold within the State, but where a package is sold by an organiser established outside the State and by an agent within the State, then it merely includes the retailer. This is for the obvious good reason that this jurisdiction, where the contract was made by the consumer, solely covers the retailer and so it is easier for the consumer to enforce any breach of the Act and in particular for any contractual liability that may arise by virtue of the Act against the package provider, which can easily be enforced against the retailer within the jurisdiction of the State. This has the important consequence, that a foreign-based retailer or package provider is not subject to the application of the Act.

This view is supported by section 2(3) which provides that the Act only applies to packages offered for sale or sold within the State and hence, is not to apply to packages offered for sale outside the State (for example, by means of magazine or newspaper advertisements for such packages), particularly in terms of UK offers. This would only be altered if the UK package provider had some link with the State, for example, a place of business or agent within the State.[39] However, this does not affect the application of the Act to the place of destination of the package (i.e. the Act and Directive naturally includes both national and international packages), but only is limited by virtue of the residence of the actual package provider providing the package. The retailer in section 2(1) naturally, is defined merely as the person who sells, or offers for sale, a package put together by the organiser, and hence would be known in ordinary parlance, as the travel agent.

The Brussels Convention on International Travel Contracts

It should be noted that the terms used in the Act and in the Directive have a historical provenance dating well before the adoption of the 1995 Act or the Directive in 1989, as the terminology used is the same as used in the Convention on International Travel Contracts of 23 April 1970 adopted at Brussels.[40] This being the much overlooked precursor to the regime now found in the Directive and the Act. The main difference between the terms used in the 1970 Convention and the Directive is with regard to a package; the limitation of 24 hours imposed by the Directive was not part of the Convention in Article

---

39. This is in order to ground jurisdiction under Articles 2 and 5 of the Brussels Convention, if he complied with the definition of domicile for a company in Part 3 of the Fifth Schedule to the 1988 Recognition and Enforcement of Judgments Act.
40. See, for the text of the 1970 Convention, *International Legal Materials* (1970) Vol. 9, p. 699.

1(2), however the influence that this Convention had in forming the background to the Directive cannot be underestimated.

On the face of it, both the Act and Directive are quite precise in their definitions. However, there are certain ambiguities which should be taken into account. For example, the fact that the third element of a package of the provision of tourist services which must be "a significant element, but not an ancillary element to the provision of transport or accommodation", by definition can only be adjudicated on a case by case basis, even though initial illustrations can be given, as already done previously.

Thus, a strict reading of that part of the definition of the package may on its face exclude certain services, such as transport and attendance at an opera or concert. However, it has been said that it would be unacceptable to deprive such consumers of the protection of the Directive or the Act in such circumstances despite the strict wording of the definition. As Zunarelli comments, the determination of whether a particular consumer deserves protection should rest on a judicial interpretation of the consumer's principal interest under the Act despite the strict terms of the Act.[41]

This interpretation would be consistent with taking a purposive view of the principal consumer protection objective of the Directive, as implemented in the Act that would support such a view. Comparing the 1970 Convention and the Directive in relation to tour organiser, it is in essence the same in both documents but, the notion of a retailer in the Directive is different to that of what is called 'the intermediary travel agent' in the 1970 Convention. With regard to the retailer, it should be noted that there is no requirement that the retailer should not be engaged in occasional activity, as is required for the tour organiser in section 3 of the Act. However, in the 1970 Convention, the limitation on occasional activity is included for both the travel agent and the organiser, resulting in a disparity between the Directive and the Convention.

Other Definitions

The only other basic definitions which need to be considered are firstly that of the 'contract' in section 2(1) which is defined as "an agreement linking the consumer to the organiser (whether dealing directly with the consumer or through a retailer)". This appears to be self-explanatory, yet has the slightly broader definition with regard to the linking element, above and beyond the stricter formal requirements of the common law for a binding contract so as to include the strict rules of offer and acceptance, consideration, intent to create legal relations and evidentiary requirements.[42] The other, final definition which

---

41. See Zunarelli, "Package Travel Contracts: Remarks on the EC Legislation" in *Fordham Int. Law Journal* (1994) Vol. 17, No. 3, p. 489 *et seq.*
42. See generally Clark, *Contract Law in Ireland* (3rd edn, 1992) Chapters 1-4; Chitty, *On Contracts* (27th edn, 1994) Vol. 1, Chapters 2-3.

is included is that of an 'offer', which is stated to be "an invitation to a person, whether by means of advertising or otherwise, to make an offer to buy a package". This again is, in itself, self-explanatory and is primarily relevant with regard to the obligations imposed by the Act in terms of information which must be contained in brochures prior to the conclusion of the contract.

ISSUES OF INTERPERTATION

On the scope of the definition of a 'package',[43] it has been commented that the various guidelines show extreme differences as to the extent of the definition of a package and whether they include tailor-made packages, as opposed to the usual more conventional mass package holidays.[44]

One of the difficulties with regard to the definition of a 'package' concerns the meaning of 'pre-arranged'. The difficulty is whether it means to be pre-arranged by the tour operator before the client enters a travel agency or does it just mean that all components of the package are in place before the client travels. Further, it is possible that it could be interpreted as meaning merely that the elements should all be put together before the actual contract is concluded. If it is either of the latter two, then it is possible that for *ad hoc* travel accommodation components organised by a travel agent, that the agent could become liable for the proper performance of the whole contract. Therefore, it is vital that the meaning of 'pre-arranged' is clarified by means of guidelines or judicial decision to ensure that *ad hoc* travel packages are either expressly included or excluded from the scope of the Act. This would put individual travel agents at the risk of the uncertainty of whether to try and comply with the provisions of the Act or presume that they do not apply to such arrangements.

The prevalent view in the UK seems to be that 'pre-arranged' does not mean only packages, which can be bought off-the-shelf, but also includes all packages put together before the conclusion of the contract.[45] This on its face, will naturally include the *ad hoc* type of arrangements to which reference has already been made, in order to broaden the scope of the Directive more than perhaps was intended. However, it may be the case that due to the very purpose and nature of the Act, that any interpretation of 'pre-arranged' which would exclude such tailor-made packages to the detriment of the consumer would be unlikely to be followed both by the legislature and more importantly by the courts.

With regard to accommodation, it should be noted that as long as there is some accommodation, which does not necessarily have to be a significant

---

43. See, for example, the UK Guidelines of the DTI and of ABTA.
44. See Grant & Mason, *Holiday Law* (1996) pp. 31-36.
45. See *ibid.* p. 33.

element of the package, then the accommodation element of the definition of a package will be fulfilled. Therefore, it is not just the traditional holiday package which is included by the Act, but also the more broader concept of tourism and business travel which inevitably includes accommodation.

Another question arises with regard to the significant element of the tourist services, which are not ancillary to transport or accommodation, is whether there is a difference between a service, such as fishing rights or skiing, and the provision of facilities which are incidental to the accommodation or transport, such as access to a swimming pool or gym. It could be argued that such access is not a service, but a facility and hence would not be within the package. The significance of this issue, as with all possible ambiguities with regard to a package, is the fact that if a strict view is taken then it may exclude certain packages from the Act and so exclude the strict liability of the organiser or agent for the consumer's loss.

Overall, it can be said that the definitions both in the Directive and as implemented in the Act are, in general, sufficiently clear. However, there are certain aspects of the definitions which still need to be clarified and which are of critical importance in determining the scope of the Act, and hence the contractual obligations and liability of the tour organiser and travel agent. It can be expected that both in this jurisdiction and in the UK that there will be sustained argument on these issues in the future, which we would hope will achieve a definitive interpretation.

CHAPTER TWO

Pre-contract Obligations on Tour Organisers

BROCHURES

Prior to the conclusion of the contract, the tour organiser is under certain specific obligations relating to the information provided to the consumer, upon which he makes his decision in concluding the contract. This is to ensure that the consumer is not misled in any way with regard to the type of package holiday for which he has contracted and that he has all the adequate information in order to make an informed choice about the package.

This is in line with the general consumer rationale of both the Directive and the Act that the most effective way to protect the consumer fully, is to ensure that he has adequate and accurate information available to him, before entering into a legally binding contract. The area of brochure content has long been one of difficulty where eloquent language and creative pictures can often mislead a consumer about the quality of the resort and package that he has chosen. This aim is achieved in the Act by section 10 which lays down certain specific minimum details which must be included in a brochure: these must be laid out for the consumer in a legible, comprehensible and accurate manner. The basic details include the price and adequate information about a range of matters which are listed in section 10. These include details about the destination, the transport used, the type of accommodation most importantly, detail regarding its location, the category of accommodation, its main features and also whether it's approved in that Member State by a tourist authority or has a tourist classification.

These first two categories are obviously the most important and in particular, the detail now required with regard to the accommodation is a vast improvement upon the previous position of the consumer. The other details required include the meal plan, the itinerary, passport and visa requirements, the amount to be paid on account and the timetable for the payment of the balance of that amount, whether a minimum number of persons are required for the package to take place, any tax charges and the arrangements for the bonding of the organiser, if the tour organiser becomes insolvent. Finally, where the package is offered by an organiser outside the State, then it must include the place of business of the nominated agent within the State who will accept service of any proceedings arising out of the contract.

This last requirement supplements the consumer's position with regard to packages offered for sale by an organiser outside the State (e.g. by advertisement in UK newspapers). A tour organiser is deemed not to be bound by the Act if he is not resident within the State, so it is necessary that an agent on behalf of the foreign tour organiser must have a registered place of business for the service of proceedings in this jurisdiction. These requirements are an important part of what should be included in the brochure and not only must they be included but also, as section 10 points out, it must be in a legible, comprehensible and, most importantly, an accurate manner. It is important to note that these obligations primarily and necessarily relate to the tour organiser, being the one who actually compiles the brochure in the first place. However, there is also a related obligation on a retailer or travel agent, that he shall not supply a brochure either knowing, or having reasonable cause to believe, that it does not comply with the requirements in section 10(1).[1]

Therefore, there is a joint obligation on both the tour organiser in the first place and the retailer in the second place, to ensure that all brochures contain the necessary information in an accurate manner. These obligations are enforced under the Act by the creation of an offence under section 10(3) for both a retailer and an organiser. It should be noted that although the matters in section 10(1)(a) to 10(1)(g) are required by Article 3 of the Directive, the requirement to give information on taxes, nominated agents and insolvency arrangements are additional information required only under the 1995 Act, as permitted under Article 8 of the Directive for a Member State to take more stringent measures for consumer protection.

During the Dáil Debates, there was concern about the adequacy of the requirement to give information about accommodation, for example, with regard to safety concerns. There were concerns with regard to the safety of certain Spanish resorts, which led to recent tragedies, and also to the fact that the requirement to give information about health formalities did not include the requirement to give information about any health risks in that resort or in that area.[2] Minister Stagg alleviated these concerns, by saying that:

> I am aware that concern has been expressed regarding the safety of Irish holidaymakers overseas. There have been cases of tragic accidents abroad in recent years resulting in injuries and the death of Irish holidaymakers. While these have, fortunately, been small in number to the relative numbers holidaying abroad, I fully understand the concerns raised. This Bill provides, in line with the EU Directive, that where a package in the Member State includes accommodation, the contract with the consumer must state the compliance of the accommodation

---

1. See s. 10(2), the breach of which gives rise to an offence under s. 10(3).
2. 143 *Seanad Debates* Col. 1689; 44 *Seanad Debates* Col. 682.

with the laws of that Member State. This puts an onus on the tour organiser to ensure that all accommodation, which they provide for Irish
holidaymakers, is of an extensively safe standard.[3]

With regard to section 12(1)(b), and the requirement that as part of the essential terms of the contract information about health formalities required by
national administration for the journey and the stay must be inserted in the
contract. It was commented by Deputy Brennan that:

> The Bill requires intending passengers to be given information on a
> range of issues including health formalities for their journey and holi-
> day stay. That requirement is onerous and could result in many legal
> actions being taken. If a person contracted the AIDS virus during a stay
> abroad, there could be considerable scope for legal action as the Bill
> requires the travel agent to indicate in advance to the traveller all nec-
> essary health formalities.[4]

It was further commented by Deputy Brennan that:

> The Bill requires travel agents to have expertise and competence in the
> area of health when surely a small travel agents could not be expected
> to have such competence. The Bill is still somewhat loose in that travel
> agents must make the traveller aware of the health requirements of the
> national administrations. I can only assume the travel agent must con-
> tact the Department of Health in the country to which a person is trav-
> elling to establish its health requirements. Would a small travel agents
> in, say, Ballinasloe or Naas booking a ticket for a person to travel to
> Greece have to telephone the Greek Embassy in Dublin to obtain a
> copy of the health requirements in Greece or are they expected to have
> an up to date copy of such information in their offices? Will it suffice if
> they merely refer the person to a leaflet and leave it to that person to
> obtain it?[5]

This concern was countered by the Minister for State, by emphasising that the
obligation in this regard was primarily on the tour organiser. The retailer was
merely a form of communication to provide that information either as an indi-
rect way of communicating or as a direct means from the organiser to communicate such requirements of the national administration regarding health. It
was concluded by the Minister that:

---

3. 451 *Dáil Debates* Col. 320.
4. 453 *Dáil Debates* Col. 832.
5. 453 *Dáil Debates* Col. 833.

We have achieved a fair balance by not requiring organisers to provide large volumes of information on health centres in every country in the world but simply the health formalities required by national administration. People are not allowed to enter certain countries without being inoculated against yellow fever and tour operators inform people travelling to such countries of the requirement to have such inoculation. There is no particular health requirement of which I am aware for people entering this country, but that does not apply to all countries. Information in this regard should be supplied to travellers by the organisers of package holidays and my amendment meets this requirement.[6]

The requirements to include this basic information in brochures is reinforced by the statutory offence and also by the civil liability imposed by section 11 of the Act[7] as it seeks to impose a uniform standard for brochure content for which consumers from all Member States can judge accurately the quality and true nature of the package being offered.

FURTHER INFORMATION TO BE PROVIDED BEFORE THE CONCLUSION OF THE CONTRACT

As well as the provisions regarding the content of the brochure, there are, under the Directive, certain other types of information which must be provided to the consumer by the tour organiser through a retailer prior to the conclusion of the contract. This information must be in written form and must include four basic types of information: general information about the passport and visa requirements, health formalities required by the national authorities, the minimal level of insurance cover stipulated by the organiser for either cancellation or repatriation in the event of accident or illness and the arrangements with regard to security in the event of insolvency of the tour organiser. Again, these requirements, provided in section 12(1), are reinforced by the fact that it is an offence for either the organiser or retailer to fail to disclose such information to the consumer. The only defence for an organiser is if the failure is due to the retailer and not for himself.

It is apparent that some of this basic information has also been covered in the brochure, so section 12(3) makes it possible for the informational requirements of section 12 to be fulfilled, if reference is made to a non-amended brochure which contains the same information (such as, for example, passport and health formalities which are required to be in the brochure in the first place). This in itself would not be sufficient, if there were any relevant alterations to the basic requirements in the information required in the brochure. In

---

6. 453 *Dáil Debates* Col. 835.
7. This is dealt with in Chapter 3 below.

that case, the new information and amendments must be given in writing to the consumer above and beyond what is contained in the original brochure.

In relation to insurance, the consumer is required as a term of the contract to take out insurance and under section 12(1)(c), he must be informed of the minimal level of cover that is necessary. There is an important proviso in section 12(1)(c), that the Act does not authorise an organiser to make it compulsory for the intending consumer to purchase any specified insurance policy. Therefore, the consumer may be required to take out insurance, but he may not be required to take the specified policy of the tour organiser. Thus, it can be some other individually negotiated policy chosen by the consumer himself, so that although insurance may be required to be purchased on the part of the consumer, under the terms of the contract to cover the cost of cancellation by the consumer or the cost of assistance, including repatriation in the event of accident or illness, the consumer cannot be compelled to take out any specific policy of insurance offerered by the tour organiser or associated insurance company, which are invariably offered as part of the contract under section 12(1)(c).

This is an important provision, as it prevents the all too common modern practice of tying a consumer in to a specific insurance policy of a certain insurer who has an agreement with the tour organiser. It allows true freedom of choice for the consumer in choosing his holiday insurance. However, despite this freedom, the reality is usually that a consumer will partake of the insurance policy offered by the tour organiser at the time of the contract for the sake of convenience. If the position is that it is a discretionary matter to take out insurance for cancellation and repatriation in the event of illness which is not required under a specific contract, section 12(4) again provides that the organiser must provide the consumer with information about the optional conclusion of such an insurance policy. Therefore, he must provide either his own chosen policy on behalf of the tour organiser, where optional and the details of same.

Section 12 reflects Article 5 of the Directive. It is important to note that although it is required to be in writing, the information may also be given in some other appropriate form. This may include for example, a holiday video or information pack or by some other permanent means, which would often be the case in practice, therefore easing the burden on the organiser. The other practical possibility with regard to the provision of the information is the reference merely to the original unamended brochure for the information required under sections 12(1)(a) to 12(1)(d), so long as it is in unamended form and reflects the current position, which will be the most common course for the tour organiser to take.

INFORMATION TO BE PROVIDED BEFORE THE
START OF THE PACKAGE

There are other types of information which the tour organiser must give to the consumer at a time prior to the start of the package, when both the brochure requirements and the extra requirements in section 12 have been fulfilled.

Section 13 sets out three further types of information which must be provided in writing, or in some other appropriate form, to the consumer. These include: the times and details of the transport component of the package, including the place to be occupied by the traveller (for example a cabin or berth), the name, address and telephone number of the actual representative of the organiser in the locality where the consumer is staying or the agency in that locality who can assist if the consumer is in difficulty, or at the very least, the telephone number which will enable the consumer to contact the organiser and retailer. Finally, with regard to a journey or stay by a minor outside the State, information enabling direct contact to be made with the minor or the person responsible for the minor's place of accommodation.

Again, these basic three elements of information, prior to the commencement of the package are another advance from the information already required to be provided by the tour organiser. They relate to more specific details of the actual implementation of the package (for example, in the transport component) and most importantly, to the consumer's ability to contact the tour organiser's representative in the locality of the destination. This latter requirement is an essential part of any package in terms of protecting the consumer in case of accident or general difficulty or complaints concerning the quality of the package, as the tour organiser's representative is usually the only point of contact the consumer has in the package destination.

Again, as with section 12, it is an offence for either an organiser or retailer to fail to provide the required information. Further, this information can be provided validly by means of reference to a brochure, if the details required are contained in a non-altered form in that brochure or by some other appropriate form as in a video information pack. As well as the possibility of referring the consumer to the brochure, it is also possible to provide this information by reference to the terms of the actual contract between the tour organiser and consumer – as long as that contract and the information is provided in good time before the commencement of the package. It is most likely that the information would not be contained separately to the brochure, but either by way of the brochure or by way of the actual contract. In practice, unless there happened to be some change in arrangements in the time between the signing of the contract and the start of the package, which can happen, especially where holidays are now booked many months in advance, the required information would be contained in the original brochure.

ESSENTIAL TERMS OF THE CONTRACT

The next logical step with regard to the consumer information objective of the Act and the Directive is that of the essential terms which must be included in the actual contract concluded between the tour organiser and the consumer. Section 14(1) sets out the basic elements, where relevant to the particular package, which must be included in the contract. These essential terms set out in section 14(1)(a) to 14(1)(l), being the terms already referred to concerning the terms of the brochure and the required terms which must be communicated before the conclusion of the contract under sections 11 and 12.

There are also certain additional elements which must be included in the contract (such as the itinerary of the package, if relevant, any visits, excursions, etc.) which are included in the total price for the package. The three most important elements which must be in the contract, and to which reference has not yet been made, include firstly the price of the package, and also most importantly if any price revisions may be made in accordance with the terms of the contract, and secondly any additional fees etc. for services at post and airports (such as landing, embarkation, etc.), the costs of which are not included in the cost of the package. Thirdly, the contract must also include any special requirements which the consumer has communicated to the organiser or retailer when booking and which have been accepted. Furthermore, in terms of the legal redress available both under the Act or the common law for the consumer, the period within which the consumer must make any complaint about the failure to perform or the inadequate performance of the contract provided by the tour organiser, is within 28 days from the date of completion of the package.

These final three elements are probably the most important elements to be included in the contract, which are additional to the information provided prior to the contract both in the brochure and otherwise. It is particularly important to note the requirements with regard to price revisions which can often be hidden in a package contract and consumers may not be aware that there are additional costs with regard to taxes, landing costs and so on, which are not included in the contract. Naturally, it follows that any special requirements above and beyond the basic terms of the contract must be included in the contract for the package with that particular consumer. It must be the case that such special terms are actually agreed by the tour organiser or retailer and not just merely a case of the tour organiser undertaking to employ best efforts, or reasonable endeavours, to provide a certain standard of accommodation, for example a ground floor apartment where a child is part of the group. Therefore, in order to protect the tour organiser in failing to meet such specific special requirements, the best efforts term, which is a common term of most contracts, would not be covered by section 14 and so would not be required to be included in the contract.

It is important to note that these terms are not necessarily found in all package holiday contracts, as section 14 makes clear, since it is only where they are relevant to the nature of that particular package that they must be included. For example, it may be the case that for certain bargain packages, that the accommodation is not specified prior to arrival, so upon arrival the accommodation is then allocated to each consumer depending on what is appropriate and available at that time.

The other important requirement to note in section 14 concerns the time limit for complaining by the consumer to the tour organiser, about non-performance or inadequate performance. It is provided in section 14(2) that any such time limit, as long as it is beyond 28 days, is without prejudice to the liability of the organiser. Hence, it cannot be the case, as it was previously, that if a consumer did not complain within a specific time period, that his complaint or his entitlement to pursue legal redress would be then barred. Therefore, the mere fact of non-communication cannot now bar the liability of the organiser under the Act. Despite the fact that the consumer is now under an express time limit in which he must complain, this must be at the earliest available opportunity and in writing to either the organiser, retailer or local supplier of the services about the failure of the services involved. The fact of not meeting this time limit in itself, could only damage the credibility of the complaint under the Act and not affect the actual liability of the organiser itself.

This is also relevant in terms of any arbitration provisions included in the contract, as they invariably stipulate a strict time limit within which a complaint must be made, so initiating the arbitration procedure. Provisions with regard to a strict time limit, as long as it is over 28 days, could then, if not complied with, bar the arbitration provisions in any one contract, if the consumer did not comply with them. However, this still would not affect the liability of the organiser under the Act, merely the fact that the arbitration provisions could not, strictly speaking, be initiated and the only redress therefore would be by means of court proceedings.

Section 14 is significant in understanding the essential terms which must be included in the contract. However, for practical purposes, the most significant element is that with regard to making any complaints: firstly the complaint period must not be less than 28 days and secondly, that it must be made in writing at the earliest available opportunity by the consumer, but without prejudice to the liability of the organiser. The other element to the complaint provisions is the fact that although writing is stipulated, it does allow for communication in any other appropriate form which can be by means of an oral complaint, which would be the most obvious and natural way to complain in the first instance as long as that complaint is confirmed in writing, if the consumer fails to obtain a satisfactory response to his complaint.

Therefore, it allows a written record of the complaint which benefits both the consumer and the tour organiser to know exactly what happened and when, for the purpose of any redress which may be sought after the package has been concluded. At the same time, it provides sufficient flexibility for the consumer's complaint in terms of time and the manner of complaint, which would necessarily be required in the context of a holiday situation. The other useful and important obligation which is imposed on the organiser in cases of a complaint, is by virtue of section 14(4) that he shall make prompt efforts to make appropriate solutions. It imposes an obligation upon the tour organiser to try and resolve the complaint as soon as possible and as best as possible, which naturally would be related to any contractual liability for the cause of the complaint by virtue of the other provisions in the Act or by virtue of the common law.

FORM OF THE HOLIDAY CONTRACT

The next provision, which takes the consumer information objective further, is section 15, which concerns the form of the actual contract. This section mandates that all the terms of the contract should be set out in writing or in such other form as is comprehensible and accessible to the consumer and communicated to the consumer before the contract is made, as well as providing a written copy of these terms to the consumer. Therefore, there are two obligations which are distinct: with regard to the terms being concluded in writing or some other form and a copy of the terms to be supplied to the consumer.

The only qualification of the obligation to record the terms in writing is in relation to last-minute bookings. Section 15(2) provides that the obligation under section 15(1)(a) with regard to a written form of the contract does not apply for last-minute bookings which are made not more than fourteen days before the date of departure. Naturally, in that situation it would be impractical for a written form of all the terms of the contract to be given to the consumer before the contract is actually made. However, even in this situation the tour organiser is still required to provide to the consumer a written copy of the contract, even if that is naturally after the commencement or departure by the consumer on the package. Again, the failure to provide either the written terms or a copy of the written terms is both an offence by the retailer and the organiser under sections 15(3) and 15(4).

TRANSFER OF BOOKINGS

As well as imposing obligations for the provision of consumer information, there are certain other obligations and rights conferred on the consumer, the first of which is the right to transfer a booking. Section 16(1) implies a term that when the consumer is prevented from proceeding with the package, he may transfer the booking to a person who satisfies all the same conditions required of the original consumer, provided that the consumer gives reasonable notice to the organiser or retailer of his intention to transfer the booking before the specified departure date.

This is a major improvement on the consumer's position from the previous common law position. Previously most package holiday contracts were non-transferable or non-assignable and in the event of someone being unable to proceed with the package even for a good cause, there could be severe penalties in terms of cancellation charges. This was compounded by the fact that the cancellation insurance available was often restrictive against the range of circumstances that it would include for protection. This is now remedied by the provisions of Article 4(3) of the Directive as implemented by section 16. It should be noted, both from the Directive and from section 16, that some stated cause must be necessary before a transfer could be completed under this section. Therefore, a mere change of mind or lack of enthusiasm for the particular place of destination would not be sufficient to enable the consumer to transfer the booking. For example, circumstances of family bereavement or impending marriage of a family member may be such to permit the transfer of the holiday.[8] The other condition necessary for a valid transfer is that a transferee must satisfy all the same conditions as the original consumer, so for example, for an under-30 holiday, it could only have been transferred to a person who is under 30.

The consequences of payment for the transfer is dealt with in section 16(2), which provides that both the transferor and the transferee shall be jointly and severally liable to the organiser or retailer for the price of the package and for any additional fare and reasonable costs incurred by the organiser as a result of the transfer. Therefore, both the principal contractor and the assignee are jointly and severally liable for any balance due on the package, as well as for any extra additional fare and the reasonable costs incurred by the organiser for the implementation of the transfer, such as administration costs or supplementary payments that have to be made consequent upon the transfer, including re-booking fees for different accommodation or dietary requirements for the transferee.

CONTRACT PRICE REVISION

The consumer's interests are further protected in terms of any alterations or revisions to the price by the tour organiser under the contract by virtue of section 17(1), which provides that any term in the contract which allows the price to be revised shall be void, unless it allows for upward or downward alterations and satisfies several conditions set out in section 17(2). There are two conditions set out, namely that the manner of the price revision will be

---

8. See Clark, *I.C.L.S.A.* (1995) p. 1715.

calculated as described precisely in the terms of the contract and that the circumstances in which the price may be revised shall be described in the terms and shall be such as to provide that price revision may be made only to allow for variations in three types of situations. These charges include: transport costs, dues, taxes or fees chargeable for services (such as landing taxes or embarkation or disembarkation fees at ports and airports) and the exchange rates which apply to the particular package. Therefore, it can be seen that any alteration in the price after the contract has been concluded can only be for the purpose of giving credit for those three types of particular charges, which by definition, can vary from time to time from the conclusion of the contract to the date of departure and over which the tour organiser has no direct control.

The condition under which any price revision may be made, is that it must not be made later than a date specified in the contract, which shall not be less than twenty days before the specified departure date. Therefore, any price revision, in order to comply with the above condition, must be made, at the latest, twenty days before the departure date. This section, as with Article 4(4) of the Directive, seeks to address a problem of consumers that last-minute, additional surcharges would be imposed by the tour organiser onto the contract price, which has often been a problem in the past. It was often the case that, in pre-1995 package contracts, a right would be automatically given to the operator to implement such a price variation and also as to what level of variation or surcharge could be imposed.

It can be seen that the scope for tour operators to include any price variations is now very limited and could not include such things, as in the past, as additional bedroom charges or other cleaning charges. Such charges could not include any profit margin element, but merely reflect the actual charge incurred between the date of conclusion and the date of the variation with regard to those three specific types of situations which are beyond the control of the tour organiser. It is often the case that tour operators will build into the contract a 2 per cent tolerance level, so that only when the increase or the decrease exceeds that 2 per cent level, does the price variation come into play. This is part of the UK Regulations to implement the Directive,[9] Regulation 11(3) of which, describes such variation as non-eligible variations and so they are not within the scope of the Act.[10]

ALTERATION OR CANCELLATION BY TOUR ORGANISER

There is further protection within the 1995 Act to cover any alteration or

---

9. The UK Package Travel, Package Holidays and Package Tours Regulations 1992, S.I. 1992 No. 3288.
10. See Clark, *I.C.L.S.A.* (1995) p. 1716.

cancellation of the package by the actual tour organiser itself by virtue of section 18 which implies two terms in the package contract. Firstly, where the organiser is compelled before departure to alter significantly an essential term of the contract, the consumer will be notified as soon as possible in order to enable the consumer to take appropriate decisions and in particular, to withdraw from the contract without penalty or to accept a variation to the contract specified, the alterations made and their impact on the price. This may particularly apply to a situation, such as the implementation of price surcharges by the tour organiser, being related to the previous provisions in section 17 concerning the revision of the price.

It allows the consumer firstly, the right to be notified and secondly, the right to take whatever decision he deems appropriate on foot of the alteration, being either to withdraw from the contract completely or to accept a variation of the contract on the altered basis. The second implied term, which is related to the first, is that a corresponding obligation is imposed on the consumer to inform the organiser or the retailer of his decision as soon as possible. The problem regarding this subsection is the lack of definition regarding when the tour operator is compelled to alter significantly an essential term, as to what circumstances would justify such significant alteration of an essential term.[11]

The Directive itself does not prove entirely helpful in explaining this. It should be noted that the provision regarding the essential terms of the contract which have been included in the contract and section 14 are naturally essential. Therefore, a significant alteration of one of those terms would naturally come within section 18. However, it should be noted that these terms in the context of alteration and cancellation are not exhaustive. This is due to the particular nature of the individual package, there could be other essential terms which could be liable to be altered in order to justify protection under section 18.

The other aspect of section 18 is contained in subsection (2), which sets out the implied remedies for the consumer where the consumer either withdraws from the contract under section 18(1)(a) or the organiser cancels for any reason the package before the date of when it is due to start. The first right of the consumer in section 18(2)(b)(i) is the right to take a replacement package of equivalent or superior quality, if the organiser is able to offer such a replacement. Alternatively, the consumer may choose to take such a replacement of a lower quality and therefore be repaid the balance of the difference in price between the two packages. Finally, the consumer may elect to be repaid as soon as possible all the monies paid under the contract. Therefore, the consumer has two basic choices: firstly, whether to take a replacement of a lower or higher quality and secondly, not to do so and just be repaid all the monies paid under the contract. As well as these rights, the

---

11. See Clark, *I.C.L.S.A.* (1995) p. 1717.

consumer is entitled to further compensation by the organiser for the non-performance of the contract under section 18(2)(c).

There are two possible situations where this additional compensation will not be available under the Act. Firstly, where the package is cancelled because the minimum number of persons required for the package are not available and the consumer is informed of the cancellation in writing within the prescribed period in the contract and secondly, if the package is cancelled by virtue of *force majeure*. This term *force majeure* is explained in section 18 as being by reason of unusual and unforeseeable circumstances beyond the control of the organiser, the retailer or other supplier of services, the consequences of which could not have been avoided even if all due care had been exercised.

This *force majeure* provision reflects Article 6 of the Directive, as well as the well established jurisprudence of the European Court of Justice on the meaning of the term in EU law.[12] The very nature of *force majeure* as with frustration at common law, is that the contract has become impossible to perform and hence, all rights and obligations under the contract are discharged. However, it should be noted that with regard to the definition under the Act *force majeure* may not, even if satisfied by the cumulative conditions under the Act, discharge the contract depending on the nature of the breach in question, as it may be just a breach of one particular, fairly limited and small provision under the contract, as in for example, a facility or service and so not discharge the whole contract.

Therefore, unless these two conditions are both fulfilled, the consumer will always be entitled to compensation above and beyond a replacement or repayment of monies paid under the contract from the organiser. This compensation would include such damage as the basic waste and expenditure above and beyond any balance paid, as well as the mental distress and disappointment of the holiday being cancelled. The way that this compensation provision is diminished by virtue of contractual practice is that the standard form, package contract will inevitably provide for a set scale for compensation or a set sum for cancellation within a set number of weeks before the departure date with the highest amount payable the closer the cancellation to the departure date (i.e. within two weeks).

It should be noted with regard to the requirement that all terms of the contract should be reduced to writing under section 15, that if this is not done, it merely means that there is a breach of section 15 and that the retailer or organiser will be guilty of an offence. It does not have the result that the fact that just because some terms are not reduced to writing in the contract, that

---

12. See in particular, *Firma Schwarzwaldmilch GmbH v. Eindfuhr und Vorratstelle fur Fette* C–4/68; [1968] E.C.R. 377 and *Einfuhr und Vorratsteel fur Getreide v. Pfutzenreuter* C–3/74; [1974] E.C.R. 589. Also see generally, Schwarze, *European Administrative Law* (1992) pp. 463-469 and Grant & Mason, *Holiday Law* (1996) p. 212 *et seq.*

they are not therefore terms of the contract either expressly or impliedly which are legally binding and enforceable. Of course, the implied terms of the Act are often reduced in writing as a matter of standard form, but by definition do not per se have to be reduced to writing in order to be relied upon by the consumer.

CHAPTER THREE

Civil and Statutory Liability for Misleading Statements by a Tour Organiser or a Retailer

LIABILITY FOR MISLEADING BROCHURES

The primary ground of the liability for a tour organiser or retailer for any misleading statements in holiday brochures is contained in section 11 of the 1995 Act which reflects Article 3 of the Directive. The basic principle is that no misleading information shall be supplied to a consumer either in a brochure or in other descriptive matter relating to the package, the price or any conditions applied to the contract. Therefore, it reiterates the basic requirement that all information in brochures and other related promotional material must be true and accurate, either when it is produced by the organiser or when supplied by the retailer.

With regard to section 11 and the liability to retailers for false and misleading brochures, the point was made by the Minister for State[1] that the intention of the legislature was to make it easier for the consumer to seek redress in the event of, for example, a brochure being false and misleading. Therefore, he would not accept that an unfair onus should be placed on a consumer by having to prove that the retailer knew that the information was false or misleading, but only that he should have reasonable cause to believe that it was so. This was countered in view of the liability on the travel agent by allowing a defence that he did not know and had no reason to suspect that a brochure was false or misleading. This was aimed at allaying the fears expressed by Deputy Brennan that it would impose unfair liability for a small travel agent to be responsible for all statements made in a brochure issued by a multinational firm. For example, he made the point:

> . . . that there are 300 or more small travel agents around the country, each employing two or three persons who would find it extremely

---

1. 453 *Dáil Debates* Cols 827–828.

difficult, if not impossible, to stand over every line of every brochure produced by a multinational company.[2]

He further made the point with regard to the liabilities and burdens imposed on small travel agents by virtue of this legislation and other consumer protection legislation that:

> I want to highlight on this date the large number of small travel agents who are affected by additional consumer protection legislation. I know there must be a fine balance and we must have the consumer protection, but it must be reasonable and sensible. Given that we have a few hundred travel agents, each employing two or three people, it is not reasonable to expect them to be familiar with the minutiae of international travel brochures and to check them out. Should they be expected to fly to destinations to check on information in a brochure or should they accept the organiser's word? I am extremely anxious that retailers should be only held liable for information of which they can reasonably be expected to be aware given their size. It is one thing to expect a large travel agency employing a few hundred employees with legal and other specialist departments to know about these things, but another for a small travel agency employing two or three people to take brochures at face value.[3]

With regard to the position of the retailer, it is set out that it can be a defence under section 11(2) that the retailer did not know and had no reason to suspect that the brochure or other descriptive matter concerned contained any false or misleading information. This naturally follows, as only the tour organiser has the sole and direct control over the production and accuracy of the brochure, which cannot be within the knowledge of the retailer, unless he has a reason to suspect it was false or misleading.

The section then goes on to set out the conditions under which a consumer may recover compensation for any misleading information contained in material supplied to him by the tour organiser or the retailer.

Firstly, with regard to the tour organiser, who provides a brochure which is supplied to the consumer, either directly or indirectly through the retailer, he shall compensate the consumer for any damage caused as a direct consequence of, and attributable to the consumer's reliance on, the information which is false or misleading. The information concerned can either be contained in the actual brochure or other descriptive matter such as leaflets, advertisements etc. This can relate to any oral explanation or emphasis put upon the brochure by the organiser. It should be noted that the essence of the basis of the compensation is by virtue of statutory tort under sections 11(3) and

---

2. 453 *Dáil Debates* Cols 829–830.
3. 453 *Dáil Debates* Cols 830–831.

11(4), but it is not a criminal offence, as usually provided for various other breaches of the Act. It should also be noted that this statutory tort should be seen as complementing the consumer's general range of other existing contractual and tortious remedies available for reliance on such misleading information.

With regard to the retailer's liability, he is liable to compensate the consumer for any damage caused as a result of the direct consequence of, and attributable to the customer's reliance on, such false and misleading information either in a brochure or descriptive matter supplied by the retailer or given by the retailer in respect of the brochure or descriptive matter. The retailer's liability under section 11(4) should be read in the context of his defence under section 11(2) that he either did not know or had no reason to suspect that such material was false and misleading. This defence is one that is going to be raised by the retailer in circumstances of any such proceedings under the section, as it is likely that if there is loss resulting from false or misleading information, that the consumer will sue both the tour organiser and the retailer. It would therefore leave it up to the retailer to raise the statutory defence and so it would be an open issue for the court as to whether he did or did not know, or had no reason to suspect, that the information was false or misleading. In most cases under this section, it is likely that as long as it is proved that the brochure contained false or misleading information, judgment can easily be recovered against the tour organiser. However, the retailer's defence would be an open issue which naturally would be fought keenly during the proceedings, with the difficult issue of proving the retailer's knowledge either way.

Recoverable Loss

The loss which can be recovered by the consumer under this section is an area which naturally could be the subject of substantial argument as to what is meant by "damage caused to the consumer as a direct consequence" of the misleading information. Prima facie it can include loss such as wasted expenditure, personal injury or illness, physical discomfort, mental distress and disappointment occasioned by the substandard nature of the holiday which are the basic heads of loss for any substandard holiday under ordinary common law principles.[4]

This now well recognised principle on which all the subsequent common law approach to damages in holiday contracts rested was first developed in the leading case of *Jarvis v. Swan Tours*[5] where a unanimous Court of Appeal decision allowed damages for mental distress caused by the disappointment of a substandard holiday, summed up by Lord Denning M.R. as follows:

---

4. See *Jarvis v. Swan Tours* [1973] 1 All E.R. 71; *Kemp v. Intasun Holidays Ltd* [1987] 2 F.T.L.R. 234 at 237E-238E *per* Kerr L.J. [1987] C.L.Y. 1130 and *Davey v. Cosmos* [1989] C.L.Y. 2561. See Chapter 8 below.
5. [1973] 1 All E.R. 71.

In a proper case damages for mental distress can be recovered in contract, just as damages for shock can be recovered in tort. One such case is a contract for a holiday, or any other contract to provide entertainment and enjoyment. If the contracting party breaks his contract, damages can be given for the disappointment, the distress, the upset and frustration caused by the breach.[6]

In the case of *Kemp v. Intasun Holidays Ltd*[7] it was further recognised that damages would flow from a breach of contract for distress and disappointment suffered by a substandard holiday for breach of the booking arrangements themselves, but also for any breach of additional information given of additional requirements by the consumer and communicated to either the travel agent and/or the tour operator. In this case, an asthmatic was given a substandard and unsalubrious room which gave rise to an attack of asthma by the plaintiff for the day and a half in which he and his family were accommodated in that room before being moved. The issue was whether that distress could be remedied in damages for breach of the requirement that a room would be fit for the habitation of an asthmatic. To succeed on that basis, the plaintiff had to show that the tour operator had knowledge of his condition to enable the consequences of the substandard room on his health to be a foreseeable consequence of that breach to be recoverable in damages. It was emphasised by Kerr L.J.:

> That it is clear that the foreseeable consequences of a breach of contract of this kind, as has been decided in many cases, will always include any distress, discomfort, disappointment, or as Mr Lowe puts it, loss of enjoyment of the actual holiday in comparison with the contractual holiday which should have been provided.[8]

It was found that the defendant tour operator could not have reasonably contemplated that the conditions in the room provided might foreseeably be injurious to the health of the plaintiff and his family. The second ground on which recovery was sought was whether this finding of the foreseeable consequences of the plaintiff inhabiting this room was mitigated by the fact that in a casual conversation with the travel agent before the holiday was booked, the plaintiff's medical condition was indicated. This was relied upon to possibly indicate that the tour operator had knowledge of the special circumstances of the contract, which gave an additional contractual consequence to the booking conditions already agreed between the parties.

It was found on the facts that the travel agent in question, was not at that

---

6. [1973] 1 All E.R. 71 at 95.
7. [1987] 2 F.T.L.R. 234.
8. [1987] 2 F.T.L.R. 234 at 238(d)-(g) *per* Kerr L.J.

time an agent on behalf of the tour operator and so any knowledge which may have been communicated at that stage, even though an agency may have been created later, could not be found to have any contractual consequences.[9] It was interestingly left open as to whether there was any duty on the agent to communicate such information to the tour operator.[10]

The causal connection between the loss and the misinformation is based on what is meant by a direct consequence of that particular breach of duty. This seems to be closely related to the basic contractual rule of remoteness of damage, although another interpretation could be made. Therefore, it seems that a consumer could recover for whatever loss is a natural and direct consequence of the misleading information. For example, if the accommodation was represented to be hygienic, but turns out to be the contrary, causing illness, that would be a natural direct consequence of the breach of duty, premised on the contractual test of remoteness of damage. It is also possible to broaden the view of misleading information, if it was known by the tour organiser or retailer that the consumer had special needs or expectations above and beyond what was contained in the actual brochure, but the service actually provided by the organiser or retailer did not conform to these special needs or expectations, which would also result in liability under this section.[11]

OFFENCES

The other statutory liability with regard to misleading information relates to the content of brochures.[12] Under section 10 it is an offence for an organiser or retailer to supply a brochure knowing or having reasonable cause to believe that it does not comply with the necessary elements required under section 10. This is a major offence for both an organiser and a retailer under section 10(3).

With regard to the offences, the penalty is outlined in section 6, as being on summary conviction the possible imposition of a fine not exceeding £1,500. This penalty applies both to individuals and corporate bodies. Further, section 6(3) provides that, where an offence has been committed by a corporate body, with the consent or connivance or facilitated by any neglect by any director, manager, secretary or other officer of such body or any person who is purporting to act in any such capacity, that officer or person shall be guilty of an offence and shall be liable to the same penalty, namely a fine of £1,500. This is a general standard provision with regard to making company officers liable for the offences of the company.

---

9. [1987] 2 F.T.L.R. 234. at 237(a).
10. [1987] 2 F.T.L.R. 234 at 239(d)-(f) *per* Parker L.J.
11. See Clark, *I.C.L.S.A.* (1995) p. 1711 and *Kemp v. Intasun Holidays Ltd* [1987] 2 F.T.L.R. 234.
12. See Chapter 2, p. 27 above.

The summary proceedings may be prosecuted by the Director of Consumer Affairs under section 7(1). There is a 12-month time limit for issuing proceedings under the Act as section 7(3) amends the Petty Sessions (Ireland) Act 1851, whereby there was normally a 6-month time limit. Section 6(4) also goes on to deal with the service of proceedings on persons resident outside the jurisdiction, whereby service can be effected on a person ordinarily resident in the State in lieu of service on the named defendant, such as any representatives, solicitor or agents. Section 7(7) also provides that upon conviction, the court shall, unless there are special substantial reasons for not so doing, order the convicted person or company to pay to the Minister or Director of Consumer Affairs the costs and expenses as a result of the investigation and prosecution of the offence.

It should be noted that the offence committed by the organiser under section 10 is one of strict liability as naturally, the tour organiser should be able to verify the matters in the brochure prior to releasing it onto the market, and even if requirements change, the organiser would still face conviction unless the brochure is withdrawn. If there is any correction in the brochure and the travel agent is told by the tour operator of this, then the brochure must either be withdrawn or amended, by such as in an erratum slip, otherwise the offence will be committed by both the organiser and the retailer. It should be noted however, that the prosecution still has to prove, for the purpose of the retailer's conviction, that he either knew or had reasonable cause to believe that it did not comply with the requirements of the section.[13] With regard to the function of the Director of Consumer Affairs, Minister Stagg stated:

> The Director of Consumer Affairs will be responsible for implementing the legislation. It will be his job to ensure that either the organiser or the travel agent does not issue brochures containing false information and he will have the resources which will not be available to the ordinary consumer to check that.[14]

As well as the statutory offences under the section, the section also allows similar recovery on the basis of the ordinary common law by virtue of sections 10(4) and 10(6) whereby the essential terms of the contract, which must be implemented by virtue of section 10(1), are deemed to be warranties whether express or implied as to the matters to which they relate, unless the consumer and the tour organiser directly, or through a retailer, agree that certain terms should not form part of the contract on or after the date the contract is made. Consequently, the consumer also has the option of recovering damages for breach of warranty for the breach of any of the terms of the brochure upon which he enters into the contract. If, for any reason, any of the requirements set out in a brochure (as to accommodation etc.) are not complied with or are

---

13. See Clark, *I.C.L.S.A.* (1995) p. 1710; 453 *Dáil Debates* Col. 828.
14. 453 *Dáil Debates* Col. 831.

not satisfactory to the consumer, then they are treated as warranties and therefore he has a remedy in damages for the breach of same.

There are two provisos to this general rule of recovery in sections 10(5) and 10(6). Firstly, the implied or expressed warranties do not apply in respect of particulars where the brochure contains a clear and legible statement that changes may be made in the particulars contained therein, before a contract is concluded and such changes in those particulars are clearly communicated to, and accepted by, the other party before a contract is concluded. Therefore, the consumer could not recover for breach of warranty where the particulars concerned are allowed to be changed and have so been changed and accepted by the consumer before the contract has actually concluded, so that the brochure would not reflect accurately the current position by virtue of the change at the date the contract is concluded.

There is a further proviso in section 10(6), whereby particulars of the contract will not be deemed to be warranties where both consumer and organiser or retailer agree, on or after the date on which the contract is made, that those particulars should not form part of the contract. This naturally refers to any particular terms which cannot be complied with and it has been agreed that they cannot be complied with or alternatively, that it is merely a case of using the best efforts or the reasonable endeavours of the tour organiser in order to accommodate the requirements of the consumer. Therefore they should not be deemed to be breach of warranties which sound in damages.

The importance of this deeming of terms as warranties is the fact that it deprives the retailer or tour organiser of the ordinary common law defence that any such warranty or representation was merely an advertising puff or a bare representation which is not answerable in damages.[15] It has been commented that the post-contractual variation provision in section 10(6) is unfortunately much weaker than the pre-contractual variation provision in section 18 of the Act governing alteration or cancellation by the tour organiser.[16] However, it can be argued that section 10(6) should be read in conjunction with the Unfair Contract Terms Regulations 1995[17] which in general invalidates clauses that allow the unilateral variation of contractual terms where agreed in a standard form.[18]

It should be noted that the commencement of the Act was by virtue of Statutory Instrument, which has a particular consequence for any of the offences and liabilities created by the Act, when the Act commenced, as naturally, a lead-in period would be necessary to allow organisers and retailers an opportunity to comply with the new provisions of the Act and avoid accidental criminal liability by virtue of immediate implementation of the liabilities

---

15. See Clark, *Contract Law in Ireland* (3rd edn, 1992) pp. 229-234 and Clark, *I.C.L.S.A.* (1995) p.1710.
16. See Chapter 4 below.
17. S.I. No. 27 of 1995, see Appendix 7.
18. See Clark, *I.C.L.S.A.* (1995) p. 1711 and in particular Chapter 11 below.

under the Act.[19]

With regard to the travel agent's liability for misleading brochures, it is fair to say that responsibility should still be imposed on the agent, even though he is not the originator or publisher of the brochure, since he does supply the consumer with the brochure and more than that, he does not do so as a mere passive agent, but as one who exercised judgement in terms of with which tour operators he will deal and hence which brochures and holidays he will sell, being the primary point of contact and adviser of the consumer with knowledge and experience of the tour organisers and destinations.

There is a difficulty insofar as there is no express defence under section 11, as opposed to section 10. Therefore, travel agents would be strictly liable for the supply of misleading brochures, especially in the circumstances where in the ordinary course, you would expect the agent to be the first to be sued as he is the direct link with the consumer, is local and is personally known to the consumer as opposed to the remote tour organiser. However, it must be remembered that a retailer is only liable if he knows or has reasonable cause to believe that the contents of the brochure are not accurate or do not contain the required matter under section 10(1). The onus is on the prosecution, which may ameliorate the liability of the retailer, as being insignificant hurdle to overcome. The agent or the consumer naturally could blame the operator, but that may not always be possible, for example, if an operator becomes insolvent or is a non-resident company. It follows from this that the only certain way a travel agent can protect himself is by ensuring that the agency agreements he has with the tour organisers contain indemnity clauses for any liability arising out of false or misleading brochures either under section 10 or section 11. This is, in essence, the most obvious and easy remedy of the statutory liabilities incurred both under sections 10 and 11, being matters of commercial judgement and bargaining power but may not always be possible in reality.

COMMON LAW REMEDIES

Misrepresentation

It should be remembered that despite section 11, the basic common law still provides a remedy to supplement the liability under sections 10 and 11 for misleading information in brochures, by way of an action in negligent misrepresentation, where the consumer relies on a misrepresentation which is false, in a contractual or fiduciary relationship, thereby causing him loss.[20]

---

19.   144 *Seanad Debates* and also S.I. No. 235 of 1995, The Package Holidays and Travel Trade Act 1995 (Commencement) Order 1995 commencing s. 5 with regard to the setting of fees payable under the Act on 1 September 1995 and the remainder of the provisions of the Act on 1 October, 1995. See Appendix 3.
20.   See *Hedley Byrne v. Heller* [1964] A.C. 465, applied in this jurisdiction in cases such

It should be noted that the traditional remedy of negligent misrepresentation might not apply to a pre-contractual misrepresentation, as the misrepresentation would not be a term of the contract. This difficulty was relieved by means of statutory intervention in section 45(1) of the Sale of Goods and Supply of Services Act 1980, which provides:

> Where a person has entered into a contract after misrepresentation has been made to him by another party thereto and as a result thereof he has suffered loss, then, the person making the representation would be liable to damages in respect thereof had the misrepresentation been made fraudulently, that person shall be so liable notwithstanding the misrepresentation was not made fraudulently, unless he proves that he had reasonable grounds to believe and did believe up to the time the contract was made that the facts represented were true.[21]

This supplements the range of common law remedies available, as it allows recovery of damages for pre-contractual representations, which are innocent and not fraudulent, and imposes the onus on the representor to prove that he had reasonable grounds to believe the facts of the representation were true. It is important to remember that prior to this section, innocent misrepresentation in general could not provide a remedy for the injured party.[22] There has been some doubt as what the measure of damages is under the section, as if it is the tort or contractual measure.[23] It now appears to be the case that the tortious measure should be applied, being that for deceit rather than that for negligence, so it allows a plaintiff to recover for all loss flowing from the misrepresentation, even when it is unforeseeable.[24] Thus, Balcombe L.J. stated:

> In view of the wording of the subsection it is difficult to see how the measure of damages under it could be other than the tortious measure and, despite the initial aberrations referred to above, that is now generally accepted.[25]

---

as *Hazylake Fashions v. Bank of Ireland* [1989] I.R. 601; *Kennedy v. AIB* unreported, Supreme Court, 19 October 1996; *McCullagh v. Gunne (Mcnaghan)* unreported, Carroll J., 17 January 1997 and *Tristan v. Mayo County Council*, unreported, Moriarty J., 6 July 1998 and see generally, Clark, *Contract Law in Ireland* (3rd edn, 1992) pp. 236-237 and Chitty, *On Contracts* (27th edn, 1994) Vol. 1, Chapter 6.

21. For a recent application of s. 45(1), see *O'Donnell v. TMS* [1997] 1 I.L.R.M. 466 (HC) and unreported, Supreme Court, 1 April 1998.
22. See *Nocton v. Lord Ashburton* [1914] A.C. 932.
23. See Clark, *Contract Law in Ireland* (3rd edn, 1992) pp. 240-241.
24. See the Court of Appeal in *Royscot Trust Ltd v. Rogerson* [1991] 3 All E.R. 294, contra the earlier broader approach taken in the holiday context by Lord Denning M.R. in *Jarvis v. Swan Tours* [1973] 2 Q.B. 233.
25. *Royscot Trust Ltd v. Rogerson* [1991] 3 All E.R. 294 at 398.

The consumer can also recover for fraudulent misrepresentation whereby a false representation is made by the tour operator or retailer knowingly, without belief in its truth or recklessly or carelessly as to whether it is true or false.[26] This in essence is the tort of deceit which naturally includes the element of deliberate and knowing misrepresentation as to the falsity of the statement, which is a higher hurdle for a consumer to overcome and it may be unlikely that a tour operator or organiser would be liable under this head, unless in the most exceptional circumstances.

Therefore, not only could the consumer recover damages for both types of misrepresentation, but also potentially achieve rescission which may be unlikely in a holiday context, since it is most likely that the damage or the breach will occur, when the actual holiday is undertaken, then damages would be the most likely remedy. It should be noted that although the action is for misrepresentation, the liability under section 11 for misleading brochures is similar, as they both require reliance. It is possible that liability under the Act would be broader, because it covers any misleading information concerning a package, which could give a very wide interpretation, so as to include basic resort and hotel descriptions, for example.

Misrepresentation at common law is a narrower cause of action, because it only covers false statements of fact, it does not include mere statements of opinion or statements as to the future, whereas such statements of opinions and descriptions, for example in brochures, would incur liability under the Act. Such statements would not in general be amenable to the ordinary common law action of misrepresentation. The only exception to this is where the statement of opinion is the result of an utterance by a person who knows it to be false or had the opportunity to check its accuracy.[27] The other point with regard to the interrelationship of section 11 and misrepresentation is the level of damage recoverable. As under misrepresentation, damages would be assessed on basic tortious grounds, so both the rules as to causation and remoteness of damage in tort will apply.[28]

However, the problem with regard to contractual liability under section 11, is that it is not clear whether the tortious or contractual rules regarding causation and remoteness apply, analogous to the uncertainty surrounding section 45(1) of the Sale of Goods and Supply of Services Act 1980[29] which is another matter which would only be resolved by virtue of a definitive judicial pronouncement.

---

26. *Derry v. Peek* [1889] 14 A.C. 337 and see generally, Clark, *Contract Law in Ireland* (3rd edn, 1992) p. 234.
27. Clark, *ibid.*, p. 229.
28. See Chapter 7 below.
29. See above p. 49.

CHAPTER FOUR

Post-departure Responsibilities of Tour Organisers

The most important part of the 1995 Act is the implementation of the Directive with regard to strict liability on tour organisers in respect of the improper performance of the obligations under the contract, irrespective of whether such obligations are to be performed by the organiser himself, the retailer or other supplier of services.[1] The intent behind this provision is to ensure that the tour organiser is subject to the same kind of strict liability to a consumer in the travel industry as already is the case as a result of other statutory provisions, in particular, section 39 of the Sale of Goods and Supply of Services Act 1980.[2]

POSITION AT COMMON LAW

Apart from the Directive and the Act, the traditional common law view with regard to the tour organiser's liability for the defective performance of the contract, as well as any other supplier of services abroad in pursuance of the contract, has been narrow. This is particularly exemplified by the English case of *Wall v. Silver Wing Surface Arrangements Ltd*[3] whereby an English tour operator avoided liability, because a reputable, local service provider had failed to perform the contract adequately. Since, in the absence of an express term, the tour organiser is under no liability to properly select independent contractors.

The problem with regard to the liability of a tour organiser for the services supplied abroad is obviously the fact that the tour organiser cannot effectively supervise independent contractors of services while abroad, so allowing the previously narrow common law attitude to the tour operator's liability. The consequence of this is naturally that the only remedy left to the consumer is to bring a foreign action in tort against the service provider which inevitably

---

1. See s. 20.
2. See 143 *Seanad Debates*, Col. 1627, per the Minister for State.
3. Unreported, UK High Court, 18 November 1981.

would be in the jurisdiction where the package was provided, for example, see Article 6 of the Brussels Convention.[4]

This has also been reiterated more recently in the English case of *Wilson v. Best Travel*[5] where it was held that the duty of care owed by a tour operator to its customers in accordance with section 13 of the UK Sale of Goods and Supply of Services Act 1982[6] was a duty to exercise reasonable care to exclude from the accommodation offered any hotel, the characteristics of which were such that guests could not spend a holiday there in reasonable safety. The duty to ensure reasonable safety was discharged if the tour operator checked that local safety regulations had been complied with and the duty did not extend to excluding a hotel whose characteristics, so far as safety was concerned, failed to satisfy the current standards applying in England (provided always that the absence of the relevant safety feature was not such that a reasonable holidaymaker might decline to take a holiday at the hotel in question, e.g. if a hotel included in a brochure had no fire precautions at all). Accordingly, since the defendants had inspected the accommodation offered in their brochure as part of their services, since the patio doors complied with Greek safety regulations and since the degree of danger posed by the absence of safety glass in the patio doors was not such that the plaintiff would have declined to stay at the hotel, the defendants had discharged the duty of care owed to the plaintiff, whose claim therefore failed.

Mr Justice Philips rejected the first basis of the claim on an implied term in the contract to inspect the accommodation offered in the brochure, saying:

> The defendants would not have considered it either obvious or reasonable that they should give a warranty of this kind. Mr Burton referred me to the transcript of a decision of Hodgson J. in *Wall v Silver Wing Surface Arrangements Ltd* in which, in a case of very different facts, the plaintiff sought to establish a similar implied term in a contract for a package holiday. After a careful analysis of the relevant law, the judge rejected the term alleged on the ground that the implication of such a term was neither necessary nor obvious nor reasonable. I share both his reasoning and his conclusion.[7]

He went on to say with regard to the duty of care required under the duty to provide reasonable care and skill under the Sale of Goods and Supply of Services Act 1980, which would also apply in negligence, that:

---

4. See Clark, *I.C.L.S.A.* (1995) pp. 1719-1720.
5. [1993] 1 All E.R. 353.
6. Equivalent to sections 39(a) and 39(b) of the Irish Sale of Goods and Supply of Services Act 1980.
7. [1993] 1 All E.R. 353 at 355.

> The nature of the services provided by a travel agent when arranging a holiday can vary enormously, depending on the nature of the holiday. I am satisfied, having read their brochure, that the service provided by the defendants included the inspection of the properties offered in their brochure.[8]

He concluded by taking the view that:

> In my judgment, one of the characteristics of accommodation that the defendants owed a duty to consider when inspecting properties included in their brochure was safety. The defendants owe their customers, including the plaintiff, a duty to exercise reasonable care to exclude from the accommodation offered any hotel whose characteristics were such that guests could not spend a holiday there in reasonable safety. I believe that this case is about the standard to be applied in assessing reasonable safety.[9]

The traditional common law approach has been lessened certainly in England in recent years particularly in the case of *Wong Mee Wan v. Kwan Kin Travel Services Ltd*[10] whereby the Privy Council imposed primary liability on the tour operators and a duty of care in order to take reasonable care in selection of those who provide those services on their behalf.[11]

Strict Liability

With regard to the common law duties of tour operators, it is important to note that section 20(1) imposes not only strict liability, but also liability on the organiser regardless of the fact that the services are to be performed by another. This is the most usual case of a supplier who provides the actual service in situ at the destination of the actual holiday for and on behalf of the organiser. The duties which must be observed are the express duties or implied duties imposed by the Act. Where such implied duties are at issue above and beyond the statutory implied duties, it will be necessary to establish in every case whether they have been breached.

The liability is further reiterated by virtue of the fact that under section 20(2), the organiser is liable to the consumer for any damage caused by the failure to perform the contract or the improper performance of the contract. Therefore, the organiser can be either liable for the absolute failure to perform the contract in the first place or by virtue of the improper performance of

---

8. [1993] 1 All E.R. 353 at 356.
9. [1993] 1 All E.R. 353 at 358.
10. [1995] 4 All E.R 745.
11. See Chapter 5, p. 65 below.

the contract. It is likely that the improper performance ground of liability is the most common, as the holiday naturally would be provided, but it would be below the standard expected or contracted for.

With regard to the liability imposed on the tour organiser under the Act, the Minister for State, Mr Stagg said:

> I am aware that there is much concern in the travel trade industry regarding the extent to which organisers could be held liable to the consumer following the implementation of this legislation. In this regard, I would like to clarify that the retailer's liability to their customers will not be dramatically increased following the Bill's enactment. Under the Sale of Goods and Supply of Services Act 1980, the seller, or retailer in the case of the travel trade, is already responsible in almost all cases for the performance of their side of the contract. The effect of the Bill will be to place responsibility on the organiser similar to that which is already on the retailer under the Sale of Goods and Supply of Services Act.[12]

Defences

Although it is stated to be strict liability, there are three defences open to the organiser under section 20(2)(a) to 20(2)(c). The first of these is where the failure in the performance of the contract is attributable to the consumer, reflecting the basic contributory negligence defence of ordinary tort. Secondly, that the failures are attributable to a third party unconnected with the provision or the services contracted. Therefore if the failure is due to some unconnected party and such failure is unforeseeable or unavoidable, then there will be no liability attaching to the organiser for the said failure. This is a fair and reasonable defence, so as to allow liability only in situations in which the organiser can lawfully be deemed to be in control, directly or indirectly, of the supplier or agent acting for and on behalf of the organiser, which would not be the case in the terms of this defence. The final defence reflects this point, as where the failure is due to *force majeure*, which is defined under section 20(2)(c) as being that of unusual and unforeseeable circumstances beyond the control of the organiser, retailer or other supplier of services, the consequences of which could not have been avoided, even if all due care had been exercised.

There are two points to this defence of *force majeure*: firstly, the circumstances must be unusual, unforeseeable and beyond the control of the organiser. Secondly, which is an additional and cumulative condition, the consequences could not have been avoided, even if all due care, i.e. there was no

---

12.   451 *Dáil Debates* Col. 318.

negligence, had been exercised. There is also a second heading of *force majeure*, defined as as an event which the organiser, retailer or other supplier of services, even with all due care, could not foresee or forestall. This again reflects the fact that the degree of control over the provision of the service is the key element in triggering liability on behalf of the organiser. Again, there must be not only an unforeseeable event, but also it could not have been avoided, even if all due care had been exercised. Therefore, being unforeseeable in itself is not sufficient, but it must also be unavoidable, even if there was no negligence on behalf of the organiser or its agents.

Compensation

The section therefore, having set out the basic principle of liability and the damage for which the organiser would be liable and the defences open to him, then goes on in subsection 3 to indicate the circumstances in which the compensation, for which the tour organiser would be liable, can be limited by virtue of the terms of the contract. Section 20(3) allows limitation of the amount of compensation payable apart from the cases of death or personal injury and where damage is caused to the consumer by the wilful misconduct or gross negligence of the organiser. Therefore, in any other circumstance, the contract can validly limit the amount of compensation payable for example, with regard to property, loss or destruction.

Having set out the types of case in which compensation can be limited, section 20(4) then goes on to state the limit of quantum below which the compensation cannot be limited, which in the case of an adult is to an amount equal to double the inclusive price of the package to the adult and in the case of a minor, the amount equal to the inclusive price of the package of the minor concerned. Therefore, the bare minimum of compensation for any circumstance other than death or personal injury or acts of gross negligence, is double the price of the holiday for an adult. This is the most usual case even if, for example, in property destruction cases, the loss of the property may not be as great as that of the amount of the actual holiday in question. It ensures that a minimum base level of compensation is given to the consumer and therefore it cannot be limited to insignificant or minimal amounts in the contract, which would not truly reflect the loss suffered by the consumer. It is now common for the terms of this limitation from section 20(4) to be expressly included as part of the standard booking conditions.

This allowance of certain basic compensation limits for cases other than cases of death or personal injury or gross negligence, must also be read in the light of any international conventions in force which relate to such services. Such conventions allow similar limitations which are also expressly allowed by virtue of section 20(5) with regard to being in force and governing such services in the place where they are performed or are due to be performed. This relates to the Warsaw Convention on Travel by Air 1929, the Berne

Convention on Carriage by Rail 1970, the Athens Convention on Carriage by Sea 1974 and the Paris Convention on the Liability of Hotel Keepers 1962.[13] The intention behind this provision is to allow the organiser to step into the shoes of a service provider, so that if a hotel keeper, for example, is allowed to be protected by the 1962 Convention, the limit of the liability of the organiser in the shoes of the hotel keeper applies to the liability of the service provider. Therefore, any provisions in the conventions which apply to such service providers will also apply to the tour organiser,[14] giving the explanation to this otherwise cryptic subsection.

The other Act which is relevant in terms of limitation of liability, is referred to in section 20(8), as the Hotel Proprietors Act 1963 which is deemed to apply to such situations for limitation of liability section 20. It therefore allows a hotelier to limit his liability to £100.[15] This limit of liability applies to a guest for damage to or loss of property of any one person, if the following conditions were satisfied, namely: the act was not due to the wrongful act of the proprietor or a servant, the property was not expressly deposited for safe keeping with the proprietor, or the proprietor in default was unable to keep it on deposit and the required notice under the Act was displayed at or near the main reception.[16]

It should be noted that with regard to the 1963 Act which applies to all hotel proprietors in this jurisdiction, it imposed a statutory duty to take reasonable care of the person of the guest and to ensure that, for the purpose of personal use by the guest, the premises are as safe as reasonable care and skill can make them.[17] There is a further statutory liability for loss or damage to property received by the hotel proprietor where sleeping accommodation is provided.[18] This statutory liability is on its face quite stringent, especially as it is not possible to contract out of the provisions of the Act, but it often seems to be overlooked as a basis for a plaintiff's claim.[19]

These implied terms with regard to the liability and the limitation of the liability of the tour organiser cannot be excluded by any contractual term. Therefore any exclusion clause which would purport to limit the liability or exclude the liability under sections 20(1) and 20(2) would be void under section 20(6). Further, there is a final implied term on the tour organiser, that when the consumer is in difficulty, he must give prompt assistance to that consumer when the difficulty arises by virtue of a *force majeure* or third-party

---

13. See Chapter 8 below.
14. See Clark, *I.C.L.S.A.* (1995) p. 1720 and Grant & Mason, *Holiday Law* (1996) pp. 162-4.
15. See s. 7 of the 1963 Act.
16. For the text of the required notice, see the First Schedule to the 1963 Act.
17. See s. 4.
18. See s. 6.
19. See s. 9 and see McMahon & Binchy, *The Irish Law of Torts* (2nd edn, 1990) pp. 215-216.

default events, for which he would otherwise not be liable under section 20(2). Therefore, although he would not bear liability for such events, he is still subject to an implied contractual term to assist the consumer in difficulty when such circumstances arise. This reflects the pivotal position of the local representative of the tour organiser in the event of problems in the holiday destination.

It must be remembered that in practice tour oranisers will either seek to encourage consumers to use the small claims procedure in the District Court up to £500 or to use the arbitration scheme organised by the Irish Branch of The Chartered Institute of Arbitrators on behalf of tour organisers.[20]

Effects of Strict Liability

The imposition of the strict liability of section 20 has its historical foundations in the 1970 Brussels Convention on International Travel Contracts (CCV) which imposed liability for the non-performance of the tour operator's duties even when non-performance depends on his employees.[21] The CCV also imposed liability for the damage suffered by the consumer because of the non-performance of the service, even for services that should have been performed by third parties chosen by the organiser.

It is fair to say that section 20 does impose strict liability in the true sense for the failures of or non-performance of the package or services on the tour organiser.[22] It is framed in a way that presumes fault by the organiser subject to the positive defences which can be pleaded on his behalf, but those defences also reflect an element of the concept of fault liability which is most common in the common law jurisdictions with regard to negligence. These positive defences invariably relate to the inability to foresee or the lack of control over certain other third parties or events which cause the failure or non-performance of the service in question. These positive defences can be criticised, in so far as the wording is less than totally consistent. For example, a failure cannot be unforeseeable or be unavoidable and an event cannot be forestalled.[23]

It should be noted that with relation to the tour organiser's position and the retailer's position, the strict liability under section 20 only applies to the tour organiser, regardless of the fact that the obligations under the contract are to be provided by the retailer or some other supplier. Therefore, one could only rely on section 20 against the tour organiser and not against the retailer or any other supplier. However, as is provided for in section 20, all the other

---

20. See Chapter 11 below.
21. See Article 12, reproduced in *International Legal Materials* (1970), Vol. 9, p. 702.
22. See Article 5(2) of the Directive.
23. See Zunarelli, "Package Travel Contracts: Remarks on the EC Legislation" in *Fordham Int. Law Journal* (1994) p. 499.

usual rights of action will still subsist against the retailer or the other suppliers of services so they can be sued as well. Consequently, one can sue the tour organiser under section 20, but would have to rely on either some other failure under the Act against the retailer and/or the usual common law rights of breach of contract, misrepresentation and negligence etc. It has been argued whether such liability should be joint and several or alternative. For example, the fact that the same obligation is imposed on both the retailer and the organiser to provide prompt assistance in the event of a consumer getting into difficulty indicates such liability should be joint and several.[24]

With regard to the limitation of the liability of the organiser it is important to note that, despite all the international conventions to which reference is made, which can also apply under section 20, there is no mention of the CCV which specifically governed the uniform application in this area prior to the adoption of the Directive and has specific limitations on liability referred to therein. So reference cannot be made to the most uniform application of limitation prior to the Directive for the purpose of limiting a tour organiser's liability. It can be seen that the strict liability under section 20 in the Act is really a form of qualified strict liability, by which tour organiser's liability has extended beyond the usual fault liability, but with significant exceptions to full, strict liability.

It can be suggested that the exceptions in section 20(2) to the strict liability are either exclusive or merely examples of the usual type of situation whereby no liability will result. However, it seems to be a better interpretation that they are purely an exclusive list of situations where no liability will result by virtue of the use of the word "because".[25] It can also be said that the defence fault caused by the consumer's acts would on its face, be unnecessary to include due to the simple fact that under the ordinary rules of causation, such liability would not attach, because the cause of whatever damage would be the consumer and not any failure on behalf of the tour organiser.[26] Thus, in *Hartley v. Intasun Holidays Ltd*[27] it was held that if the consumer received inferior accommodation, which was not in accordance with the contract at common law but was part of alternative arrangements made by the tour organiser, as a result of the consumer arriving a day after the intended departure date, due to his confusion (particularly where the then standard trading conditions allowed such a change in departure date to incur 100 per cent cancellation charges) the organiser was under no obligation make alternative arrangements for the consumer.

There are also other issues with regard to the defences, for example, with regard to failures attributable to an unconnected third party. Would that

---

24. See s. 20(7), Article 6 of the Directive and Zunarelli, *ibid.*, pp. 500-502.
25. See for example, Grant & Mason, *op. cit.*, pp. 1-15.
26. See for example, *Hartley v. Intasun* [1987] C.L.Y. 1149.
27. [1987] C.L.Y. 1149.

defence include, for example, an employee or more commonly, or would it include the results of an air traffic controllers' strike which can often cause massive disruption? It clearly can be said that an employee would normally impose liability on his employer by virtue of vicarious liability doctrine. Therefore, it is unlikely that the tour organiser would escape liability by virtue of a failure on behalf of an employee in ordinary circumstances, except perhaps in a case of a disaffected employee acting outside the scope of his employment.[28]

The reverse is also true, where the failure is due to an unconnected third party but it also has to be unforeseeable or unavoidable. Hence, if the hotel was booked in the middle of a city which was frequented by criminals and drug addicts, with a consumer being injured as a result of this by virtue of the acts of one of them, it was still an event caused by an unconnected third party. However, it would be difficult to say that it was foreseeable in the context of that situation.

It has been suggested that the width of the three positive defences in section 20 dilutes too much the theoretical strict liability under the section, so as to ensure that they encompass just about all that could go wrong with the package which was not the fault of the organiser or supplier. However, it should be pointed out that the interpretation and application of these defences would undoubtedly be viewed in a strict sense by the courts in order to preserve the consumer protection rationale of both the Directive and the Act. Therefore, they would be likely to be interpreted in a strict way against the interests of the tour organiser and in favour of the consumer and his ability to recover damages.

It is also to be noted that liability will only occur where the failure results in a failure of an obligation under the contract. So, if an event occurs which causes injury or damage and does not breach an obligation on the contract in terms of accommodation or provision of services etc., then section 20 strict liability would not apply. The only remedy for the consumer in those circumstances would be the ordinary common law remedy of negligence and breach of contract etc. However, it can be pointed out that because of the defences, it would only apply to events which are unforeseeable or are unavoidable, which again would limit the scope of these defences to the tour organiser. It is possible therefore, that events which relate not directly to the holiday contract, but in more general terms relate to the safety of the resort or the health standards employed in the resort with regard to sanitary provision etc., which caused damage or injury to the consumer, then it is still possible that section 20 would apply and the defences would not be applicable and so such events would be unforeseeable and the liability would be avoided.[29]

---

28. See generally, McMahon & Binchy, *op. cit.*, pp. 753-760.
29. See *Davey v. Cosmos* [1989] C.L.Y. 2561.

In *Davey v. Cosmos*,[30] the consumers were allowed to recover by virtue of illness caused by raw sewage being pumped into the sea at the resort, because it was held that it was an implied term in the contract and a common law duty of care, that the tour organiser should take all reasonable steps to avoid exposing the customers to any significant risk of danger or injury to their health. Therefore, the tour organiser should have warned the plaintiff of the danger prior to departure. This reasoning would also apply, for example, to the duty the disclose or warn of criminal dangers in terms of muggings etc., in large, international cities. This duty of disclosure which could be an implied term the breach of which, could see liability arise under section 20 because such an event would not be unforeseeable or avoidable even though it was done by an unconnected third party.[31]

Significant Failure of Performance after the Start of the Package

The other significant imposition of civil liability on a tour organiser, as well as section 20, is set out in section 19 that relates to the significant failure of performance after the start of the package. This relates to the stage prior to when section 20 covering defective performance or inadequate proper performance is in issue, as it relates to the situation where a significant proportion of the services contracted for are not provided for or the organiser becomes aware that a significant proportion of the services cannot be provided.[32] Where this occurs, section 19 imposes two implied terms on the tour organiser in that situation. The first is section 19(2) whereby it is implied that the organiser shall make suitable alternative arrangements at no extra cost to the consumer for the continuation of the package and shall compensate the consumer for any difference between the services to be supplied on the contract and those actually supplied. It would appear under this section that the consumer is under an obligation to accept whatever arrangements are made by the tour organiser, if they are reasonable alternatives to those contracted for. The reasonableness of the alternative would be naturally a matter of fact to be decided in each particular case.

The other implied term in this situation is section 19(3), whereby if it is impossible to make the necessary alternative arrangements or either the alternative arrangements are not accepted by the consumer on reasonable grounds, the organiser will, where homeward transport arrangements are a term of the contract, provide the consumer at no extra cost with equivalent transport back to the place of departure or to another place to which the consumer has agreed. He shall also compensate the consumer for the proportion of services not

---

30. [1989] C.L.Y. 2561.
31. See generally with regard to the duty to disclose, Dickerson, "Dangerous Holiday Destinations – A Duty to Disclose" [1995] T.L.J. 11.
32. Section 19(1).

supplied. This imposes the extra obligation on the tour organiser of repatriation of the consumer either when the holiday cannot be continued by virtue of
the lack of an alternative arrangement or when the alternative arrangements
are made they are not reasonable and so the consumer rejects them, and so
naturally, should be allowed to be repatriated as soon as possible at no extra
cost.

It must be remembered that if the consumer has a reasonable alternative
with which to continue the holiday, then he cannot rely on the implied term in
section 19(3) for repatriation. Therefore, if the holidaymaker is homesick or
merely unsatisfied for other reasons, that will not permit him to avail of the
obligation to be repatriated under the section. This is reasonable insofar as
repatriation with regard to charter flights are inevitably difficult, since they
are naturally only chartered on a set basis either weekly or even fortnightly for
smaller tour operators. Thus, it would be difficult and expensive for an alternative flight to be arranged outside the normal charter flight schedules.

The other natural and important obligation concerns compensation, so
that if a holiday cannot be completed or the services which have been contracted cannot be provided, then naturally compensation should arise. This
would be either the balance of the purchase price or a total refund to be paid
to the consumer.

An important point arises with regard to this implied term as neither the
Act or the Directive requires that notice be given to the consumer in the contract, brochures or otherwise of these implied terms. Therefore, though they
are implied terms, it would be difficult for the consumer to be aware of them,
since they are usually not included in the booking conditions.[33] This problem
arises with most of the implied terms under the Act and therefore their use
and effectiveness is lessened by virtue of the fact that they may only come to
the attention of the consumer when he seeks legal or other advice with regard
to his position after the event or after the failure to provide certain services
under the package. Although, in practice, the standard booking conditions do
reflect the implied terms under the Act, insofar as the obligations of the tour
organiser are concerned at least. It would undoubtedly have improved the
consumer's position, if such conditions were obliged to be included in either
the brochures or the booking conditions, so that in the event of this situation
arising, the consumer himself would be fully aware of all his rights under the
Act and therefore, could ameliorate his position considerably. As has been
pointed out, it is often the case that tour organisers will rely and emphasise the
exclusion clauses in order to limit the efficacy of these terms and in terms of
making the consumer aware of them.[34]

It should also be noted that in section 19(1) these terms either apply when
a significant portion of the services contracted for are not provided or if the

---

33. See Clark, *I.C.L.S.A.* (1995) p. 1718.
34. *Ibid.*, p. 1718.

tour organiser becomes aware that they cannot be provided. Thus, it only will apply if the tour organiser becomes aware of the failure of the performance. This should be read in the light of the fact that it is the standard condition that consumers bear the onus of notifying the tour organiser of any failure or any complaints they may have and only when that is done,[35] would the tour organiser become aware under section 19(1) of the failure to provide a certain proportion of the services.

Further remedies, for which provision is made under the Act above and beyond mere compensation in damages, are also provided for under section 19. All relief referred to in section 19 whereby the consumer has a right to an alternative package if the tour organiser becomes aware that a significant proportion of the services contracted for cannot be provided or such services are not provided. Under section 18 where the organiser significantly alters essential terms of the contract the consumer also has a right to take a replacement package of equivalent or superior quality.

Issues of Interpretation

It has been pointed out,[36] that there is a difficulty with regard to the scope of what an essential term is for the purposes of these two sections, as obviously the essential terms required to be in the brochure under section 14 will be essential. However, it can depend on the particular circumstances and nature of the holiday in question that there may be other agreed essential terms in the package holiday. For example, if it was on an unaccompanied singles holiday that would be in itself an essential term in the contract.

The other qualitative interpretation that needs to be looked at in this context is that of what a significant alteration of the essential term is. It has been the practice for some time that in standard booking conditions, tour organisers classify changes to details such as airlines, hotels, resorts, etc., as either minor or major changes by means of lists in the booking conditions to which a consumer is bound. However, despite these pre-emptive qualitative definitions of whether it is a minor or major change in any booking conditions, it naturally follows that again, depending on the circumstances of the holiday, a particular alteration of a particular service or facility, which was due to be offered in the package, may in the circumstances of any particular case be considered to be a significant alteration above and beyond the classification of the tour organiser in their booking conditions.

The other point of definition concerns section 18(1)(a) as it only applies where the organiser is compelled to alter significantly an essential term of the contract. The other point of interpretation with regard to section 18(1)(a) is with regard to the use of the word 'compel', as the right of a consumer to an

---

35. As imposed by ss. 14(1) and 14(2).
36. See Grant & Mason, *op. cit.*, p. 255 *et seq.*

alternative package only applies where the organiser is 'compelled' to alter significantly an essential term of the contract. The use of the word 'compel' naturally implies compulsion and necessity on behalf of the tour organiser in effecting this change and hence, it narrows the scope of the applicable circumstances where a consumer has a right to an alternative package. Therefore, the consequence for the tour organiser is that he can then, legitimately and without having to provide an alternative package, alter terms of the contract in a wider range of situations. However it should be noted that these rights only apply to significant alterations of essential terms by virtue of section 18(2)(a), which result in the consumer withdrawing from the contract or it leads the tour organiser to cancel the package before departure. They will only not apply if the cancellation is due to the fault of the consumer.

The implementation of the Directive in the UK, Package Travel Regulations in 1992 Regulation 12, use the word 'constrained' to alter the essential terms of the contract.[37] Therefore, in the UK a tour organiser is subject to a wider duty, as 'constrain' implies that a wider range of circumstances will trigger this requirement to provide an alternative package where there is a significant alteration in the essential terms of the contract. With regard to section 18(2) and the obligation to offer alternative packages on cancellation by the tour organiser, this has long reflected the traditional practice of tour organisers in their standard booking conditions.

With regard to section 19 and the significant failure of performance after the start of the package, the issues of interpretation that arise with regard to this are similar to those under section 18. Firstly, with regard to what is a significant failure of a performance of a service of the contract. Obviously, if the combination of the elements of the package was not provided in accordance with the contract, that would be a significant failure. Otherwise, the degree of failure depending on the service or facilities not provided is very much a matter of degree depending on the circumstances of the case. With regard to the arrangement of the suitable alternative arrangements, it can be said that as long as it is suitable to the consumer, the fact that the alternative arrangement may be more expensive than the original package should not prevent it being implemented, as it would not be impossible to do so, but only more expensive for the tour organiser so to do. Therefore, on a purposive of interpretation it should be allowed for the consumer to take a suitable, more expensive alternative arrangement, if it was possible to do so.[38]

The other issue of interpretation that arises in section 18(2) concerns the value of the equivalent package, as being either equivalent or superior quality,

---

37. Grant & Mason, *op. cit.*, p. 256.
38. *Ibid.* p. 261 *et seq.* and with regard to examples of suitable alternative arrangements under s. 19, see the English cases of *Harvey v. Tracks Travel* [1984] C.L.Y. 1006; *Rhodes v. Sun Spot Tours* [1983] C.L.Y. 984 and *Wheelhouse v. CIT* [1994] 10 C.L.Y. 128.

which naturally will give rise to the issue of what alternative is either superior or equivalent. For example, a 3-star hotel must be replaced by an equivalent 3-star hotel or a 4-star hotel. It is unclear from the Act or the Directive whether a consumer is offered and takes a superior quality replacement, whether the difference in price between the original price and this superior replacement will have to be borne by the consumer. However, it can be implied from section 18(2)(b)(ii) that since the consumer has a right to take a lower quality package and recover the difference in price between that and the original package then the reverse should also apply. Thus, if a superior quality package is offered and accepted, the difference in value should not be borne by the consumer but by the tour organiser. If these real remedies of substitution of a package are not accepted by the consumer, then he is entitled to damages and compensation by the organiser for the non-performance of the contract.[39] However, it is unclear again as to what measure of damage should be included in this, but it would be the general breach of contract rules and damages[40] subject to the two express defences in sections 18(2)(c)(i) and 18(2)(c)(ii) namely, if it is cancelled because of lack of numbers or cancelled by virtue of *force majeure*.

CONCLUSION

It could be said that the imposition of strict liability is a major improvement on behalf of the consumer, which imposes an infinitely higher standard of liability on tour organisers and their negligence. It remains to be seen how strict the courts will be in applying the defences and how effective they will be in preventing liability being imposed under section 20 in the future. It is to be hoped that they would be interpreted in a strict fashion by virtue of the consumer protection rationale under the Act and therefore, would be weighted fully in favour of the consumer rather than the tour organiser. It is true to say that section 20 and the liability imposed therein is diluted by the fact that amount of liability can be limited, but at least only in terms of property damage and not in terms of personal injury.[41] It will be examined later whether these limitations for liability are as effective as they appear under the section when read in the context of the Unfair Contract Terms Regulations 1995.[42]

---

39. See s. 18(2)(c).
40. See Chapter 7 below.
41. See s. 20(3).
42. See Chapter 11, p. 128 below.

CHAPTER FIVE

Common Law Duties of Tour Operators

At common law, the usual duties of a tour operator in tort are the first to arise, namely that of negligence, to take reasonable care in the provision of the package holiday. Prior to the introduction of the 1995 Act, the common law approach to the liability of a tour operator for a defective performance of the contract was in general narrow.

This is evidenced by the leading English case of *Wall v. Silver Wing Service Arrangements Ltd*[1] which held that in the absence of an express term, the tour operator would be liable for properly selecting independent contractors to provide a service, so that the liability of the tour operator, when a reputable local service provider fails to adequately perform the service, is avoided. This has recently been reapplied in England in the case of *Wilson v. Best Travel*.[2] The basic rationale behind this limited common law duty is the fact that the tour operator has limited powers of supervision and control over contract providers in another jurisdiction who are providing the actually holiday service. However, this causes additional difficulty for the consumer, who is then only left with the remedy of suing in the foreign jurisdiction in tort against that service provider, which would be a very difficult and expensive exercise for most consumers, especially when the loss may be small.

However, since 1995 in the UK, the balance seems to have been redressed in favour of the consumer by virtue of the Privy Council decision in the case of *Wong Mee Wan v. Kwan Kin Travel Services Ltd and Others*.[3] This decision paves the way for the tour operator to be personally liable for the default of independent contractors in the provision of holiday services abroad. The circumstances in this case were that fact that the plaintiff's daughter contracted in Hong Kong for a package holiday in China with the first defendant, the tour operator. A tour guide was employed by the second defendant who supervised an onward tour to a lakeside resort to be provided by the third defendant. As a result of the negligence of the third defendant in allowing an unqualified person to drive the speed boat transporting the tour party, the

---

1. Unreported, UK High Court, 18 November 1981.
2. [1993] 1 All E.R. 353 and see generally Clark, *I.C.L.S.A.* (1995) p. 1719.
3. [1995] 4 All E.R. 745.

plaintiff's daughter was drowned. The Court of Appeal in Hong Kong overturned in the first instance, the decision which had found the first defendant responsible for not taking adequate measures to protect the party while being transported by the speed boat. The Court of Appeal was of the view that tour operators would be under an intolerable burden if held liable for the default of the negligent transport operator in another country for breach of non-contractual duty.

However, the Privy Council reversed this decision relying on a Canadian case of *Craven v. Strand Holidays (Canada) Ltd*[4] which drew a distinction between the tour operator, who contracts with the consumer intending certain primary duties to be undertaken by the tour operator, with cases where the tour operator only puts the consumer into the hands of a competent service provider. In *Craven v. Strand Holidays* the plaintiffs claimed damages for personal injury when a bus in which they were travelling in Colombia overturned due to the negligence of the driver. The driver was not the employee of the defendant, but the bus trip had been arranged as part of a package tour sold by the defendant to the plaintiffs. The Ontario Court of Appeal held that there was no implied term that the plaintiffs would be carried safely (a claim in respect of which would in any event be excluded by the exemption clause in the contract), and that the defendant would be liable only if it had been negligent in the selection of the bus operator. Lacourciere J.A. in *Craven v. Strand Holidays* said:

> If a person agrees to perform some work or services, he cannot escape contractual liability by delegating the performance to another . . . But if the contract is only to provide or arrange for the performance of services then he has fulfilled his contract if he has exercised due care in the selection of a competent contractor. He is not responsible if that contractor is negligent in the performance of the actual work or service, for the performance is not part of his contract.[5]

Lord Slynn in *Wong Mee Wan* was therefore of the view that:

> It is thus clear that the fact that it is known that another person will or may perform the services or part of them does not mean that the contract is one of agency. In each case it has to be asked as a matter of construction into which category the contract falls. This may not always be easy.[6]

The Privy Council was of the view that the central question was whether the

4. [1982] 142 D.L.R. (3d) 31.
5. [1982] 142 D.L.R. (3d) 31 at 36.
6. [1995] 4 All E.R. 745 at 750 *per* Lord Slynn of Hadley.

first defendant was, in reality, doing no more than arranging the tour so that they undertook no liability for any default by those providing the service, or at the most, a liability to take reasonable care in the selection of those who provided the service. On considering the brochure, Lord Slynn said:

> It was clearly always the first defendant's intention that parts of the package tour would be carried out by others and, in particular, in their respective spheres, by the second and third defendants.[7]

The Privy Council therefore concluded that the first defendants were under a contractual duty to perform the services with reasonable care and skill, even if some of those services were to be provided by others. They would point out the limits of the duty in the following terms:

> The plaintiff's claim does not amount to an implied term that her daughter would be reasonably safe. It is a term simply that reasonable skill and care would be used in rendering the services to be provided under the contract. The trip across the lake was clearly not carried out with reasonable skill and care in that no steps were taken to see that the driver of the speedboat was of reasonable competence and experience and the first defendant is liable for such breach of contract as found by the trial judge.[8]

The policy objection that this liability would impose an intolerable burden on tour operators was rejected by virtue of the example of the 90/314 Package Holidays, Package Travel and Package Tours Directive, as follows:

> Their Lordships of course appreciate the desire of the Court of Appeal to avoid imposing a burden which is *'intolerable'* [my emphasis] on package tour operators. It must, however, be borne in mind that the tour operator has the opportunity to seek to protect himself against claims made against him in respect of services performed by others by negotiating suitable contractual terms with those who are to perform those services. He may also provide for insurance cover. He may include an appropriate exemption clause in his contract with the traveller. It also has to be borne in mind, in considering what is 'tolerable' or reasonable between the parties, that a traveller in the position of Miss Ho Shui Yee could have no influence on the terms negotiated by the tour operator with third parties, and if injured by their lack of care would, if having no right against the package tour operator, be obliged to pursue a claim in a foreign country. The difficulty involved in doing so does not need to be elaborated. In considering what is or is not tolerable as

---

7. [1995] 4 All E.R. 745 at 752.
8. [1995] 4 All E.R. 745 at 753-754.

between traveller and tour operator it is of some relevance to note the Package Travel, Package Holidays and Package Tours Regulations 1992, S.I. 1992/3288, made pursuant to Council Directive (EC) 90/314.

In particular, the Privy Council relied on Articles 15(1) and 15(2) of the Directive, as in section 20 of the 1995 Act, with regard to the liability for the improper performance of the contract, and continued:

> There is an obligation under the Regulations for the person providing the package tour to ensure that a bond is entered into in respect of monies paid for services not provided and to provide insurance under which the insurer agrees to indemnify the person who takes or agrees to take the package, or the person on whose behalf the package is being purchased, against the loss of money paid over by them under or in contemplation of contracts in the event of the insolvency of the contractor. These terms do not of course apply to the present contract but they do throw some light on the contention that an unreasonable burden would be imposed if the contract were held to contain a term that reasonable skill and care would be used.[9]

It is important to note that prior to *Wong Mee Wan*,[10] the position resulting from *Wall v. Silver Wing Service Arrangements Ltd*[11] was well established in England. In a string of cases,[12] for example, where a hotel room for a family was invaded by cockroaches for three nights, interrupting sleep, the fumigation of the room affected their clothes for the rest of the holiday, it was held that the duty of the tour operator was to use skill and care in the choice of hotels and to take reasonable care to monitor the state of repair thereafter. Since the evidence was that no cockroaches were found before or after the complaint, the defendant tour operator had taken reasonable steps, and it was not the correct approach to say that the mere existence of the cockroaches meant that they were not able to enjoy the standards of a 4-star hotel.

This theme can also be seen in *Toomey v. Intasun Holidays Ltd*[13] and *Usher v. Intasun Holidays Ltd*.[14] In the latter case the plaintiffs booked their honeymoon with the defendant tour operator, but due to industrial action and technical problems their flight was over a day late arriving in Tenerife, being a bitterly upsetting start to the honeymoon with no information or reassurance from the defendants. It was held that a tour operator is not liable for the acts of

---

9.   [1995] All E.R. 745 at 754.
10. [1995] 4 All E.R. 353.
11. Unreported, UK High Court, 18 November 1981.
12. Including *Gibbons v. Intasun Holidays Ltd* [1988] C.L.Y. 168 and *Kaye v. Intasun Holidays Ltd* [1987] C.L.Y. 1150.
13. [1988] C.L.Y. 1060.
14. [1987] C.L.Y. 418.

a carefully chosen subcontracting airline, as they have no control over the airline. In the alternative, the defendant's exclusion clauses would be effective, as they were not unfair within the meaning of the UK Unfair Contract Terms Act 1977, as the plaintiffs had a large range of tour operators from which to choose. However, the defendant should have done more to reassure the plaintiffs and so to that extent were in breach of contract.

However, there were some notable exceptions such as *Tucker v. OTA*[15] where the consumer booked a family holiday on the basis of direct daytime scheduled flight and a specific 3-star hotel in Majorca. However, the scheduled flight was overbooked, refused an unscheduled night flight, and so lost two days of his holiday. The hotel was also overbooked, requiring the plaintiff to spend two nights in an inadequate apartment. The defendants argued that it was only obliged to use its best endeavours to arrange the flight and hotel was rejected, and damages were awarded since, the contract was to provide the flight and hotel accommodation, and there was no failure to mitigate the consumer's loss as his refusal to take the unscheduled flight was not unreasonable.[16]

For an Irish example of the difficulties of proving negligence against a tour operator under conventional principles, see the case of *Kavanagh v. Falcon Leisure Group (Overseas) Ltd.*[17] In this case, the plaintiff fell on a ramp in the hotel bar while on an all-inclusive holiday in Spain, sustaining a severe ankle injury, caused by the slippery ramp. It was held that the duty of the tour operator is not the same as that of an occupier, as the duty of an occupier in the circumstances was to protect people from unusual danger, and the slippery ramp was an unusual danger. In contrast, the duty of the tour operator did not extend to the everyday management and maintenance or regular supervision of the hotel, and so the plaintiff's claim was dismissed.

The limitations of suing in negligence has been graphically illustrated by a recent decision of *McKenna v. Best Travel Ltd and Others*.[18] This case involved a consumer who booked a package holiday in Cyprus via the first defendant. She also booked a mini-cruise to Egypt, which could only be booked in Cyprus. For the purpose of the cruise, she had to undergo a coach tour in Israel, which includes both Jerusalem and Bethlehem. While on such a coach, close to Bethlehem, a stone was thrown through the window striking the plaintiff on the mouth, as a result of which she sustained serious injury. Therefore, she sued for personal injuries against the tour operator and the travel agent in contract and in tort. The High Court found in favour of her in the terms of negligence, but dismissed her claim on the breach of contract. The issue on

15. [1986] C.L.Y. 383.
16. See also *Cooke v. Spanish Holiday Tours* as reported in *The Times*, 6 February 1960 and Grant & Mason, *Holiday Law* (1996) p. 113.
17. [1995] I.L.T. 211. Circuit Court *ex tempore* decision of Smith J., 20 July 1994, as noted by Skeffington in "Liability of Tour Operators for Injury Abroad".
18. Unreported, Supreme Court, 18 November 1997.

appeal was whether or not a warning should have been given to the plaintiff concerning the state of unrest, which then existed in and around Bethlehem. Barron J. pointed out:

> . . . that although the ultimate responsibility for the safety of tourists must lie with the tour operator, the travel agent must also familiarise itself with the conditions likely to be met by such person Although the mini-cruse was not booked through the second-named defendant, the travel agent was aware that the plaintiff and her sister intended to travel on it. In these circumstances, its duty of care was the same as if the tour had been booked through it.[19]

The duty of care of the tour operator was reiterated by Barron J. in fairly broad terms, where he held:

> The duty of care extends to all matters concerning the safety, well-being and comfort of the tourist which by the nature of the relationship between the tourists and those providing the service would or should be known to the latter but not to the former.[20]

He then, importantly, went on to point out the standard of knowledge which should be required by both the tour operator and of the tourists. Firstly, with regard to those in the travel industry, the level of knowledge must be attributable to the person on the spot providing the service, not merely the organiser or travel agent based in Ireland upon that level of knowledge. With regard to the tourists, it must the level of knowledge of someone who, having decided to go on holiday to a particular country, might be expected to have gained information from advertisements or news items relating thereto.

It seemed to be the case that there were no particular warnings with regard to unrest in the area either in the travel industry generally or in Ireland at the time. However, it was pointed out that the bus company would make enquiries daily as to whether it was safe to run the service. Hence, it was argued that this was an indication that there should be a warning as to the dangers involved in travelling in the area at the time. However, that was rejected as being too broad a proposition, as there are many dangers in ordinary day to day living as well as foreign travel. Therefore, to impose such a duty to warn of such otherwise minimal risks would be to make life practically impossible, both for those providing the services and those accepting them.

Mr Justice Barron concluded that in the circumstances there should be a duty to warn on behalf of the tour operator, as he pointed out:

---

19. Unreported, Supreme Court, 18 November 1997 at p. 9.
20. *Ibid.* at p. 11.

The defendants in this case were not insurers that nothing would happen to injure the plaintiff. Their obligation stops at taking all reasonable steps to ensure the safety and well-being of their customer. The fact of unrest in certain parts of Israel at the material time was well known and the tour operator is entitled to assume such knowledge on the part of its customers. What it is not entitled to assume is knowledge on the part of its customers in its capacity as a tour operator. The test is when a reasonable prudent tour operator exercising reasonable care considers it necessary to inform those travelling with it.

Therefore, he concluded that, since on the evidence there was no high risk of danger to tourists in Bethlehem apart from one incident involving a tourist nine months previously, it did not in the circumstances warrant any particular knowledge of danger which must be passed on to a tourist who must be presumed to be aware of the general conditions in the area in which they were travelling. Therefore, it can be seen that despite the Package Travel Directive, the liability in negligence is still weighted heavily in favour of the tour operator in terms of the width of the duty of care owed to consumers with regard to the conditions in a foreign country. Although it is fair to say that the duty to warn is a duty which is slightly more broad in its terms of the ordinary duty to provide reasonable care in the actual provision of the services in a physical sense.

There is also another related issue with regard to the loss or damage to luggage or property particularly in transit. It can be argued, on behalf of the consumer, that the tour operator's independent subcontractors are bailees of the luggage with an obligation of safe-keeping. This was considered in *Gibbons v. Intasun Holidays Ltd*[21] where luggage was lost in transit and the claim for the loss was on the basis of bailment. It was held that the defendant tour operator was not a bailee of the cases, since it employed independent subcontractors of the airline's local agency, who further subcontracted the transfer coaches. This was despite the fact that the tour operator's representative gave instructions to the coach driver and worked with him in the transfer of the luggage.

It ought also to be noted that, naturally, the breach of a duty of care and negligence is also supplemented by an action in contract for the breach of the duty, which is a breach of a specific duty as provided for in the contract and which gives rise to a reasonably foreseeable damage as a result. The defence that can succeed in such breach of contract cases is that of the tour operator using all reasonable endeavours to rectify the breach, as inserted in the booking conditions. This is especially if the breach (such as overbooking) is due to the fault of the hotel then it maybe found to be no breach of contract on behalf

---

21. [1988] C.L.Y 168.

of the tour operator.[22] This is much closer to the strict liability of the tour organiser under the 1995 Act. However, there would still be an issue as to causation and more importantly, the resulting losses consequential upon the breach. The issue would be whether the losses would be recoverable or be too remote as a result of the breach, as either not being considered as fairly and reasonably arising naturally from the breach in the usual course of things or that such loss was in the contemplation of the both parties at the time the contract was made.[23]

The other major liability at common law is by virtue of misrepresentation[24] whereby, particularly in the pre-contract stage and by virtue of advertisements and brochure statements, a consumer could be misled by reliance upon a particular representation which proved to be untrue, thus leading to loss, unless the tour operator could prove that he had reasonable grounds for making that representation.[25] This could undoubtedly be the case where he is relying on a source of knowledge in the holiday destination of which he has no direct knowledge.

Therefore, this basic claim of misrepresentation is one of negligent misrepresentation. If there was negligent misrepresentation, or even if there could be proved to be fraudulent misrepresentation, it would be infinitely be more difficult, as one has to prove that there is a false representation which has been made knowingly, or without belief in its truth or recklessly or carelessly whether to be true or false.[26] It would, therefore, be much more difficult to prove fraudulent misrepresentation on behalf of a tour operator with regard to pre-contract statements or statements in a brochure unless there was clear knowledge or proof that he did not believe in its truth or was reckless as to whether it was true or false.

The basic remedy would firstly be one of damages, if it was after provision of the contract, for the law is separate both for personal injury and any consequential and other economic loss which may result. Alternatively, if the misrepresentation was prior to departure and was realised by the consumer then he would be able to rescind the contract and be returned to the position to where he was before the contract was made. This would mean that, naturally, any balance or monies due would be repaid by the tour operator.

It should be noted that it is important in terms of pleading misrepresentation that the terms relied on were actually part of the contract. Firstly, they should be part of the written contract and if not, and were merely oral statements that they can be proved by evidence. Secondly, and more importantly,

---

22. See for example, *Toomey v. Intasun Holidays Ltd* [1988] C.L.Y. 1060.
23. See *Hadley v. Baxendale* [1854] 9 Ex. 341 at 354-355 per Alderson B. and generally, Clark, *Contract Law in Ireland* (3rd edn, 1992) Chapter 19; Chitty, *On Contracts* (27th edn, 1994) Vol. 1, Chapter 6 and, in particular, see Chapter 7 below.
24. See Chapter 3, above, pp. 48–50.
25. See for example, *Wilson v. Pegasus Holidays* [1988] C.L.Y. 1059.
26. See *Derry v. Peek* [1889] 14 A.C. 337 per Lord Herschell.

that they should not be considered to be mere puffs for the purposes of advertising the services involved which have been consistently held as not to be a term of the contract, breach of which would give rise to any remedy in law.[27]

---

27. See generally, Clark, *Contract Law in Ireland* (3rd edn, 1992) pp. 229-234.

CHAPTER SIX

Jurisdiction for Consumer Claims under the 1995 Act and at Common Law

It must be remembered that although direct and strict liability is imposed on the tour organiser by virtue of section 20 of the 1995 Act, the Act still does not govern the determination of jurisdiction for such claims. Therefore, the rules on jurisdiction under the Brussels Convention on the Recognition and Enforecment of Judgments 1968 with regard to the Member States of the EU, the traditional conflict of laws rules[1] (where the place of destination is not a Member State of the EU) still apply for both the claims under the statutory liability for the Act and for the ordinary claims in tort and contract at common law.

COMMON LAW

The common law rules as to jurisdiction in relation to contracts are that, where a defendant is within this jurisdiction and can be served personally with an originating summons, that in itself will deem jurisdiction on the Irish courts simply by virtue of the personal service of the summons on the defendant who happens to be physically present within the jurisdiction at that time.[2] Otherwise, at common law where the defendant service provider is not domiciled within the contracting state of the Brussels Convention, namely is not an EU resident, then the only means by which a consumer plaintiff can assume the jurisdiction of the Irish courts is by virtue of the original procedure under Order 11 of the Rules of the Superior Courts 1986 as amended. This, in relation to contract, will allow service out of the jurisdiction on a foreign defendant when the action is one brought to enforce a contract or to recover damages or other relief for and in respect of the breach of contract where are of the following three conditions is fulfilled.

---

1. See generally Binchy, *Irish Conflict of Laws* (1988) p. 123 *et seq.* and Order 11 of the Rules of the Superior Courts 1986 as amended.
2. See Binchy, *op. cit.* p. 124.

1. Firstly, that the contract was made within the jurisdiction. This on its face would be the most normal ground for such a jurisdiction under the common law rules, as the contract with an Irish consumer and a foreign, non-EU package service provider would most likely be concluded within this jurisdiction either by the signing and returning of the booking form as in a telephone/credit card transaction or by virtue of the signing of the contract in the presence of an agent on behalf of the foreign national.[3]

2. The second condition, which could be fulfilled for the purpose of service outside the jurisdiction in terms of breach of contract, is where the contract was made by or through an agent trading or residing within the jurisdiction on behalf of a principal trading or residing out of the jurisdiction. Hence, if the terms of the contract of the package holiday were concluded by virtue of a travel agent resident here on behalf of a non-EU holiday package provider then that in itself would be sufficient to ground jurisdiction under Order 11 and allow a summons to be issued outside the jurisdiction for the purpose of granting the Irish courts jurisdiciton.

3. The final condition which may be fulfilled under this head of Order 11 is that the contract is, by its terms or by implication, to be governed by Irish law. This is by its nature, a question of interpretation of the contract as to whether there is either an express or implicit choice of Irish law to determine the rights and obligations arising from the contract. Hence if it was Irish law that should be applicable it should be the Irish courts which are in the best position to apply and interpret Irish law in the circumstances of any one case.[4]

The final heading for the purpose of the contract jurisdiction under Order 11, rule 1 is with regard to a breach of the contract being committed within the jurisdiction, even though such a breach was preceded or accompanied by a breach out of the jurisdiction, which rendered impossible the performance of part of the contract which ought to have been performed within the jurisdiction. This means that regardless of whether the contract has been frustrated or repudiated by virtue of a breach outside the jurisdiction, as long as there is a breach of contract within the jurisdiction, that in itself would be sufficient to allow the Irish courts to have seisin of the matter.[5]

With regard to the rules of founding jurisdiction in common law for tort, the basic rule required for service out of jurisdiction under Order 11, rule 1 is that the action is founded on the tort committed within the jurisdiction. This, on its face, would obviously apply to torts causing loss or damage occurring within the jurisdiction. However, in the package holiday context the tort is

---

3. See generally, Binchy, *op. cit.* pp. 139-142.
4. *Ibid.* pp. 142-143.
5. *Ibid.* pp. 144-147.

invariably going to occur outside the home jurisdiction either in transit or in the place of destination whereby the loss or damage is caused. So, on the face of it, jurisdiction for torts committed in the package holiday context which inevitably are committed in the place of destination of the holiday will invariably not be within this head of Order 11 to found jurisdiction for the Irish courts.[6]

The important difference that the imposition of this direct liability makes is that a consumer can sue a tour organiser directly for the non-performance, or the improper performance, of the provision of the services of the holiday contract, even if the services are being provided by a service provider in the holiday destination, such as a person running a hotel or accommodation complex etc. The service provider is in the nature of a subcontractor to the actual tour organiser who is resident in this jurisdiction, so providing a direct cause of action against the tour organiser which previously did not exist.

The previous position without this direct cause of action against a tour organiser, was that the only cause of action in basic contract and tort was against the foreign service provider under the subcontract. Hence, this would be normally in the jurisdiction where the tort occurred or where the defendant service provider was domiciled. In either of these cases, the jurisdiction would be the actual destination of the holiday. This naturally would pose difficulties in practical and legal terms for an ordinary consumer trying to proceed with a foreign claim in a foreign jurisdiction and so, it rarely happened. Naturally, there are no jurisdictional problems with regard to an Irish package holiday taking place in this jurisdiction, but only with regard to a foreign holiday. It is on this point of the direct liability being imposed on the tour organiser resulting in the basis of jurisdiction being that of Ireland, that is a significant improvement for the consumer.

THE BRUSSELS CONVENTION ON THE JURISDICTION OF COURTS AND THE ENFORCEMENT OF JUDGMENTS 1968

The primary rule of jurisdiction as applicable in this context is that of under Article 2 of the Brussels Convention,[7] where a person who is domiciled in the contracting State shall, whatever their nationality, be sued in the courts of that State. Therefore, the first rule is that where a person is sued as a defendant, he must be sued in the courts of his residence under the rules of jurisdiction in force in that State. Once the tour organiser is domiciled in the State, he can be

---

6. See generally, Binchy, *op. cit.* pp. 147-153 and *Grehan v. Medical Incorporated and Valley Pines Association* [1986] I.L.R.M. 627.
7. As implemented by the Jurisdiction of Courts and Enforcement of Judgments (European Communities) Acts 1988 and 1993.

primarily sued within this jurisdiction by virtue of the direct liability imposed under section 20 of the 1995 Act.

CONSUMER CONTRACTS: ARTICLES 13 TO 15

It will be seen that the general jurisdiction provisions under the Brussels Convention, as they may apply to the package holiday context, can be often a problem for a consumer suing either by common law or by virtue of the breach of the terms of the Act. This is often because whatever rule is applied by virtue of the Brussels Convention, the jurisdiction is likely to be the jurisdiction of the defendant, if he is not domiciled in this State or the jurisdiction of the destination of that package holiday where the incident occurred. These difficulties are expressly ameliorated by Articles 13 to 15 of the Convention which deal expressly with the position of the consumer.

Article 13(1) provides that proceedings concerning a contract concluded by a person for a purpose which can be regarded as being outside his trade or profession, hereinafter called 'the consumer', jurisdiction shall be determined by this section, without prejudice to the provisions of Articles 4 and 5 if it is:

13(3) any other contract for the supply of goods or contract for the supply of services, and

  (a) in the State the consumer is domiciled the conclusion of the contract was preceded by a specific invitation addressed to him or by advertising; and

  (b) the consumer took in that State the steps necessary for the conclusion of the contract.

This Article was intended to allow for the extended consumer protection legislation in the Member States, so the Convention would afford the consumer the same protection in the case of transport of frontier contracts as he receives under national legislation.[8] Article 13 is the threshold provision for determining jurisdiction in the case of a consumer that is then dealt with expressly in Article 14. Therefore to have the advantage of Article 14 one has to comply with the requirements of Article 13.

In the package holiday context, this means that it is inevitably a contract for the supply of services and as long as the contract was concluded in the State of the consumer's domicile by virtue of specific invitation addressed to him or by advertising (which advertising would be the normal way by which means package holiday contracts would be concluded in general terms), there would be little difficulty in establishing that requirement for the purposes of Article 13, even if there is no specific invitation addressed to him prior to the conclusion of the contract.

---

8. Byrne, *The European Union and Legano Conventions on Jurisdiction and the Enforcement of Judgments* (1994) p. 100.

The second requirement under Article 13(3) is that the consumer took in that State, i.e. the State of his domicile, the necessary steps for the conclusion of the contract. Thus all requirements for the signing and actual formal conclusion of the contract must have been taken in that State. This again would be the normal course of events for all consumers. The only potential difficulty here is with regard to dealing with non-domiciled companies by virtue of telephone bookings. So that if the telephone booking was made to a company in England and concluded over the telephone, it may be said that the conclusion of the contract and the steps necessary to do that by the consumer were taken in England and not in the State of his domicile. However, this would very much depend on the nature and manner in which such credit card telephone bookings were considered to be formally concluded, as the final conclusion of the contract may be a signing of the actual booking forms by the consumer in his own domicile to be returned to the non-domiciled package provider.[9]

The only limitation of the provision of the special jurisdiction for consumer contracts under Article 13 in the context of package holidays is that Article 13(3) expressly states that the section shall not apply to contracts of transport. Therefore, in relation to purely transport arrangements and incidents of breaches of contract or tort relating to same, either under the 1995 Act or at common law, (for example damage or personal injury caused while travelling on an airline or for any other form of air or sea transport even though that was part of the actual package holiday contract), jurisdiction will not be governed by virtue of the special jurisdiction for consumer contracts under Articles 13 to 15, but the general rules of jurisdiction both in relation to contract in Article 5 and tort will apply. The basis for this exclusion was explained in the preparatory work prior to the adoption of the 1978 provision of the Convention, that transport arrangements in general are subject to other international conventions and agreements, such as the Warsaw Convention.[10] However, this means that the difficulties with regard to jurisdiction both at common law and under claims under the 1995 Act still apply for incidents occurring purely on the use of transport, which is something that should be borne in mind in dealing with such a claim in the context of an overall package holiday contract.[11]

The substance of the jurisdiction rules for consumer contracts lies in Article 14 which provides that a consumer may bring proceedings against the other party to a contract either in the courts of the contracting State in which that party is domiciled or in the courts of the contracting State in which he himself is domiciled. Proceedings may be brought against a consumer by the

---

9.   See generally *Shearson Lehman Hutton Inc. v. TVB* C–89/91; [1993] E.C.R. I–139 and *Brenner and Nuller v. Deanwhitter Reynolds* C–18/93; [1994] E.C.R. I–4275.
10. See Chapter 8 below.
11. See Byrne, *op. cit.* p. 106.

other party to the contract only in a court of the contracting State in which the consumer is domiciled. These provisions shall not affect the right to bring a counter-claim in the court in which in accordance with Article 14, the provisional claim is pending.

Therefore, it can be seen the consumer has the option of either suing in his own home jurisdiction or in the jurisdiction of the defendant package provider. This naturally means that this discretion for the consumer is inevitably exercised by means of suing the defendant in the consumer's own home jurisdiction for the purposes of speed, efficiency and general convenience on behalf of the consumer. This avoids any jurisdictional difficulties caused by reliance on the general rules and provisions of the Brussels Convention which often would lead to jurisdiction only being founded in the foreign jurisdiction of the place of destination. Therefore, by virtue of Article 14, the consumer has the right always to sue in his home jurisdiction for any breach of contract or tort committed against him by virtue of the tour organiser or travel agent.

The other provision of Article 14 which is relevant, provides that if a consumer is in breach of any contract and is sued himself by a service provider or package holiday provider, then he can only be sued in his home jurisdiction where he is domiciled. Therefore, it can be seen that the whole purpose of this provision is to ensure, in the specific context of consumer contracts, that the consumer has the best protection afforded to him and hence, ease of access to his home jurisdiction regardless of where the breach of contract or other tort occurs. This is even in the case where jurisdiction under the general rules of the Convention would be outside his home jurisdiction. The final provision of Article 14 merely states that a counter-claim can still be brought by either the consumer or the service provider in the court in which the original claim is pending in order to avoid separate but related claims in different jurisdictions. The final provision in this section is Article 15 which allows for the alteration of the basic rule under Articles 13 and 14 by an agreement. This agreement can only be valid to alter the basic terms of Article 14 if three conditions are satisfied. These three conditions require that the agreement must:

(a) be entered into after the dispute has arisen;

(b) allow a consumer to bring proceedings in courts other than those indicated in this section; or

(c) be entered into by the consumer and the other party to the contract, both of whom who were at the time of conclusion of the contract domiciled or habitually resident in the same contracting State, and which confers jurisdiction on the courts of that State, provided that such an agreement is not contrary to the law of that State.

Therefore, these three conditions are alternative, not cumulative, and allow an agreement to alter the consumer's discretion as to jurisdiction under Article

14. It cannot be included purely in standard form conditions prior to the contract being concluded, or the dispute arising, unless it would allow the consumer to sue in other jurisdictions as well as those indicated in Article 14 or allow the consumer to confer jurisdiction on the State of domicile of both himself and the other contracting party, as long as that agreement complies with the law of that State.

Such an agreement cannot restrict the jurisdiction available to the consumer, namely his home jurisdiction, under Article 14. It can only do so in principle, if it arises after the dispute has arisen and hence then the consumer can choose whether to change his jurisdiction or, not being aware of the provisions of Article 14, being in an informed position to do so and hence would not be restricted, precluded from relying on the mandatory provisions of Article 14 prior to the conclusion of the contract by agreeing to standard form booking conditions.

The other two conditions allow the preservation of the basic rule of the consumer's home domicile jurisdiction, but allow him specifically to confer jurisdiction on that court if both he and the other service provider are domiciled in that State specifically, which naturally cannot adversely affect the consumer's rights as to jurisdiction under Article 14. The other provision reflects this basic rationale as it allows the consumer still to sue in his home jurisdiction, as under Article 14, but allows jurisdiction to be conferred on other courts for the purpose of instituting proceedings. This would, naturally, be to the benefit of a consumer in that circumstance, as he would have a greater choice of jurisdiction and if the jurisdiction chosen was more beneficial than his home jurisdiction, then that allows that choice to be implemented by virtue of an agreement under Article 15. The important provision with regard to Article 15 that, as with all agreements on jurisdiction, the formal evidential requirements of Article 17 must be complied with.[12]

TORT

If a plaintiff was suing the tour organiser in tort on the ordinary common law principles of negligence for loss or injury that occurred while present in the location of the holiday (namely in some foreign jurisdiction), Article 5(3) of the Brussels Convention provides that in matters relating to tort,[13] delict or quasi-delict, jurisdiction is in the courts of the place where the harmful event occurred.[14] This allows the plaintiff to sue in the place where the harmful

---

12. Namely that it is in writing or evidenced in writing. Thus an oral agreement would not be sufficient. See generally with regard to Article 17, Byrne, *op. cit.* p. 126 *et seq.*
13. Aside from the consumer jurisdiction in Articles 14 and 15.
14. For a recent consideration of this issue in the package holiday context, see *McGee v. JWT Ltd* unreported, High Court, 27 March 1998, per O'Sullivan J.

event occurred, as opposed to the general rule under Article 2 of the Convention that the defendant is entitled to be sued in the courts of his domicile which, for the purposes of a package holiday contract, may often be the domicile of a non-resident corporation. In principle, under Article 2, the package holiday provider would only be sued in the courts of his jurisdiction and not in the courts of the plaintiff's home jurisdiction.

This naturally has the effect that, for the purpose of a consumer suing in negligence as opposed to breach of contract under the Act, jurisdiction in principle would lie firstly, with the courts of the defendant's domicile, which would have the obvious practical consequences of compelling a consumer plaintiff to sue in a foreign jurisdiction with foreign law and possibly a foreign language which would be beyond the cost and means of most plaintiffs especially where the loss incurred is small.

Therefore, Article 5(3) relating to tort is a special jurisdiction, which is an exception to the general rule of Article 2 for the benefit of the plaintiff, to enable them to sue in the place where the harmful event occurred and not the place of the defendant's domicile. The issue with regard to Article 5(3) is what is constituted by the place where the harmful event occurred. The established case law with regard to Article 5(3) provides that the place where the harmful event occurs, for the purposes of tort, can possibly mean two places: firstly, the place of the happening of the event which gives rise to liability in tort and, secondly, the place where that event results in the actual damage occurring to the plaintiff. It is possible that these places may be identical depending on the nature of the tort in question, but they also may be different especially in terms of cross-border, transnational torts, for example in water pollution cases where the act giving rise to liability occurs in one State and the actual loss or damage occurs in another.

It has therefore been held that where these two places are not identical, Article 5(3) allows the plaintiff at his own option to either sue the defendant in the courts of the place where the damage occurred or in the courts of the place of the event which give rise to and is the cause of that damage.[15] The consequence of this, in the context of the package holiday industry, is that where an action in tort is commenced by the plaintiff, on the basis of either personal injury or property damage which occurs in the place of the actual holiday destination, Article 5(3) would allow the plaintiff to sue in that destination. It can be seen that for practical purposes, this may be not of great benefit to a plaintiff, as a plaintiff ultimately wants to sue the courts of his own jurisdiction, namely Ireland, and if the place where the harmful event

---

15. See *Handelswerkerij GJ Bier BV v. Mines de Potasse Dalsace SA* C–21/76; [1976] E.C.R. 1735 at 1748. See also *Grehan v. Medical Incorporated and Valley Pines Association* [1986] I.L.R.M. 672 and *McEhinney v. Williams* [1994] 2 I.R. 215. See generally Byrne, *op. cit.* (1994) pp. 71–79.

occurs for the purpose of personal injury is the place of the destination, then he will only be allowed to sue by virtue of Article 5(3) in the place of the destination, namely the foreign jurisdiction. Secondly, the general rule with regard to Article 2 and the suing of a defendant in his own domicile, may also lead to that same conclusion and suing in a foreign jurisdiction, if the package holiday provider is neither domiciled in this jurisdiction as an individual person or as is more likely, is not incorporated in this jurisdiction.[16]

Therefore, for practical purposes, if the consumer is only relying on the tort of the negligence or some other tort by virtue of the fault of the travel agent or the tour organiser, the key issue for the purpose of trying to claim the Irish courts jurisdiction on behalf of the plaintiff, revolves around the domicile of the defendants. The defendants domicile is governed by the tests laid out in the Fifth Schedule to the 1988 Enforcement of Judgments and Recognition of Judgments Act (for the purpose of trying to ascertain jurisdiction for the purpose of Article 2 of the Convention) to sue the defendant in the courts of his domicile, which for the purposes of an individual, means ordinary residence in the State by virtue of Part I of the Fifth Schedule.

Therefore, for the purpose of suing a travel agent, this would often be easy to establish, as he would ordinarily be resident in this jurisdiction. For the purposes of suing a corporation (in terms of a package holiday provider) by virtue of Part III of the Fifth Schedule, it will be domiciled in the State via its seat in the State, which either means it was incorporated or formed under the law of the State or its central management and control was exercised in the state. Therefore, the company should be incorporated under the Companies Acts 1963 to 1990, which would establish sufficient domicile to be sued in the courts of his own domicile for the purpose of being a defendant under Article 2. Therefore, there would be no great jurisdictional problems in suing an Irish package holiday provider which would invariably be incorporated in the State, but the difficulty would arise with regard to a foreign package holiday provider whose packages were brought by virtue of an agent in this jurisdiction selling to the general public, but who was not incorporated in this State. Therefore, there may often be problems in acquiring a home jurisdiction for the plaintiff in terms of suing in tort for the loss or personal injury incurred while in the place of the holiday destination, which by virtue of Articles 5(2) and 5(3) may often result in the only jurisdiction being available in tort, being that of the defendant's domicile namely, the place of the holiday destination.

---

16. See for the purposes of the rules as to domicile, Part III of the Fifth Schedule to the 1988 Enforcement of Judgments and Recognition of Judgments (European Communities) Act.

CONTRACT

However, the more usual circumstance is of suing in contract for either breach of the express or implied terms under the 1995 Act and, in particular, section 20 with regard to the tour organiser's liability to the consumer for the improper performance of the obligations under the contract, either by virtue of an express term or by virtue of any implied terms in the contract under the Act. The basis for this claim is one in contract and hence, for the purpose of jurisdiction, will be governed by Article 5(1) of the Brussels Convention which provides that a person domiciled in a contracting State may be sued in matters relating to a contract, in the courts of another contracting State for the non-performance of the obligation in question.[17]

The difficulty with this provision is which conflict of laws rules are used to determine what is the place of performance of the obligation in question, as the obligation in question can be obviously determined as obvious to both parties. For example, in the obligation to pay or in a package holiday context, the obligation for the proper performance of the obligations under the contract under section 20.

In the package holiday context, there would seem to be little difficulty with determining the place of performance as, obviously, the place of performance under any type of conflict of law rules will be the place of the holiday destination itself, where the services are to be provided for the fulfilment and performance of the package holiday which has been contracted. However, it must be remembered that it has been held, for the purpose of Article 5(1), that the place of performance of the obligation in question is to be determined in accordance with the rules of conflict of laws of the court before which the matter is brought.[18] This means that the conflict of laws rules, which will determine where the place of performance under contract is, will be determined in accordance with the rules of the court before which the matter is to be heard in that jurisdiction. Presuming that a plaintiff, sued by virtue of Article 5, won in this jurisdiction, it would be the Irish conflict of laws rules that would determine where the place of performance was for the purposes of Article 5, and for the purposes of confirming jurisdiction in Ireland under Article 5(1).

It should be noted that if the parties, for example, in a general package holiday contract, specify where the place of performance is by express agreement, that will also be a factor in determining where the place of performance is, but may not be sufficient to merit it being an exclusive jurisdiction agreement for the purposes of Article 16(1) of the Brussels Convention. Therefore, the place of performance can be specified in the contract, and the court in examining where the place of performance was, would have high regard to

---

17. See generally Byrne, *op. cit.* pp. 43-70.
18. See *Tessili v. Dunlop* [1976] E.C.R. 1473 at 1486.

that agreement and would more than likely follow it.[19] It is also important to note that if, as may often happen in a case, the contract, under which Article 5(1) is alleged to confirm jurisdiction, is disputed by the defendant, that in itself does not destroy the jurisdictional basis under Article 5(1). This is because the jurisdiction of the courts of the place of performance can still be invoked even if the existence of the contract on which the claim is based is in dispute between the parties.[20]

This is the primary basis for jurisdiction of the contractual claim under the Act by virtue of which a contractual claim for breach of section 20(1) of the 1995 Act on the basis of the place of performance of the obligation in question would, more than likely, mean that the plaintiff would have to sue in the place of destination of the holiday where the services were actually provided. This naturally depends on the type of obligation in question. For example, if it is an obligation which could be performed here, such as informational requirements prior to departure, not the actual provision of the services themselves at the place of destination (or the actual provision of services here in terms of departure facilities and arrangements for departure on time), it would likely mean that the plaintiff is still faced with suing in the foreign jurisdiction. However, it must be remembered that the primary claims are brought against travel agents which are by definition invariably domiciled here for the purpose of Article 2 and secondly, that tour organisers again, when they are an Irish-based company, invariably are domiciled here in terms of being incorporated under the laws of the State and hence being domiciled for the purpose of Article 2 in this jurisdiction. Therefore, for the bulk of consumer claims under the Act, there is often no dispute as to jurisdiction when the action is against an Irish tour organiser or Irish travel agent, even though the breach of the contract occurred in the place of destination.

BRANCH OR AGENCY

There are two further possible grounds of jurisdiction upon which a consumer can rely in terms of a breach of contract claim, which may enable him to sue a non-domiciled foreign package provider in this jurisdiction. The first of these is provided for in Article 5(5) of the Brussels Convention with regard to disputes arising out of the operations of a branch, agency or other establishment, in the courts of the place in which the branch agency or other establishment is situated. This allows a plaintiff to sue for disputes arising out of the operations of an agent in the courts where the actual agent is established. This has the benefit in terms of package holiday cases insofar as where a travel agent is

---

19. See *Zelger v. Salanitri* [1980] E.C.R. 89.
20. See *Effer v. Cantner* [1982] E.C.R. 825 at 835 and *Barclays v. Glasgow City Council* [1993] Q.B. 429.

the intermediary between the package holiday provider and the consumer, which is usually the case, then any dispute about the contract can be said to be a dispute arising out of the operations of the agency and hence, would be a good ground for founding jurisdiction in the State.

However, Article 5(5) has been interpreted in a very restrictive manner by the European Court of Justice which indicates that to establish an entity as an agent for the purpose of Article 5(5), it is required that he acts virtually solely on behalf of the parent company and is under the direction and control of that parent company.[21] It has been further held that as a result of this view of Article 5(5) in the character of a branch or agency to come within Article 5(5) an independent commercial agent who works for other firms and is free to arrange his own work among those firms and the undertaking in question is not a branch or agency within the meaning of Article 5(5).[22] Therefore, it is a narrower definition than mere common law agency[23] under which a travel agent would be included, and in reality requires that virtually a subsidiary company or agent is established, which works solely and exclusively for the parent undertaking in the transaction of their business. Therefore, unless the foreign package holiday provider had a subsidiary company acting solely on its behalf in this jurisdiction, as opposed to the ordinary travel agent, then it would be unlikely that a claim under Article 5(5) for jurisdiction in Ireland would succeed. This would often be the case where, for example, a foreign package holiday provider has an actual subsidiary company in this jurisdiction or in terms of subsidiaries of airlines having branch offices in this jurisdiction, that would be sufficient for the purposes of Article 5(5).

EXCLUSIVE JURISDICTION CLAUSES

The next avenue to define jurisdiction in Ireland for the purpose of a package holiday contract is by virtue of an exclusive jurisdiction clause under Article 17 of the Brussels Convention. This provides that where there is an agreement on jurisdiction evidenced in writing, that a specific court is to have jurisdiction in any particular legal relationship and any dispute arising thereafter, then that court shall have exclusive jurisdiction over the dispute. This allows the parties to confer jurisdiction exclusively and specifically on a specific court by virtue of the agreement. This is usually the case in a standard form package holiday contract, as the jurisdiction will often be the jurisdiction in which the contract is entered into which would both be the jurisdiction of the defendant tour organiser or travel agent and the plaintiff consumer.

---

21. See *Somafar v. Fern Gas* [1978] E.C.R. 2183 at 2193 and *Cleveland Museum of Art v. Capricorn International*, as reported in *The Financial Times*, 17 October 1989.
22. See *Blankart v. Trost* [1981] E.C.R. 819 at 830.
23. See Clark, *Contract Law in Ireland* (3rd edn, 1992) p. 388 *et seq.*

It is important to note that where the clause is concluded in a standard form printed conditions of a contract, then it must be obvious that the agreement of both parties to the condition containing the clause has been expressed in writing and therefore general agreement to the conditions and not to that specific clause will be insufficient for the purposes of Article 17.[24] The issue with regard to Article 17 jurisdiction clauses is invariably whether they comply with the formal requirements necessary under Article 17 with regard to being evidenced in writing and have a specific agreement invariably included in the general standard printing conditions.[25]

HOLIDAY HOMES

There is the interesting issue of the letting of holiday property in another jurisdiction, particularly in relation to the letting of villas or apartments as opposed to traditional packages offered in hotels or apartment blocks.

This involves the case of *Hacker v. Euro-Relais*[26] whereby it was held that, for the purpose of grounding jurisdiction in relation to a letting agreement with the defendant (a tour operator of a holiday home in another jurisdiction), Article 16(1) which gives exclusive jurisdiction for disputes arising out of the immovable property to the courts where that immovable property is situated, did not apply on the basis that such lettings were different to those originally contemplated by the Convention. This was because they were not substantial, long-term lettings and were different to the ordinary tenancy agreements which would usually cover such lettings, as opposed to the short-term travel contracts applicable in this case. This was supported by the fact that the principle object of the agreement was of a different nature, namely for the purpose of a holiday, and not for the purpose of the letting of the property in question. Therefore, a strict interpretation of the provision in the case of *Sanders v. Van Der Putte* was followed.[27] As a result of this decision, Article 16(1)(b) was inserted and amended to provide that, in regard to letting disputes, proceedings which have as their object tenancies of immovable property, include for a temporary private use for a maximum period of six consecutive months the courts of the State in which the defendant is domiciled shall also have jurisdiction provided that the landlord and tenant are natural persons and are domiciled in the same contracting State.

This provides a slight lessening of that strict interpretation of Article 16(1)(a) whereby there is the alternative jurisdiction of the defendant's domicile, namely the landlord's, where is it for temporary private use for a period

---

24. See *Ross v. Houtte* [1984] E.C.R. 2417 at 2436.
25. See generally, Byrne, *op. cit.* pp. 126-144.
26. C–280/90; [1992] E.C.R. 111.
27. C–73/77; [1977] E.C.R. 2383. See generally, Byrne *op. cit.* pp. 114-116.

less than six months which on its face would include most, if not all, package holiday contracts in terms of the letting of apartments or villas for such use and for such short periods. The only difficulty in applying this fully to the package holiday context is the fact that the landlord and tenant must be natural persons whereby it would normally be the case that the landlord of the actual apartment building or villa in a commercial, package holiday context would invariably mostly be an incorporated person. However, it could still apply to small apartments or villas which are hired out by private individuals and in that case the defendant's domicile would be an alternative jurisdiction. There is a further limitation with the requirement that both landlord and tenant must be domiciled in the same contracting State and it is only then that the defendant's domicile is in the alternative choice as well as having a choice of the jurisdiction where the property is situated. This would mean that, for example, if both landlord and tenant were Irish then the Irish courts would have jurisdiction, but if there were a foreign national involved, this amelioration of Article 16(1)(a) would not apply.[28]

APPLICABLE LAW

The other related issue to that of jurisdiction concerns the applicable law. Again, this would normally be covered by virtue of a clause in the standard conditions that Irish law would be the applicable law of the contract and so, the issue as to what the applicable law is, rarely arises. This has been reinforced firstly by virtue of the Directive, as implemented in Irish law, which gives harmonisation with the laws of the other contracting States. The Directive is, in essence, the law which governs the contract and even if the applicable law was other than Irish law, required provisions of directly or by implementing measures, the Directive would still be in effect. Secondly, it is reinforced by virtue of the Rome Convention on the Law Applicable to Contractual Obligations 1980, which is implemented in this jurisdiction by virtue of the Contractual Obligations (Applicable Law) Act 1991. Articles 5(2) and 5(5) of the Rome Convention, as outlined in the First Schedule to the 1991 Act, expressly provide that a consumer in a package holiday contract shall not be deprived of the protection of the mandatory rules of the State of habitual residence, where the contract is concluded by one of three particular methods. These are transnational canvassing and advertising, through an agent in the country of habitual residence for a foreign principal or through cross-border excursion selling. Therefore, the mandatory rules of consumer protection would for an Irish consumer in this instance be the 1995 Act and hence that could not be ousted by any other provision of another applicable law applying to the contract by virtue of Articles 5(2) and 5(5).

---

28. Byrne, *op. cit.* p. 108.

On the face of things, the 1995 Act and the rules contained therein, relating to the protection of the consumer will apply in most circumstances where the three types of methods of conclusion of the contract are provided for in this jurisdiction. Specifically, the most notable conclusion of the contract would be that contained in Articles 13(3)(a) and 13(3)(b) namely, where the conclusion of the contract was preceded by a specific invitation addressed to him or by advertising and he had taken in that country all the steps necessary on his part for the conclusion of the contract and he has his official residence in that country.

Therefore, an Irish consumer who responds to advertising in this jurisdiction and is habitually resident and concludes the contract here will be able to rely on Article 5(2) of the Rome Convention and the 1995 Act even if the applicable law is different to that and does not contain provisions implementing the 1990 Directive. The other way that the consumer can rely on the mandatory rules is simply by virtue of the fact that the other party, namely the package holiday provider or his agent, received the consumer's order in that country (namely, the country of his habitual residence) then again, he cannot be deprived of the protection of the mandatory rules of the 1995 Act. This would be the normal way that a consumer would conclude a contract for the provision of a package holiday in this jurisdiction and would include most, if not all, of package holiday contracts concluded in the State.

Therefore, Article 5(5) expressly provides that the protection under Article 5 does apply to such package holiday contracts, as defined under the Directive namely, as a contract which, for an inclusive price, provides for travel and accommodation. This is on the basis that such packages are invariably concluded and contracted for, entirely in one country even though the package provides for a performance abroad. It is also suggested that this protection could also apply whereby a package holiday is purchased from a foreign package provider and the transportation commences in that foreign country (for example, England) and the rest of the performance is in the State of destination.[29] Therefore, it can be seen that on any reading of the contract or whatever the applicable law is deemed to be by virtue of the rules under the Rome Convention or expressly provided for in the contract that on either reading, the Directive and hence the 1995 Act by virtue of Articles 5(2) and 5(5) of the Rome Convention will inevitably always apply for the protection of the consumer.

---

29. See the Gulliano & Ricard, "Report on the Rome Convention 1980" p. 24 and Clark, *I.C.L.S.A.* (1995) pp. 810-811 and see generally, Byrne, *The Rome Convention on Applicable Law to Contracts* (1998).

CONCLUSION

Jurisdiction is rarely in dispute in the ordinary standard condition package holiday contract, as either jurisdiction is provided for by virtue of an exclusive jurisdiction clause for the Irish courts, or the package holiday provider or travel agent are both domiciled by virtue of being ordinarily resident and incorporated in this jurisdiction and hence, can be sued as their defendants domiciled in Article 5(2) of the Rome Convention supported by the consumer's entitlement to his home jurisdiction under Article 14 of the Brussels Convention. It is only in the more unusual cases that there may be a problem with regard to jurisdiction for a contractual claim, as breach of the express and implied terms both under the contract and by virtue of the 1995 Act, in particular section 20(1). However, it is necessary to be aware of the various potential bases of jurisdiction where jurisdiction is in dispute or the usual of consumer jurisdiction or an exclusive jurisdiction clause or the defendants being domiciled in this State are not available to the plaintiff.

CHAPTER SEVEN

Damages in Contract and Tort

DAMAGES IN TORT

The purpose of damages in tort is to restore the plaintiff (as far as is possible with an award of money) to the position that he would have been in had the tort never been committed. Therefore, the two key elements in establishing liability for loss in tort is that there is causation between the tort of the loss incurred either directly or indirectly and secondly, that the loss was reasonably foreseeable.[1] Therefore, this principle of *restitutio in integrum* is easily ascertained where there is actual pecuniary loss resulting from the tort in question, as in loss of profits or loss of part of the price of the holiday. However, where the loss incurred is non-pecuniary in terms of personal injury, mental distress etc., the compensation can only be notional compensation for the injuries sustained as to what is fair and appropriate in all the circumstances of the case, as actual compensation is not possible.[2]

For the tort of negligence, which is the tort most likely to be an issue in a package holiday context, it is now generally accepted that in principle, the tour organiser is responsible for any type of damage which should have been foreseeable by a reasonable man, as being something of which there was a real risk. This applies even though the risk would only eventuate in very exceptional circumstances or in the most unusual case, unless the risk was so small that the reasonable man would feel justified in neglecting it or brushing it aside as far fetched.[3]

Therefore, in negligence the degree of likelihood relevant to the measure of damages is the same as the degree of likelihood relevant to the existence of a duty of care in the first place.[4] It can be summed up that a plaintiff can recover damages in respect of a foreseeable accident, even though only an accident of that type and not the precise circumstances of the accident were foreseeable, for a non-foreseeable form of a foreseeable type of injury and for

---

1. See generally, McMahon & Binchy, *The Irish Law of Torts* (2nd edn, 1990) p. 769 *et seq.*; Halsbury, *Laws of England* (4th edn) Vol. 12, p. 411 *et seq.*; McGregor *On Damages* (15th edn, 1988) and *The Wagonmound* [1961] A.C. 388.
2. See generally, McMahon & Binchy, *ibid.*, Chapter 44.
3. See Halsbury, *op. cit.* Vol. 12, para. 1139 and *The Wagonmound* [1961] A.C. 388 at 640 *et seq.*
4. See *The Wagonmound* [1961] A.C. 388 at 424-425.

unforeseeable consequences of a foreseeable type of injury.[5] Therefore, the plaintiff can only recover foreseeable damages when the wrong in question has been caused by the tort, but that cause does not necessarily have to be the sole or dominant cause of the loss of injury sustained. It is of course well accepted that the plaintiff's acts or omissions in the context of contributory negligence may serve to extinguish or reduce the damages recoverable.

DAMAGES IN CONTRACT

By virtue of the provisions of the 1995 Act and in particular section 20, damages in contract and the measure of same are those that are most likely to be an issue in the usual package holiday case. It is well established that the purposes of damages for breach of contract is to put the plaintiff, as far as money can, in the same situation as if the contract had been performed.[6] This basic rule is supported by the rule as to remoteness of damage recoverable for breach of contract under the rule in *Hadley v. Baxendale*.[7] The rule that stems from *Hadley v. Baxendale* is, that damages can be recovered for the breach of contract which are fairly and reasonably to be considered arising naturally according to the usual course of things, from such breach or such damages as may reasonably be supposed to have been in the contemplation of both parties at the time they made the contract as a probable result of the breach of it.

Therefore, one can recover damages which are either easily foreseeable as being the consequences of the breach of the contract in the ordinary course of things. The second element goes further and allows recovery for damages which were in the contemplation of both parties, even though such damages may not be reasonably foreseeable, apart from that special state of knowledge of the parties, in the ordinary course of things. Therefore, the rule presumes, in the first place, that the parties have a reasonable person's knowledge of the consequences of the breach and secondly, that there are special circumstances indicating that there is a special knowledge which is actually possessed by the parties regarding the consequences of a breach that will also lead to recovery of damages flowing from same.[8]

The scope of this test has been slightly narrowed by virtue of the case of the *Koufos v. Czarnikow Ltd*[9] whereby knowledge of the special consequences of a breach must be within the reasonable contemplation of the parties, as opposed to reasonably foreseeable as a result of such knowledge. This was applied in the package holiday context in the case of *Kemp v. Intasun*.[10] In

---

5.   Halsbury, *op. cit.* para. 1139.
6.   See *Robinson v. Harmon* [1848] 1 Ex. 850 at 855.
7.   [1854] 9 Ex. 341.
8.   See *Victoria Laundry (Windsor) Ltd v. Newman Industries Ltd* [1949] 2 K.B. 528.
9.   [1969] 1 A.C. 350.
10. [1987] C.L.Y. 1130; [1987] 2 F.T.L.R. 234.

this case an asthmatic suffered an asthma attack by being placed in a dirty and dusty room by the package holiday provider. It was held that the plaintiff was not to be able to recover damages on this basis, that it was not a natural consequence of the breach in the ordinary course of things of not being reasonably foreseeable. On the second limb of the *Hadley v. Baxendale*[11] test (as to whether there was special knowledge on behalf of the package holiday provider, it was held on the facts the travel agent or the package holiday provider had no knowledge of the consumer's asthma and hence, it could not be within the reasonable contemplation of the parties as a result.[12]

It is undoubtedly true that the measure of damages in package holiday cases is the one issue that causes the most difficulty in their assessment and is often the only issue in most holiday package cases. This is especially true when the loss is either minor distress and disappointment, with no personal injury element. Due to the quite specific nature of the loss involved, the loss of a disappointed holidaymaker can be difficult for the general practitioner and consumer to value accurately and so determine the appropriate level of damages to which they should be entitled.

In general terms, the damages for breach of a package holiday contract fall into two basic general headings. The difference in value between what the consumer was actually promised by virtue of the terms of the contract and that which he actually received in the provision of the services in the destination of the holiday. All consequential loss which flows from the breach of contract primarily, such as basic out-of-pocket expenses and also, more importantly and more difficulty, damages for any mental distress, physical discomfort or personal injury that may have been suffered by the consumer.

The one element in the above headings which causes the most difficulty in terms of measurements and assessment is that of damages for the mental distress of a disappointed holidaymaker, and it very much depends on the attitude of the person involved as to what degree of distress was suffered by them by virtue of the failure to provide adequate or agreed services in the holiday.

TYPES OF DAMAGES RECOVERABLE

Having set out the general rules with regard to recovery of damages both in tort and contract and the general heads of damage which arise in the package holiday context, hereafter will be set out each of the basic possible heads of damage which may be recovered in a package holiday context.

---

11. [1854] 9 Ex. 341.
12. See generally, Tomlinson & Wordell "Damages and Holiday Cases" [1988] 27 L.S. Gaz. 28.

DIFFERENCE IN VALUE CLAIMS

In this context, it is often a simple and straightforward calculation of deducting the value of the services actually received by the holidaymaker and those which he actually contracted for. For example, if the holiday cost a specific amount and the services provided reflected only half of that value in terms of accommodation or other services (such as a swimming pool, sports facilities etc.), then the difference in value is naturally one half of the value of the actual holiday.[13] In *Jackson v. Horizon Holidays Ltd*[14] it was held that where a person had entered into a contract for the benefit of himself and others who were not parties to the contract, he could sue on the contract for damages for the loss suffered not only by himself, but also by the others in consequence of a breach of the contract even though he was not a trustee for the others.[15] It followed, therefore, that the plaintiff was entitled to damages not only for the diminution in the value of the holiday and the discomfort, vexation and disappointment which he himself had suffered by reason of the defendant's breach of contract, but also for the discomfort, vexation and disappointment suffered by his wife and children. Thus, Lord Denning M.R. stated:

> If I were inclined myself to speculate, I think the suggestion of counsel for Mr Jackson may well be right. The judge took the cost of the holiday at £1,200. The family only had about half the value of it. Divide it by two and you get £600. Then add £500 for the mental distress.[16]

Therefore, he upheld the award in the following terms:

> Applying the principles to this case, I think that the figure of £1,100 was about right. It would, I think, have been excessive if it had been awarded only for the damage suffered by Mr Jackson himself. But when extended to his wife and children, I do not think it is excessive. People look forward to a holiday. They expect the promises to be fulfilled. When it fails, they are greatly disappointed and upset. It is difficult to assess in terms of money; but it is the task of the judges to do the best they can. I see no reason to interfere with the total award of £1,100.[17]

It may often be the case that the accommodation contracted for was not what was provided, for example, a difference in standard between one apartment and another. The difference in value in the standard of one apartment to more

---

13. For example, see the leading English case of *Jackson v. Horizon Holidays Ltd* [1975] 3 All E.R. 92.
14. [1975] 3 All E.R. 92.
15. See Chapter 1, p. 12 *et seq.*
16. [1975] 3 All E.R. 92 at 94.
17. [1975] 3 All E.R. 92 at 95.

luxurious apartment which may have been contracted for can easily be ascertained by virtue of the cost price of the lesser apartment in normal commercial terms.[18] The problem which may arise in terms of the difference in value between the standard of accommodation contracted for and the standard actually provided is the fact that by definition the standard of accommodation for a holidaymaker is extremely important for the overall success and enjoyment of the holiday, therefore, if the accommodation is not what was contracted for and is below standard or inadequate, then that naturally has a knock on effect on the overall success and enjoyment of the holiday. Therefore, it may not necessarily reflect the true loss of the consumer if, on a difference in value basis between the two types of accommodation, damages are awarded to reflect that difference in value between the price of the accommodation within the overall package and the value of the accommodation actually provided for. This does not take into account the effect of the lack of adequate accommodation for the overall enjoyment of the holiday and consequently this additional loss which is, in effect, the distress and disappointment of the lack of suitable accommodation, should be included in the award of damages for distress and/or physical discomfort. In this way, the total loss of the plaintiff is recovered which would not necessarily be the case, if the award was merely limited to the difference in value of the accommodation provided.

It has been suggested that perhaps another way of viewing this problem, which might be more beneficial to the consumer/plaintiff, would be to view totally inadequate accommodation as having such a detrimental effect on the holiday, that in effect the whole holiday is rendered worthless. Hence the measure of damage on a difference of value basis should be the total price of the holiday, as on the basis of a total refund, but combined with damage for the mental distress and disappointment resulting from same. This basis would naturally have the effect of increasing the overall award of the consumer/ plaintiff, as they recover not only damages for mental distress and disappointment, but also the full cost of the holiday.[19]

CONSEQUENTIAL LOSS

The damage of consequential loss essentially comprises the recovery of reasonable out-of-pocket expenses incurred as a result of the breach of contract by the tour organiser. Therefore, they are specific items of damage which can be vouched by virtue of receipt or otherwise as a specific item of expense incurred by the consumer as a result of the breach of contract. This could comprise a variety of particular expenses depending on the circumstances of any particular case, but it could include for example, the cost of meals taken

---

18. See for example *McLeod v. Hunter* [1987] C.L.Y. 1162.
19. See for this approach, generally Grant & Mason, *Holiday Law* (1996) p. 227.

out in restaurants where either the hotel food or apartment catering facilities were inadequate or unacceptable. It could also even include the cost of alternative accommodation where the original accommodation was totally inadequate or uninhabitable.

It should be remembered where there are specific items of out-of-pocket expenses resulting in the failure to provide certain services under the holiday contract, the consumer/plaintiff can only recover for the vouched out-of-pocket expense. Therefore, is precluded from recovering twice for the difference in value between the holiday contracted for with all the services agreed and the value of the holiday, minus the relevant services which were not provided, as the consumer is being compensated by virtue of the fact that the out-of-pocket expenses which he suffered as a result of that failure to provide service is reimbursed to him. This head of damage would also include loss of earnings. Naturally, a plaintiff would not be likely to succeed to a claim for loss of earnings, for that time spent on holiday, even if the time spent was alleged to be a total waste of his holiday entitlement. However, it is possible that where the consumer/plaintiff has been delayed, for example, by flight delays or overbooking and has missed a day or so of work thereafter, that he could claim loss of earnings for that time out of work.[20]

MENTAL DISTRESS

Damages for mental distress was first considered in the common law prior to the enactment of the Directive in the leading English case of *Jarvis v. Swan Tours*.[21] This case suggested that the general rule for damages for mental distress for breach of contract was that they could be recovered in an appropriate case depending on the circumstances of the case. Therefore, Lord Denning M.R. held that a contract for a holiday was one such case as with a contract to provide entertainment and enjoyment. It follows that for a break of such a contract, damages can be awarded for the disappointment, distress, upset and frustration caused by the breach. This view was also supported by Edmund Davies L.J. who stated:

> What a man has paid for and properly expects an invigorating and amusing holiday and, through no fault of his, returns home dejected because his expectations have been largely unfulfilled, in my judgement it would be quite wrong to say that his disappointment should in no way be reflected in the damages to be awarded.[22]

---

20. See for example, *Jarvis v. Swan Tours* [1973] 1 All E.R. 71 per Stephenson L.J. and *Harvey v. Tracks Travel* [1984] C.L.Y. 1006.
21. [1973] 1 All E.R. 71.
22. [1973] 1 All E.R. 71 at 75.

This was the basis on which it was established as a matter of law that damages for mental distress can be recovered in holiday cases. There is no dispute as to the plaintiff's entitlement to such damages, but there is always difficulty in ascertaining the very intangible and variable nature of what amount accurately reflects any particular plaintiff's distress or disappointment in the failure to provide certain services in the holiday contract. It is by nature an approximate exercise and very much in the nature of ascertaining damages for personal injury since there can be no mathematical rule, it is an approximate sum to reflect the distress caused by virtue of the breach in the context of the actual holiday contracted for. It is interesting to note that the Court of Appeal has recently narrowed the general recovery of damages for mental distress for breach in contract so as to be only available if the object of the contract was to provide peace of mind or freedom from distress and not purely for the anguish or vexation arising out of the breach of a purely commercial contract.[23] In *Hayes v. Dodd*,[24] Staughton L.J. with his colleagues, took a restrictive approach, saying:

> It seems to me that damages for mental distress in contract are, as a matter of policy, limited to certain classes of case. I would broadly follow the classification provided by Dillon L.J. in *Bliss v. South East Thames Regional Health Authority* [1987] I.C.R. 700 at 718:
>
>> '. . . where the contract which has been broken was itself a contract to provide peace of mind or freedom from distress. . .'
>
> It may be that the class is somewhat wider than that. But it should not, in my judgement, include any case where the object of the contract was not comfort or pleasure, or the relief or discomfort, but simply carrying on a commercial activity with a view to profit. So I would disallow the item of damages for anguish and vexation.[25]

This would not seem to affect the general principle with regard to package holiday contracts, comfort and pleasure as by their nature they are designed to provide peace of mind so it seems to be accepted that this general ruling does not affect the availability of such damages.[26] The only potential difficulty which has been suggested in this regard is in regard to flight-only holidays. Can these be said to be a contract which provides peace of mind and freedom of distress or alternatively as being purely a commercial contract for a flight from one place to another where there is no additional accommodation element

---

23. See also *Hayes v. Dodd* [1990] 2 All E.R. 815.
24. [1992] All E.R. 815.
25. [1992] All E.R. 815 at 823.
26. See for example, Grant & Mason, *op. cit.* p. 230.

involved? This on its face would seem firstly not to be within the 1995 Act and the definition of a package therein.[27] Secondly, even on the grounds of general damages for breach of contract outside the Act, it could be seen to be purely a commercial contract, particularly if it is a trip purely for business reasons and not just as a holiday.[28]

It is also the case that if the breach in question is the unavailability or lack of the agreed standard accommodation, per the holiday contract, this is the breach which causes the distress. Therefore, it is relevant in assessing distress for lack of appropriate accommodation that the nature and type of accommodation is considered, particularly in the context of a particular holiday. For example, depending on the type of holiday, a consumer may spend a lot of their time in or about the actual accommodation complex itself particularly where the hotel would have a swimming pool and sports facilities. If that is not the accommodation they receive on arrival, that will naturally have a greater impact on their holiday than on a more active, sports-based holiday (for example a skiing holiday) where the accommodation is really only relevant for the purpose of sleeping. Hence, a lower standard of accommodation will not inhibit the holiday as much as with a more conventional, pool-based holiday.[29]

It has been argued that there should be a useful guide for the award of such damages for distress and disappointment by analogy to damages for personal injury, since damages for personal injury in any particular case should not be exceeded by the damages for distress and disappointment by virtue of the similar breach in that holiday contract, but that may not always be a fair or accurate analogy.[30]

The final point to make with regard to damages for mental distress is that, by virtue of sections 20(3) and 20(4) of the 1995 Act, damages for non-personal injury cases can be limited by virtue of the contract subject to the basic limits set out in section 20(4) as to be not less than double the inclusive package price for an adult of the holiday concerned. This would, therefore, depend on the standard conditions, which now would be a normal clause in most standard contracts, as a result of the 1995 Act, that damages for distress and disappointment can be limited to a fairly small sum in relation to the package holiday price as a whole. This view is premised on the fact that damages for mental distress are not considered to be part of damages for personal injury.

---

27. In particular, see s. 20 of the 1995 Act.
28. See s. 2 of the 1995 Act and this view being upheld in the English case of *Lucas v. Avril* [1994] 7 C.L.Y. 109 and also Grant & Mason, *op. cit.* p. 230.
29. See for example, *Jones v. Villa Ramos (Algarve)* [1988] C.L.Y. 1061 where damages were awarded by reference to the diminution in value in the holiday as the consumer, due to a dispute, was not allowed to use the apartment pool and had to travel by car to the beach to swim.
30. This has been suggested by Tomlinson and Wordell, "Damages and Holiday Cases" [1988] 27 L.S. Gaz. 28.

PHYSICAL DISCOMFORT

It has long been established that a plaintiff can recover damages for physical
discomfort resulting from a breach of contract, for example, if he suffers physical inconvenience.[31] This sum varies, depending on the circumstances of the
case, but is a little more amenable to assessment in objective terms than damages for mental distress.

PERSONAL INJURY

In the most serious cases, this is the most important head of damage[32] for a
consumer who suffers personal injury while abroad such damages can now be
recovered on the basis of breach of contract by virtue of a breach of section 20
of the 1995 Act. The same basic rules as to assessment of damage and the
likely value of any particular injury apply as would be the normal case in a
personal injury action based on negligence, the same can apply in a package
holiday contract for personal injury suffered on the basis of a breach of contract.

    It is important to remember that, by virtue of section 20, no limitation can
be made on the recovery of the amount of damages for personal injury by
virtue of the standard conditions and hence, the normal value for a particular
injury applies.[33] The other important point to remember, with regard to personal injury based on the breach of contract, is that, by virtue of the arbitration scheme operated by the Chartered Institute of Arbitrators on behalf of
tour operators, the recovery of damages for personal injury is allowed which
previously was precluded by the rules of the scheme. This has meant that the
claims which go to arbitration, can also deal with the personal injury aspect,
even in the more serious cases by virtue of the quicker and cheaper arbitration
procedure with the plaintiffs can still recover the same amount of damages in
the arbitration procedure, as they would in an ordinary court action.

MITIGATION OF LOSS

Naturally, in the recovery of damages both in tort and contract, there is an
express duty on the plaintiff who has suffered loss to mitigate the damage

---

31. See for example *Jarvis v. Swan Tours* [1973] 1 All E.R. 71 per Lord Denning; *Duthie
     v. Thomson Holidays* [1988] C.L.Y. 1058; *Hodge v. London and South Western Rail-
     way Company* [1875] Law Reports 10 Q.B. 111 and *Bailey v. Bullock* [1950] 2 All
     E.R. 1167.
32. See generally, White, *On Damages* (1994) and Pierse, *The Law of Damages Relating
     to Personal Injury* (1998).
33. See generally White, *ibid.*, Volumes 1-2.

which he is suffering and thereby to take reasonable steps to reduce that loss.[34] This rule results in three consequences: firstly, that the plaintiff cannot recover for loss which he could have avoided by taking reasonable steps to do so; secondly, that the plaintiff can recover for expenses incurred in taking reasonable steps to avoid the loss suffered and thirdly, that the plaintiff cannot recover for loss which he has succeeded in avoiding.[35]

This rule impacts in the package holiday context where alternative accommodation or services are offered by the package holiday provider when the original services are not available depends as to whether any refusal by the consumer to avail of these alternatives is reasonable or unreasonable in the context of the holiday in question.[36] Therefore, when a suitable alternative is offered, it should only be refused on reasonable grounds which naturally depends on the facts of any particular case.[37]

There are several examples of the fact that if a consumer spends money on acquiring suitable alternative accommodation at his own expense then he can recoup that expense if the original accommodation was inferior.[38] It should be noted that these general principles are reflected in the Act insofar as the requirement to give notice of any failures to the tour organiser. This is as provided for expressly in section 14(2), whereby it is an essential term of every contract that a consumer must communicate at the earliest opportunity in writing, or in any other appropriate form, to the supplier of services concerned and to the organiser or local representative of any failure which the consumer perceives at the place where the services concerned are supplied. This is invariably the case anyway in the standard conditions of most tour organisers that a complaint with regard to services provided must be made within a specific time limit and if not, the remedies by way of arbitration or court proceedings are barred if that term is not complied with.

Therefore the Act will supersede any express term to that effect as the obligation is to communicate at the earliest opportunity any failure of performance of the services concerned. This will, naturally, depend on the nature of the holiday in question, the nature of the breach and the availability of communication to the supplier and tour operator. This duty to complain is part

---

34. See Halsbury, *op. cit.*, Vol. 12 and McGregor, *On Damages* para. 272 *et seq.*
35. See *British Westinghouse & Manufacturing Company Ltd v. Underground Electric Railway Company of London Ltd* [1912] A.C. 673 per Lord Haldane.
36. See for example, s. 19(2) of the 1995 Act, for the express provision of suitable alternative arrangements where there is a significant failure of performance after the start of the package requiring that compensation of the difference in value between the service supplied and as actually supplied is given to the consumer.
37. See for example, the English cases on this point of *Tucker v. OTA* [1986] C.L.Y. 383; *Rhodes v. Sun Spot Tours* [1983] C.L.Y 984 and *Toomey v. Intasun Holidays Ltd* [1988] C.L.Y 1060.
38. See for example, *Chesnow v. Intasun Holidays Ltd* [1983] 134 New L.J. 341 and *Trackman v. New Vistas Ltd The Times*, 24 November 1959.

of the duty to mitigate loss and can naturally operate to the detriment of the consumer, if not complied with either reasonably or at all prior to the 1995 Act or the Directive.[39] Therefore, in essence, section 14(2) implies a contractual express duty to mitigate the loss above and beyond the general duty in either contract or tort. However, it seems merely to confirm the duty at common law rather than to add any higher duty to that already well established duty.[40]

---

39. See, for example, *Wheelhouse v. CIT* [1994] 10 C.L.Y. 128 and *Scott and Scott v. Bluesky Holidays* [1988] C.L.Y. 943.
40. For an interesting and useful table of what generally may be the damages awarded, see Grant & Mason, *op. cit.* p. 241, which sets out for trivial complaints the award should be up to £50 per person. Where the holiday is moderately affected especially, if the accommodation is very substandard, 75 per cent to 90 per cent of the holiday price should be the amount of damages. Finally, where the whole purpose of the holiday is undermined, up to twice the price of the holiday.

CHAPTER EIGHT

Impact of the International Conventions on the Limitation of Liabilities of Tour Organisers

THE WARSAW CONVENTION ON INTERNATIONAL CARRIAGE BY AIR 1929

The Warsaw Convention in 1929, as subsequently amended, regulates the international carriage of passengers and goods by air and is implemented in Irish law by virtue of the Air Navigation and Transport Act 1936. The significance of the Convention and the Act is that strict liability is imposed on the carrier for death or injury of passengers, damage or loss of baggage and delay to passengers or baggage. However, this strict liability is ameliorated by the fact that there are two specific defences available: firstly, the defence that if the carrier can show that he took all necessary measures to avoid the damage and, secondly, if there is contributory negligence on behalf of the plaintiff.

The Warsaw Convention came into force in respect of Ireland on the 19 December 1935 pursuant to section 2 of the Air Navigation and Transport Act 1936. Section 17 onwards of the 1936 Act provided that the Warsaw Convention was the manner in which the force of law in the State with regard to the rights and liabilities of carriers, passengers, consignors, consignees and other persons in relation to any carriage by air to which the Warsaw Convention applies irrespective of the nationality of the aircraft performing that carriage.[1]

The Warsaw Convention itself is set out in the First Schedule to the Act. Article 1 of the Convention sets out the scope of the Convention by virtue of the expression 'international carriage' in Article 1(2), which is meant to include any carriage in which, according to the contract made by the parties, the place of departure and the place of destination, whether or not there be a break in the carriage, are situate either within the territories of two high contracting parties. This is the main provision for the definition of international

---

1. See s. 17(1) of the 1936 Act.

carriage and hence, it must be applied from one contracting party to the Convention to another, which invariably is the case within Europe and usually further afield.[2] It should be noted that this definition also applies to circumstances where a series of successive air carriers within the same contract is deemed to be one undivided carriage for the purposes of the application of the Convention. Thus its international character will not be lost by virtue of the fact that one flight may be solely within one contracting party before a connecting flight is taken to another high contracting party.

The liability of the air carrier is set out in Chapter 3 of the Convention in Articles 17 to 30. Article 17 states that the carrier is liable for damage sustained in the event of the death or wounding of a passenger or any other bodily injury suffered by a passenger, if the accident, which caused the damage so sustained, took place on board the aircraft or in the course of any of the operations of embarking or disembarking. This is the main basis for liability of a carrier for personal injury suffered either while on the flight or by disembarking or embarking. This, on its face, is a straightforward imposition of liability. The only difficulty which arises with Article 17 is the definition of embarking or disembarking as naturally, accidents can easily and often occur while getting on or off an aircraft.[3] This phrase has been interpreted in Irish law as having quite a wide meaning, to allow a consumer/plaintiff to recover in most circumstances for such an accident in the area of the aircraft. The liability of the carrier with regard to damage to property is set out in Article 18 which provides that the carrier is liable for damage sustained in the event of the destruction or loss of, or of damage to, any registered luggage or any goods. The occurrence which caused the damage so sustained took place during the carriage by air.

It is important to note that these basic provisions, with regard to the imposition of liability of an air carrier, only now apply at common law. For claims within the 1995 Act the air transport component, being part of the package holiday and hence part of the section 20 strict liability, is not affected by virtue of the fact that the services provided by a third-party subcontractor, namely the airline, so strict liability will still apply. Hence, Articles 17 and 18 of the Warsaw Convention will be superseded by virtue of any claim under section 20 of the 1995 Act. However, it is supplementary to the 1995 Act as, even though section 20 applies strict liability to the tour organiser alone, who would be responsible for all the components of the package including the transport component, it would also allow a consumer to sue directly the airline by virtue of sections 17, 18 and 19 with regard to damage resulting from any delay in carriage by air of passengers, luggage or goods, as an additional cause of

---

2. A full list of the high contracting parties to date can be found in Shawcross & Beaumont, *Air Law* (5th edn, 1991).
3. See, for example, *Bourke v. Aer Lingus plc* [1997] 1 I.L.R.M. 148.

action against an additional party for the benefit of the protection of the consumer. This would be in addition to, and not in substitution of, the express contractual rights against the tour organiser under section 20 of the 1995 Act. However, it may in most cases only be necessary and beneficial to sue the tour organiser by virtue of the Act and not the carrier, as well, by virtue of the Warsaw Convention as implemented by the 1936 Act.

The two defences set out in the Warsaw Convention in Articles 20 and 21 reflect the basic fault liability imposed by virtue of the Act as it allows the carrier to escape liability if he can prove that he and his agents have taken all necessary measures to avoid the damage, or that it was impossible for him or them to take such measures. This naturally reflects the duty to take all reasonable care in tort and negligence. Hence, if he took all necessary precautions to avoid the damage or injury involved then no liability would accrue, or if he proved that it was impossible to take such preventative measures to avoid the damage. Further, Article 20(2) allows no liability to be imposed if, for the purposes of damage to goods and luggage, the damage was occasioned by the navigation, piloting or negligence in the handling of the aircraft or in navigation and that, in all other respects, he and his agents have taken all necessary measures to avoid the damage. Therefore, if it can be proven that the damage was solely due to negligent piloting or navigation of the aircraft, then no liability will be imposed as long as all necessary measures were otherwise taken to avoid that damage.

The final defence provided for in the Convention is Article 21, which reflects the basic contributory negligence defence in common law is where the carrier can prove that the negligence of the person suffering damage has caused or contributed to the damage, the court may, in accordance with the provisions of its own law, exonerate the carrier or mitigate his liabilities. This allows for the implementation of the ordinary common law of contributory negligence on behalf of the passenger/consumer to be implemented in order to reduce the liability of the carrier. The other limitation with regard to the recovery for damage to goods is set out in Article 26, which in essence provides that where goods have been accepted without complaint by the consignee that, in its absence of proof to the contrary, will be evidence that the consignment was delivered in good condition in accordance with the document of carriage. Therefore, if there is damage, the consignee/consumer must complain to the carrier forthwith, at the latest within three days from the date of receipt of the luggage and seven days from the date of receipt of the goods. This must be made in writing upon the document of carriage or by separate notice dispatched within a period prescribed for such complaint. If the consignee consumer does not complain within the prescribed period an action shall be barred against the carrier except in the case of fraud. The overall limitation with regard to recovery under Articles 17 or 18 is set out in Article 29, which stipulates that there is a 2-year time limit from the date of arrival at the destination or from the date on which the aircraft should have arrived or from the date on which the carriage stopped. Therefore, it is a tight 2-year time limit depending on how the date of arrival is calculated.[4]

LIMITATION OF LIABILITY

The most important provision with regard to the 1995 Act is the application of the limitation of liability provisions under the Warsaw Convention. Otherwise the liability provisions, of Articles 17 and 18 for example, only apply at common law outside the 1995 Act. The important provision of the Act with regard to limitation of liability is contained in Article 23 which enforces this limitation under Article 22. This provides that any provision which tends to fix a lower limit than that provided for in the Convention shall be null and void, but that nullity of any such provision does not involve the nullity of the whole contract which remains valid and the subject of the Convention. The final relevant provision with regard to limiting the liability of the carrier or package provider under the Convention is by virtue of Article 25 which provides that a carrier shall be prevented from relying on the limitation of liability under the Convention, if the damage is due to malice or to such default on his part as in accordance with the law. This also applies to any of his agents, employed within the scope of the Act, who are acting with malice. Therefore, any malicious act on the part of the carrier or an agent will automatically revoke the limitation of liability and hence it will be liable for the full amount of the damage.[5]

The final point that should be made with regard to the Convention is that of jurisdiction which is provided for in Article 28. This allows that any action for damages at the option of the plaintiff can be brought to the court having jurisdiction where the carrier is domiciled or has its principal place of business or to the jurisdiction established when the contract was made or before the court having jurisdiction at the place of destination. Therefore, in general terms, jurisdiction is weighted in favour of the carrier except where he has some sort of agent acting on his behalf in this jurisdiction by which the contract was made, which would normally be the case, and hence that would be sufficient to ground jurisdiction for most international carriage claims for a domestic consumer to sue in the courts of this jurisdiction.[6]

---

4. See for example generally, Shawcross & Beaumont, *op. cit.* Chapter 1.
5. For an analysis of the concept of malice in this context, see *Goldman v. Thai Airways International Ltd* [1983] 3 All E.R. 693.
6. See Shawcross & Beaumont, *op. cit.* Chapters 1-4.

AMENDMENT TO THE WARSAW CONVENTION

The Warsaw Convention, as implemented by the 1936 Act, was amended by the Guatemala City Protocol of 1971 which came into effect in Ireland by virtue of the Air Navigation and Transport Act 1959. This amended the definition of 'international carriage' in Article 1 of the Convention as being any carriage in which, according to the agreement of the parties, the place of departure and the place of destination, whether or not there would be a break in the carriage or a trans-shipment, was situated either within the territories of two high contracting parties.

Therefore it is now interpreted in accordance with the agreement between the parties as to whether there are two high contracting parties involved between the place of departure and the place of destination. The new limitation of liability was replaced by a new Article 22, by virtue of Article 11 of the Guatemala Protocol, which increased the limit of liability to the present 250,000 French francs and 50,000 French francs. Further, the defence of the consumer for the limits of liability was altered in Article 25. This is outlined in *Goldman v. Thai Airways International Ltd*[7] whereby the limits will not apply if it is proved that damage resulted from an act or omission of the carrier, his servants or agents, done with intent to cause damage recklessly and with knowledge that damage would probably result. Thus it is required that, in the case of such act by or omission of a servant or agent it is proved that he was acting within the scope of his employment.

This means it is now a little easier to prove this defence to the limitation of liability under the Convention than was previously the case, with regard to proving malice, as now it is pure recklessness or intent to cause damage which has a lesser threshold to overcome for the consumer/plaintiff. However, it is still only in exceptional cases that one would be able to prove such culpability as required in Article 22, with regard to an intent to cause damage or recklessness with knowledge of that damage would probably result. This implies that recklessness requires a conscious disregard of a substantial, unjustifiable risk requiring, naturally, a high degree of culpability. It results in the subjective test being applied to the carrier in terms of his assessment of the risk involved in any particular act, along with knowledge of the adverse consequences.[8]

The next amendment to the Warsaw Convention was by virtue of the Guadalajara Convention of 1961, which was implemented in this jurisdiction by the Air Navigation and Transport Act 1965. The main effect of the Guadalajara Convention was to extend the Warsaw Convention to include

---

7. [1983] 3 All E.R. 693.
8. See for example the equivalent provisions under the Athens Convention on the Carriage of Passengers and Luggage by Sea 1974, Article 13 as set out in 1992 L.L.L.R. 144 and *Carrying Company v. Adriatic Petroleum Company* [1915] A.C. 705. See generally, O'hOisin [1998] *Bar Review* (Vol. 3, Issue 4) 162 at 164.

subcontracting by the contracting carrier to an actual carrier of the passengers or goods in question and so the actual carrier was also subject to the provisions of the Warsaw Convention and the liability imposed and limits of liability therein contained.

The final amendment to the Warsaw Convention was by way of the 1975 Protocols as implemented by the Air Navigation and Transport Act 1988, in Part 3, section 34 onwards. This basically allowed limitations of liabilities to now be converted in terms of special drawing rights by virtue of section 36. The Montreal Protocol of 1975, as set out in the First Schedule to the 1988 Act, amends Article 22 in terms of the limit of liability to be expressed in terms of special drawing rights as opposed to the previous limits in French francs. By virtue of the four Protocols of 1975 in Montreal, the Fourth Protocol is the final and updating one with regard to the final limit of liabilities in terms of special drawing rights, which is 100,000 special drawing rights for death or personal injury and seventeen special drawings rights per kilogram for damage to cargo and 1,000 special drawing rights for damage to the carriage of baggage of each passenger.

The definition of the special drawing rights now contained in Article 22 was further amended by the Fourth Protocol of 1975 to include reference to the International Monetary Fund which defined the substance and content of a special drawing right and the value thereof. Further, the other primary amendment which was undertaken by the Montreal Protocol and the limitation of liability provisions of the Warsaw Convention, was with regard to Article 25. This, again, reinforced the fact that the limit of liability could be revoked if there was intent to cause damage or recklessness on the part of the carrier or its servants or agents but also by virtue of a new Article 24(5)(a), the same provision applied with regard to recklessness with regard to the limit set down at 25(a).[9]

However, the most important and practical feature of the Warsaw Convention has been that, in the last 30 years, it has allowed the carrier to limit his liability to relatively small sums for any liability that can be established by virtue of the plaintiff. The limitation of the sums was originally expressed in the Convention in Poincare Francs which, unfortunately, is a form of currency which no longer exists.[10] However, this problem has been solved by virtue of the Montreal Protocols which now use the internationally recognised special drawing rights. The concept of the special drawing right for the purposes of defining value for the limited liability of carriers under the Convention, is a basket of sixteen major world currencies to ascertain an agreed value for all currency of the contracting States.[11]

---

9. See Shawcross & Beaumont, *op. cit.* Chapter 3.
10. See Article 22.
11. See generally, Shawcross & Beaumont, *op. cit.*

This has the two obvious advantages to the tour operator of a package holiday where losses are suffered by virtue of the flight or an incident happening thereon, to have both a very limited amount of compensation and certainty in that amount for which a budget can be made. It can be seen that the limitation on baggage is only nominal and would not necessarily reflect the true value of any baggage lost or damaged. Also, in the case of personal injury, the limitation would cover most minor personal injuries but if it was anything of any greater significance, or for example to include death, even including the statutory payment would not be sufficient for the sum limited.

CONDITIONS OF THE LIMITATION OF LIABILITY

These limits apply in all cases except with the specific exception where the damage or injury is caused intentionally or recklessly and with knowledge that damage would probably result. An example of this occurring prior to the Package Holiday Directive, is the case of *Goldman v. Thai Airways International Ltd*[12] where the airline was held not to be liable for the full amount of a passenger's injuries, as the limit applied. It was rejected that, the pilot omitting to switch the seat belt signs during turbulence, was not recklessness.

With regard to the Warsaw Convention, it is important to note that the application of the limitations of the Convention only apply to international carriage of persons or baggage or cargo and so do not apply to internal domestic flights. The definition in Article 11 of 'international carriage' is "any carriage in which the place of departure and the place of destination are situated either within the territories of two high contracting parties (countries) or within the territory of a single high contracting party, if there is an agreed stopping place within the territory of another State, even if that State is not a high contracting party".[13] The defences relating in Article 20 were considered in the case of *Grein v. Imperial Airways Ltd*[14] where Greer L.J. stated:

> This seems to me to amount to a promise not to injure the passenger by avoidable accident, the onus being on the carrier to prove that the accident could not have been avoided by the exercise of reasonable care.[15]

With regard to the recklessness in Article 25 as applied in *Goldman v. Thai Airways International Ltd*[16] it should be noted that the Court of Appeal held

---

12. [1983] 3 All E.R. 693.
13. With regard to the liability, see Articles 17 and 18 and the defences, to which reference has already been made, contained in Articles 20 and 21.
14. [1937] 1 K.B. 50.
15. [1937] 1 K.B. 50 at 69.
16. [1983] 3 All E.R. 693.

that Article 25 should be construed in the context and with the qualification that the act or omission had to have been done both recklessly and with the knowledge that danger would probably result, for the defence not to be available. Therefore, it was held that the test was subjective and would only apply if it was proved that the pilot omitted to order the passengers to wear seat belts, while aware the damage of the kind that did occur would probably result or was indifferent to that likelihood.

The final important provision of the Warsaw Convention is in Article 29 which imposes a 2-year time limit on a passenger's right of action under Articles 17 and 19 – namely the strict liability for loss or injury to baggage or persons from the date of arrival at the destination or from the date on which the aircraft ought to have arrived or from the date on which the aircraft carriage stopped. It should be noted that the Convention has been amended by the Guatemala City Protocol of 1971, which has only recently been implemented by virtue of their having a sufficient number of signatories to bring it into force. This Protocol limits the carrier's defence to Article 17 for personal injury or loss and increases the maximum liability.

These limitations continue to exist by virtue of the express proviso in section 20(5) of the 1995 Act. It should also be noted that this proviso regarding limitation also applies to other Conventions, particularly with regard to those concerning the similar basic principle of a limitation of liability to both rail, sea and more importantly, liability of hotelkeepers. It is premised on the basis that since the supplier of the service, namely the airline carrier in question, can, for example, limit his liability by virtue of these Conventions then the same should allow the tour operator or a package holiday provider to also limit his liability in accordance with the terms of the Conventions if he is to be held liable in the strict sense for the failure of the supplier when the supplier could, by virtue of the Conventions, limit his compensation. It would, in those circumstances, be unfair not to allow the tour organiser to also limit his liability by virtue of that failure.

THE ATHENS CONVENTION ON THE CARRIAGE OF PASSENGERS AND THEIR LUGGAGE BY SEA 1974

The Athens Convention on the Carriage of Passengers and their Luggage by Sea 1974 has now finally been implemented in this jurisdiction by virtue of the Merchant Shipping (Liability of Shipowners and Others) Act 1996 in Part 3.[17] The primary application of the Convention in the terms of the package holiday context is limitation of liability in special drawing rights as being

---

17. The Act was commenced on 6 February 1997 by S.I. No. 215 of 1997 and see generally with regard to the Convention and the Act, O'hOisin, [1998] *Bar Review* (Vol. 3, Issue 4) p. 163 *et seq.*

46,666 units in terms of damages for death or personal injury per passenger. Again, this limit of liability can only be overturned by the consumer/plaintiff by virtue of Article 13, for proving recklessness or intent to cause damage on behalf of the carrier or its servants or agents. It amends the common law outside the 1995 Act by Article 3(3), which presumes fault on the part of the carrier and all that the consumer has to prove is that there was loss or damage caused by the incident during the course of the carriage. Therefore, liability is virtually strict on behalf of the carrier in terms of carriage by sea, subject to a passenger being negligent under Article 6 liability applies not only during the carriage but also to embarking and disembarking. As with the Warsaw Convention, there is a 2-year time limit for bringing claims by virtue of Article 16.[18]

Jurisdiction is governed at common law by virtue of Article 17 which allows the consumer/plaintiff to sue in one of four jurisdictions, i.e. in either the court of the place or permanent residence or principal place of business of the defendant, or the court of the place of departure, or that of the destination according to the contract of carriage, or the court of the State of the domicile of permanent residence of the claimant if the defendant has a place of business and is subject to jurisdiction in that State, or the court of the State where the contract of the carriage was made, if the defendant had a place of business subject to the jurisdiction of that State, provided the State is a party to the Convention. Hence, in general terms, the consumer can invariably find jurisdiction in the Irish courts where he is domiciled in this State by virtue of one of the four alternative provisions for jurisdiction under Article 17.

The 1996 Act only applies to international carriage where the place of departure and the place of destination are situated in two single States or within a single State, if according the contract of carriage (or in the schedule itinerary) there is an intermediate port of call in another State. The Convention naturally relates to the carriage of passengers and luggage by ship, but not by other means, such as by hovercraft. The basic test of liability for the shipping company is for any loss or personal injury resulting from the incident, caused during the course of the carriage, which was due to the fault or neglect of the shipping company or of its servants or agents acting within the scope of their employment. Therefore, it can be seen that the onus of proof both as to the incident occurring within the course of carriage, the causation of that incident by virtue of the fault or neglect of the carrier and the extent of loss and damage lies with the claimant. However, in specific circumstances if the death or personal injury or loss of baggage is due to certain, specific events, then it is presumed that these events and the loss occurring thereby, was due to the fault or neglect of the carrier unless the contrary is proven. This relates to incidents such as shipwreck, collision, stranding, explosion or fire or defect in the ship.

---

18. See *Hyam v. Stena Sealink Ltd* [1993] 3 All E.R. 660.

THE BRUSSELS CONVENTION ON INTERNATIONAL
TRAVEL CONTRACTS 1970

As has already been mentioned this was the first major Convention on package holiday contracts in general. Though it was of limited assistance as it was only ever ratified by seven countries, with the only two EU countries being Belgium and Italy. It can be referred to by virtue of an express proviso in section 20(5) of the 1995 Act and has the importance of limitation on liability to 50,000 French francs for personal injury, 2,000 French francs for damage to property and 5,000 French francs for other damage.

Therefore, if a tour operator was within the relevant applicable definition, given in the Convention, of a tour operator he could also take advantage of this Convention. It is important to note that the applicability of the Convention refers not to the place of contracting of this jurisdiction specifically but refers to them being in force in the place where they are due to be performed which means in the place of the holiday destination. That is namely the place of the holiday destination, as being the place where the services are to be provided. It is with reference to that country's law as to whether any particular international convention relevant to the travel trade is in force or potentially applicable to the situation. Hence that is the basis for the tour operator or travel agent being able to take advantage of the limitations of a liability therein contained. For the purposes of the Berne Convention on travel contracts and the limitations on liability therein, it is only relevant to incidents occurring in either Belgium or Italy.[19]

THE BERNE CONVENTION ON THE TRANSPORT OF
INTERNATIONAL PASSENGERS BY RAIL 1970

For the transport of international passengers by rail, the relevant convention is the Berne Convention of 1970. This Convention is less far reaching than the previous Conventions as it only deals with the question of liability for death and personal injury not expressly in its provisions but by simply stating that the liability for death or personal injury the railway company is a question for the law of the State in which the incident causing death or loss occurs. However, it does relate to provisions for the loss or damage to luggage only.

---

19. See generally, with regard to the Brussels Convention on International Travel Contracts 1970, Bogdan, *Travel Agency and Commercial Private International Law* (1966) and Van Der Peren, *European Transport Law* (1968) p. 226 *et seq.*

THE GENEVA CONVENTION ON THE CARRIAGE OF PASSENGERS BY ROAD 1949

The other relevant convention in this area is the Geneva Convention on the Carriage of Passengers by Road which provides that a carrier is liable for any loss or damage resulting from the death or personal injury of a passenger to an accident which occurs while the passenger is inside the vehicle or embarking or disembarking. This also applies to any damage to luggage during the time when it is in the vehicle or being loaded or unloaded. There is a defence under the Convention that if it can be shown that the circumstances causing the accident are such that the carrier could not have avoided by exercising greater care, he will not be liable. The liability is limited for the carrier by road for death or personal injury to 250,000 French francs and for luggage to 500 French francs. For each piece of luggage there is, in general, a maximum limit of 2,000 French francs.

CHAPTER NINE

Insolvency of Tour Operators and Travel Agents

BONDING UNDER THE TRANSPORT (TOUR OPERATORS AND TRAVEL AGENTS) ACT 1982

The bonding requirements are set out at Parts 3 and 4 of the 1982 Act, and primarily in section 13, requires the tour operator or travel agent to enter into a bond before a licence is granted to him by Minister Stagg. With regard to the 1982 Act and the bonding element, the Minister stated that:

> Deputies may be aware that prior to the introduction of the 1982 Act, the Irish travel industry operated on a non-regulated basis. In December 1981 Bray Travel Ltd, then one of the largest tour operators, went out of business resulting in the loss of holiday money and the deposits of over 1,500 people and the stranding of a number of holidaymakers abroad. There were also a number of other collapses in 1981. While voluntary bonding arrangements had been introduced by the Irish Travel Agents Association and by a number of individual operators in response to these developments, it was evident that a need existed for a statutory framework to protect holidaymakers.[1]

This was done by virtue of the licensing and bonding arrangements contained in the 1982 Act. At the time, in March 1995, 300 fully licensed travel agents and 55 licensed tour operators bonded on the 1982 Act. The Minister further stated that:

> Overall, I am satisfied a system of existing licensing and bonding has worked well over the years. Where there have been a collapse of tour operators, travel agents, customers affected have been repatriated where necessary and monies passed to the operator or agent have been refunded. The Bill now before the House will operate in addition to this Act will provide added protection to the consumer.[2]

---

1. 451 *Dáil Debates* Col. 322.
2. 451 *Dáil Debates* Col. 323.

The primary purpose of the bond under section 13(3) is to provide that in the event of the inability or failure of the tour operator or travel agent concerned to meet his financial or contractual obligations, in relation to overseas travel contracts, a sum of money would become available to the Minister (or to any person nominated or approved by the Minister as Trustee) to be applied for the benefit of any customer of the tour operator or travel agent concerned who has incurred loss or liability because of such inability or failure to meet financial or contractual obligations. This can be seen to provide money for the fund in slightly broader circumstances than mere insolvency, but inevitably, any failure to comply with the contractual obligations will be due to insolvency on the part of the tour operator in question, and so it is slightly broader in its terms than the bonding arrangements under the 1995 Act. The purposes to which this sum of money under the bond can be put, provided for in section 13(4) and namely consists of four basic purposes are as follows.

1. To provide travel facilities for any customer of the tour operator or travel agent concerned who is outside Ireland and is unable to make the return journey provided for in the overseas travel contract by reason of the inability or failure of the tour operator or travel agent concerned to fulfil his financial or contractual obligations in relation to such overseas travel contract.

2. To reimburse a customer of a tour operator or travel agent for any reasonable expenses necessarily incurred by such customer by reason of the inability or failure of the tour operator or travel agent to meet his financial or contractual obligations in relation to an overseas travel contract.

3. To refund, as far as possible, to a customer of a tour operator or travel agent, any payments made by him to the tour operator or travel agent in respect of an overseas travel contract which could not be completed by reason of the inability or failure of the tour operator or travel agent to meet his financial or contractual obligations in relation to such overseas travel contract.

4. To defray the reasonable expenses incurred by the Minister or provide for any payments by the Minister on behalf of a customer of a tour operator or travel agent, in respect of an overseas travel contract which could not be completed by reason of the inability or failure of the tour operator or travel agent to meet his financial or contractual obligations in relation to such overseas travel contract.

There is a further fund to protect consumers set out in Part 4 of the Act, known as the 'Travellers' Protection Fund'. This is supplemental and complimentary to the bond entered into by the tour operator which should, on its face, cover all sums required to be paid if the tour operator or travel agent fails to fulfil his financial or contractual obligation. The Travellers' Protection

Fund is set up under section 15 is aimed at providing payments with regard to losses or liabilities incurred by customers of tour operators or travel agents who held a licence under the Act or whose licence has been revoked (and the revocation is the subject of appeal to the court), the consequence of which is the inability or failure of the tour operator or travel agent to meet the financial or contractual obligations in respect of overseas travel contracts.

Contributions to the Fund are set out by regulation of the Minister by virtue of section 16. The disbursements of the Fund are the same as under section 13 with regard to the bond and the same four categories apply by virtue of section 18(1). However, the breadth of disbursements from the Fund is slightly wider, as provided for in section 18(2), than payments with regard to loss or liability incurred in connection with an overseas travel contract to a person will be disbursed from the Fund if the tour operator or travel agent held a licence at the time of entering into the contract or the licence has been revoked and is subject to an appeal to the court.

The ancillary nature of this Travellers' Protection Fund is emphasised by section 18(3) whereby only after all monies are paid out under the bond entered into by the tour operator, will any monies be paid out for losses or liabilities incurred by the customer from the Fund. Therefore, the Fund will only apply where the monies under the bond are insufficient to cover the losses or liabilities incurred by the customer. The apparent breadth of the Fund is limited by virtue of section 18(5) which prohibits recovery of damages from the Fund in relation to the standard accommodation or service provided by an overseas travel contract, as such damages cannot be recovered from the Fund. Finally, the Act provides in Part 4 for offences to be stated under the Act namely, primarily under section 20, for failure to hold the licence where required under the Act is liable to a fine not exceeding £100,000 or to a term of imprisonment not exceeding five years.

DEFINITIONS

The 1982 Act only applies with regard to the bonding and Travellers' Protection Fund arrangements to an overseas travel contract. This is defined in section 2 as meaning a contract for the carriage of a party to the contract (with or without any other person) by air, sea or land transport to a place outside Ireland, where the provision of the carriage is the sole subject matter of the contract or is associated with the provision thereunder of any accommodation, facilities or services. It should be noted with regard to this that it can only apply to overseas travel, but is not restricted to a package holiday, as is now defined under the 1995 Act, but also simply to air or sea transport without any accommodation element.

In that regard it is slightly broader protection in its terms than the bonding required under the 1995 Act. The other definitions of note are, firstly, with regard to a tour operator, who is defined as a person, other than a carrier, who arranges for the purpose of selling or offering for sale to the public accommodation or travel by air, sea or land transport to destinations outside Ireland, or who holds himself out by advertising or otherwise as one who may make available such accommodation, either solely or in association with other accommodation, facilities or services. This is in essence very much in line with the basic definition of a tour organiser under the 1995 Act and is consistent therewith.

The definition under the 1982 Act of a travel agent is, again like the definition of a retailer in the 1995 Act, defined as a person other than a carrier who as agent, sells or offers to sell, or purchases or offers to purchase, on behalf of the public, accommodation on air, sea or land transport to destinations outside Ireland or who holds himself out by advertising or otherwise as one who makes available such accommodation, either solely or in association with other accommodation, facilities or services. It is to be noted generally with regard to the scope of application of the 1982 Act, and in particular the important provisions with regard to bonding and the Travellers' Protection Fund, that it is only referable to overseas travel contracts. This does not apply to internal, domestic flights or package holidays, which otherwise would now be covered by the 1995 Act by the bonding requirements contained therein.

The definition of a customer under the 1982 Act is interesting insofar as it is not based on any contractual obligations that have been entered into, but is achieved by virtue of deeming a person to be a customer of a tour operator if he has made any payment, either directly or indirectly, to the tour operator or travel agent, under or with the intention of entering into an overseas travel contract. This definition of a customer is primarily referable to any payment, and hence any deposit, paid for any booking of an overseas travel contract and does not require the actual conclusion of any such binding contract at the time.

The final definition in the Act covers the criteria for when a tour operator or travel agent is unable to meet his financial or contractual obligations and hence, trigger either the bonding requirement or the Travellers' Protection Fund disbursements for the protection of the consumer's losses or liabilities. There are six circumstances where this is deemed to occur: when a petition for the winding up of the tour operator/travel agent is presented, a voluntary winding up or meeting to convene same is made, a receiver is appointed over the assets of the company, the tour operator/travel agent has failed to discharge his debts or is unable to discharge his debts or has ceased to carry on business where he is not in a position to discharge his debts, an act of bankruptcy has been committed and, finally, if the Minister has reasonable grounds to believe that the tour operator is unable to or has failed to carry out his financial or contractual obligations. Therefore, it can be seen that these requirements basically refer to acts of insolvency on the part of the tour operator/travel agent. However, it is wider than that, insofar as it allows the Minister preemptively, on reasonable grounds of belief, to deem such is the case. Secondly, it allows the case where no obvious act of insolvency has occurred, but simply that the tour operator/travel agent has failed to discharge his debts or is unable so to do in the future.

THE 1995 ACT

Part 3 of the 1995 Act, in sections 22 to 25, provides for the security requirements of package holiday providers in the event of insolvency.[3] Thus ensures that consumers who have already paid monies or travelled abroad for the purpose of a package holiday have the right to obtain refunds and more importantly, repatriation in the event that the tour operator becomes insolvent. Therefore, section 22(1) requires that a package provider shall have sufficient evidence of security for the refund of money paid over and for the repatriation of the consumer in the event of insolvency. With regard to the effect of the bonding arrangements under the Act, the Minister for State stated that:

> The effect of this provision is to give to people on holiday in Ireland who are customers of Irish-based package organisers comparable protection to that which people going on holidays overseas enjoy under the Transport (Tour Operators and Travel Agents) Act 1982. It is only proper that Irish people spending their holidays at home should have this protection in the event of insolvency of the package provider or retailer. People taking holidays in Ireland who are customers of package organisers in other EU countries will, of course, be covered by the legislation implementing the Directive in this country.[4]

In order to satisfy these primary requirements, there are certain specific requirements for bonding which are provided for in sections 23 to 25. A package provider can also fulfil these requirements by complying with the licensing requirements of the Travel Agents Act 1982 and the arrangements covered therein. These requirements are in force by virtue of the fact that any package provider who does not comply with these basic security requirements will be guilty of an offence by virtue of sections 22(3)(a) and 22(3)(b). The primary intention behind these basic provisions is to allow domestic holiday-makers to benefit from security arrangements already in place by virtue of the Travel Agents Act 1982 *vis-à-vis* foreign holiday package providers. It is inevitable that these additional insurance costs would increase slightly the

---

3. See for the European Court's interpretation of the Directive's requirements and their direct effect, *Dillenkofer v. Germany* C–178/94; [1996] 10 E.C.R. I–4845.
4. 451 *Dáil Debates*, Col. 321.

cost of a package holiday, but it is forecast that such would be small.[5]

The first basic way that a package holiday provider can fulfil these basic security arrangements is by entering into a bond of an authorised institution by which the institution pays to an approved body (of which the package provider is a member) such sum as could be reasonably expected to either reimburse consumers for all monies paid under or in contemplation of contracts for packages which have not been fully performed or to enable consumers to be repatriated or to defray any reasonable expenses necessarily incurred by the approved body, in the event of the insolvency of the package provider. Therefore the basic theme under this section is that an authorised institution (such as a bank) pays to the approved body, such as a trade association (i.e. the IATA) of which the package provider is a member a sum of money that would cover any reimbursement of monies paid, the cost of repatriation and any reasonable expenses of the approved body on the insolvency of the package provider.

The second definition with regard to the approved body requires that such a body, for the purpose of approval by the Minister, must have a reserve fund or insurance cover with the authorised institution to cover the relevant costs of each package holiday if the relevant package holiday provider becomes insolvent, by virtue of section 23(2). To ensure that a bond of the appropriate sum is entered into by the package provider, the package provider must inform the approved body of the minimum sum of the bond which he considers to be appropriate to cover the costs involved on insolvency. If the approved body doesn't consider the minimum sum proposed sufficient, then it has to inform the package provider of the relevant minimum sum which will be the sum of the bond. The figures actually set for the sum of the bond as set out in the Package Holidays and Travel Trade Act 1995 (Bonds) Regulations 1995[6] which require that for a person who is an approved body, the sum is 10 per cent of the projected turnover in the period of validity of the bond and the maximum period of the bond is one year. These Regulations also set out the basic definition of the bond and also the procedure for claiming against a bond in the event of insolvency.

A bond is defined by Regulation 5 of the Bonds Regulations which states that a bond shall:

(a) in the case of a person who is a member of an approved body which has a reserve fund or insurance cover, as specified in section 23 of the Act, be for a sum of 10 per cent of the projected turnover in the period of the validity of the bond in respect of packages to which these Regulations apply;

---

5. See generally Clark, *I.C.L.S.A.* (1995) pp. 17-23 and also the Minister for State's speech, 451 *Dáil Debates* Col. 321.

6. S.I. No. 270 of 1995, See Appendix 6.

(b) in the case of a person who is a member of an approved body which does not have a reserve fund or insurance cover as specified in section 23(2) of the Act be for a sum of 15 per cent of the projected turnover in the period of the validity of the bond in respect of packages to which these Regulations apply.

The other important provision of these Regulations lies in Regulation 7 which stipulates that any demand made under a bond by an approved body shall be made in writing not later than six months after the date on which the bond ceases to have effect. If the approved body is satisfied that the package provider can discharge all obligations to consumers under the contract to which the bond relates, the approved body may, at its discretion, release the provider of the bond and any guarantor thereof from their obligations under the bond and any guarantee relating thereto at any earlier date within the period of six months. The bond may be released back to the package provider from the approved body which holds it to cover the sums expended on behalf of consumers during the period of the bond or an earlier period if the obligations are fully fulfilled on behalf of the tour organiser. The Regulations also sets out the form of the terms of the bond to be secured by a package provider with an insurance company in the First Schedule of the Regulations and, in the Second Schedule, outlines a form with the terms of bond to be provided by a package provider and guaranteed by a bank.

Finally, section 24(4) provides that it is the duty of the approved body, namely the trade association, to ensure that there are adequate arrangements for the repatriation of the consumer in the event of insolvency, so the ultimate responsibility for repatriation of holidaymakers rests with a trade association (such as the IATA) and not with the package provider. It is important to remember that with regard to this section, the fund is only to cover the relevant costs of either the reimbursement or repatriation in the event of insolvency and it does not compensate consumers for other losses such as defective performance under the contract by the package holiday provider under section 20, since section 22(4) expressly provides that the obligations and compliance with section 20 are not relevant for the purposes of this part of the Act.

There is a second alternative to the provision the relevant security in the event of insolvency when an approved body does not have a reserve fund of insurance pursuant to section 23. Section 24 allows such a body to enter into a bond with an authorised institution by which the institution will agree to pay, in the event of insolvency of the package provider, to the approved body the relevant monies to cover reimbursement, repatriation and necessary expenses of the approved body. The same basic requirements apply to such a bond with regard to the minimum amount and the duty of repatriation of the Trade Association. The specific amount is again set out in the Bonds Regulations 1995 which direct that the sum will be 15 per cent of the projected turnover for the period during which the bond is to last, which can only be a maximum period of one year.[7]

The final obligation, with regard to security in the event of insolvency, is the requirement that the package provider must have insurance under one or more appropriate policies, with an authorised insurer in respect of such business in the Member State. The insurer, under these policies, agrees to indemnify consumers as being the insured persons under the policy to cover the loss of all money paid over by them or in contemplation of contracts for relevant packages and where applicable, the cost of repatriation of consumers based on administrative arrangements established by the insured to enable repatriation of such consumers in the event of the insolvency of the package provider.[8] It further provides that the package provider must ensure that it is an essential term of every contract with a consumer, that the consumer acquires the benefit of a policy of the relevant kind in the event of the insolvency of the package provider. The requirements of the policy are further outlined by virtue of the fact that the applicability of the relevant policy for the benefit of the consumer cannot be limited by implying a condition (such as, that no liability shall arise in the event of some specified thing being done or omitted to be done after the happening of the event), giving rise to a claim under the policy for failure of the policy in order to make payments of the premium for requiring the policyholder to keep specified records to provide the insured with information therefrom. These three conditions are specifically prohibited as limiting liability under the policy for the benefit of the consumer. Therefore, it goes further than the usual standard conditions in an insurance policy insofar as it allows the consumer to recover under the policy even though there are specific acts of default either on his behalf or on behalf of the policyholder namely, the package provider.

The general requirement of section 22(1), which implements Article 7 of the Directive, to provide security for the refund of money paid over and for the repatriation of the consumer in the event of insolvency, was interpreted by the European Court of Justice with regard to the Austrian implementation of Article 7 in the case of *Verien fur Konsumenteninformation v. Osterreichische Kreditversicherungs AG.*[9] The European Court interpreted Article 7 as covering a refund for a situation where a hotelier forces a holidaymaker to pay for the accommodation provided, claiming that the now insolvent travel organiser will never pay that sum over to him, as the risk in question derives from the travel organiser's insolvency, as the guarantees afforded to consumer by

---

7. See for an analysis of this basic principle of the trade association being liable, the judgment of the Court of Appeal in *Bowerman v. ABTA Ltd*, as reported in *The Times*, 24 November 1995, which held that there was a direct contractual relationship between a customer of a failed ABTA tour operator and ABTA themselves under their protection scheme.
8. See s. 25(1).
9. C–364/96, unreported judgment of 14 May 1998.

the travel organiser, based on a broad purposive view of Article 7 in favour of the consumer.

It should be noted that since the security only covers the cost of money paid or repatriation, any claims by holidaymakers for improper performance by virtue of the contract under section 20 would not be covered by the bond. Hence, such claimants will only be unsecured creditors in the event of the insolvency of the package holiday provider for the claim for the breach of contract on the package holiday contract. It should be remembered that in recent events of travel agents or package providers becoming insolvent particularly in terms of small travel agents, the scheme has been successful and all consumers have either been reimbursed and/or repatriated where necessary.

CHAPTER TEN

Holiday Arbitration

It is a standard general condition in most package holiday contracts that all disputes will be referred to arbitration by virtue of a scheme covered by the Chartered Institute of Arbitrators, Irish Branch Arbitration Rules operated for and on behalf of tour operators. When a dispute arises after the holiday as to how to perform the obligations under the contract and loss or personal injury caused thereby by virtue of section 20, the next issue to be determined is whether the matter should go to arbitration or proceed by way of court proceedings.

Due to the fact that an arbitration clause incorporated as an express term of the contract is binding upon the consumer who has entered into that contract, then, prima facie, he is compelled to proceed by way of arbitration. This is enforced by virtue of section 5 of the Arbitration Act 1980, which provides that if court proceedings are taken in a dispute, which is governed by an arbitration clause, then the person who wishes to have the matter referred to arbitration being a defendant, package holiday provider can apply for a stay of the proceedings pending the determination of the arbitration. This is a mandatory stay as long as one can prove an enforceable agreement to arbitrate and so there is no discretion to allow the matter to proceed if section 5 applied.[1]

Therefore, the most important issue with regard to arbitration is the decision whether or not to proceed with the Arbitration Scheme, depending on the nature of the claim and the circumstances of the case. It must be remembered that now the Chartered Institute of Arbitrators, Irish Branch Scheme does include awards for damages for personal injury, whereas prior to 1994 this was excluded. Therefore, a claimant can claim for all the ordinary loss or personal injury and consequential loss incurred by means of the arbitration that he would recover in an ordinary court of law, and so the major drawback of sending major personal injury claims in a package holiday context to arbitration has now been withdrawn.

The other major issue with regard to the validity of the arbitration clause is the fact that as a result of *JWT v. McCarthy*[2] it is now required under the Sale of Goods and Supply of Services Act 1980, sections 39 and 40, that any

---

1. See *Williams v. Artane Service Station* [1991] I.L.R.M. 893; *Sweeney v. Mulcahy* [1993] I.L.R.M. 289; *Mitchell v. Budget Travel Ltd* [1990] I.L.R.M. 739 and generally, Forde, *Arbitration Law and Procedure* (1994) pp. 23-28.
2. [1991] I.L.R.M. 813 and see generally, White [1991] I.L.T. 92.

exclusion of liability or limitation of liability with regard to the arbitration scheme must be put on notice to the consumer specifically and so must be signed individually by him. In that case the limitation of liability of £5,000 under the Arbitration Scheme was held to be not enforceable by virtue of the fact that it had not been brought to the attention of the consumer as required by the Sale of Goods and Supply of Services Act 1980. Therefore, it is now the practice that all arbitration clauses do not contain any limitation of liability or of the amount that can be recovered, but still are required to be signed individually to indicate the specific agreement of the consumer to that particular arbitration clause. Agreement of the overall conditions of the contract incorporated in that clause will not now be sufficient.

The other important issue that can arise with regard to the arbitration clause is evidenced by the case of *Carroll v. Budget Travel Ltd*[3] which revolved around the issue as to whether the clause covered the incident in question giving rise to the injury claimed by the plaintiff. In that case an application under section 5 to stay the proceedings was brought by the defendant tour operator, saying they should be referred to arbitration. The issue revolved around the nature of the arbitration clauses and scope thereof. The incident involved was one of personal injury of a child which was in the company of a child-minder provided by the tour operator. The issue was if this was a service provided and/or a dispute which arose under or in connection with the contract. It was held that it was not arising under or out of the contract, but was arising in connection with the contract. As Morris J. stated:

> It would appear to me that the company provided the services of this child-minder not under any obligation which they undertook by entering into this contract, because, as far as I can see, no such obligation exists in the contract, but they undoubtedly provided this facility 'in connection with' the contract. It is reasonably clear that this facility was provided so as to make the holiday package more attractive to holidaymakers. While I can find no provision which applies to make the services available, it is nevertheless a facility which was made available to them 'in connection with' the contract. Clearly the facility would not have been available if not connected with the defendant. I am accordingly of the view that under the terms of the contract entered into between the parties the dispute that now arises, namely, whether Ingrid (the child-minder) was negligent in the performance of her duties or not and if so what damages should be awarded in negligence for which the defendants are responsible to the plaintiff, are disputes which fall to be determined by the arbitration provision of the contract.[4]

---

3. Unreported, High Court, 7 December 1995, per Morris J.
4. Unreported, High Court, 7 December 1995, per Morris J. at p. 5.

Mr Justice Morris also dealt with the interesting issue with regard to the arbitration clause under section 40 of the Sale of Goods and Supply of Services Act 1980, which arose in *JWT v. McCarthy*[5] concerning the necessity that the terms should be fair and reasonable if it varied an express term provided in the contract and must be specifically brought to the other party's attention. This arbitration clause was amended subsequent to that case and did not limit the liability or the scope of damages which could be awarded under the Scheme. It was consequently held not to fall within the terms of section 39 and so was irrelevant in the terms of the arbitration clause brought to the consumer's notice or otherwise insofar as the Sale of Goods and Supply of Services Act 1980 is concerned.

This can be very important as a dispute which arises out of or in connection with the contract in general must relate to the services actually contracted for by virtue of the holiday contract, and consequently any ancillary or corollary services, such as child-minding, may not be within the arbitration clause.

It is important to note that the arbitrator in general in domestic arbitration, such as those involving package holidays which are now administered by the Irish Institute of Arbitrators, Irish Branch, in accordance with their Arbitration Rules of 1990. These Rules give wide powers to the arbitrator to determine his own procedure in progressing the matter to the hearing, for example in Rule 22 regarding the arbitrator's power to fix the date, time and place of any meetings and hearings in the arbitration on adequate notice to the parties along with any adjournments. The powers of the arbitrators are fully set out in the Schedule of Powers and Jurisdiction of the Arbitrator in the appendix to the Rules. This, therefore, allows the arbitrator to proceed in a flexible and expeditious manner when dealing with all types of claims, in particular, holiday arbitration which can vary in their complexity and significance in terms of claims for personal injury or mere claims for damage to property or disappointment in the provision of the holiday contracted for. The arbitrator naturally has the power to examine all witnesses on oath and to order the production of documents as with court proceedings.[6] It should also be noted that the court has a supporting power prior to and including the hearing of the dispute by virtue of section 22 of the Arbitration Act 1954, which allows the court to make various orders on an interlocutory basis with regard to discovery, examination of witnesses, injunctions etc. It also makes clear by virtue of section 22(2) that the arbitrator may still have power to make such orders as well as the court orders, if such power is vested in the arbitrator by virtue of the rules of the arbitration under which he is acting.

It is important to note that the Act, as well as the common law, gives important supervisory jurisdiction to the High Court in terms of the steps to be taken prior to the award. For example section 9 of the 1954 Act provides

---

5. [1991] I.L.R.M. 813.
6. See s. 19 of the 1954 Arbitration Act.

the appointment of an arbitrator is irrevocable except where either party be allowed by the Court to revoke his own operator's authority. Also, for example, it requires that an arbitrator can be removed if he has failed to use all reasonable despatch in the conduct of the reference by virtue of section 24 of the 1954 Act. Further, the most important provision with regard to the removing of the arbitrator prior to the award is set out in section 37 which allows the High Court to remove an arbitrator who has misconducted himself or the proceedings. The degree and type of misconduct naturally varies from case to case.

There is a final supporting provision, with regard to an issue of law, which may arise in the course of the arbitration which can be referred to the High Court as to its opinion on the issue in question by virtue of section 35(1)(a). After the award, the Court's jurisdiction focuses on the actual award itself which allows it to set aside an award for the misconduct stated in section 38 (which includes, for example, breaches of a natural justice in the conduct of the proceedings as well as defects in the award), going beyond his jurisdiction or deciding in matters to which were not the subject of the reference. The Court holds the general power at common law to set aside an award for an error of law on the face of the record, namely on the face of the award purely relating to an issue of law and not an issue of fact.[7] The Court also has a power, apart from setting aside the award, to remit the award back to the arbitrator by virtue of section 36, for example, if there was a mistake by virtue of the slip rule in section 28 as to errors of calculation etc. It would also be remitted if there was a necessity to hear fresh original evidence discovered after the making of the award which might have affected the decision in the amount of the award.

The issues which arise in the context of holiday arbitration are usually straightforward in terms of the damage, loss or personal injury sustained by the plaintiff in the ordinary course. The issues which then may arise relate to the gathering of evidence in terms of summoning witnesses on behalf of the tour organiser who would have been at the destination and locus of the accident at the time, to make sure that they are within the jurisdiction but can be called by virtue of the fact that they are agents or servants on behalf of the tour organiser if necessary.

The other issue which arises due to the foreign location of the incident is that with regard to expert evidence concerning any engineering or other evidence required especially in the case of personal injury cases. The issue therefore arises, as to how any expert assessment of the accident locus, in a personal injury case, would be affected by experts resident in this jurisdiction. It would be often the case that an expert engineer would provide a joint or agreed report for both parties on the accident locus being resident in the place of

---

7. See for example, *Keenan v. Shield Insurance Company* [1988] I.R. 89 and *McStay v. Generali SpA* [1991] I.L.R.M. 237.

destination if such a report were necessary. An expert report may not always be necessary as there may be directed to be photographs taken of the accident locus by the tour organiser or, they have already been taken by the consumer at the time of the actual accident. However, it may also be the case that expert evidence may not be required in most personal injury cases suffered in a holiday context.

The other issue which arises in personal injury claims in package holiday arbitration is with regard to medical evidence and the calling and exchange of medical experts' reports on the condition of the consumer/plaintiff. This can follow different ways especially in an effort to avoid the expense and time of calling, in person, medical advisers and consultants if medical reports can be exchanged and agreed in advance of the hearing. This would be the ultimate objective of the arbitrator in order to progress matters as expeditiously and efficiently in terms of time and cost for all parties.

The Tour Operators' Scheme aims to be as cost effective as possible, so it only costs a tour organiser £250 to progress a consumer reference with the consumer/plaintiff free from any cost apart from legal representation unless costs are awarded against him. Therefore it is an efficient and speedy method to obtain the same redress as would be possible by way of a court judgment in a more informal, cost effective and speedier manner, as most consumer references, including holiday arbitrations, are commenced and projected to final award within three months unless there is something particularly complex or unusual about the circumstances or progress of the case.

A difficulty that arises in such arbitrations is that there is no power to join a third party or a co-defendant, so a travel agent could not be joined to an arbitration without the consent of both parties, even though a clear issue arises involving the agreement (such as representation made to the customer on behalf of the tour organiser), which are invariably disowned by the tour organiser. If it becomes unavailable for both parties to consent to the joining of the travel agent, then it can often be at a very late stage when the hearing has already commenced and evidence has been heard, which is highly unsatisfactory.[8] This problem has been solved in some general booking conditions by requiring the travel agent to join in the contract himself and so be part of the arbitration process. This issue also relates to the nature and degree of agency that the travel agent has on behalf of the tour operator, which usually, under the booking condition, arises on the dispatch of the invoice by the agent to the tour operator, even though the booking itself may be largely completed by that time.

With regard to the difference between arbitration and a court trial in this particular context, one should have regard to the critical comments of White:

---

8. See Fogarty, "Recent Developments in Package Holidays and Package Travel Law" I.C.E.L./Bar Council Paper, 23 November 1993.

Qualitatively, there is a difference between trial before a judge in a court established under the Constitution on the one hand and on arbitration on the other. Without questioning the benefits of arbitration as a means of dispute resolution, it is clear that it is an inferior procedure to that of a trial before a judge in court. Although a number of arguments may be made in support of this proposition, it is necessary to refer to only one of these, namely that, unlike in the case of a civil action at law for breach of duty in this jurisdiction, there is no general right of appeal for the aggrieved party form the decision of the arbitrator. The requirement to go to arbitration, therefore, deprives a party to such arbitration of rights which they would otherwise enjoy under the law, the loss of which may result in grave injustice. The argument, therefore, is that, there being this qualitative difference involving loss of rights by the consumer between trial by a judge in court and an arbitrator, a term of a consumer contract excluding recourse to the courts for breach of a term applied by section 39 by insisting upon arbitration, is a term which varies in the meaning of section 40, in as much as it has the effect of excluding or extricating the exercisable right conferred by the provisions in sections 39, namely the right to litigate before the courts a breach of the term of section 39.[9]

He went on to say that:

It may well be left to the Oireachtas to bring about the ultimate desirable reform of relieving consumers of any obligation to sacrifice their right of redress to the courts upon the alter of arbitration.[10]

This view was rejected, due to the benefits of arbitration by Deputy Brennan when he said that:

The legislation will give rise to dramatic increase in travel-related legal cases. Will the Minister consider some form of arbitration procedure for claims? If it rains all the time or someone in Spain falls into the pool having consumed too much alcohol or someone is given a brochure which does not contain the correct health information and contracts a disease, will the only remedy be to take such case to the High Court or will there be some form of instant arbitration to deal with such cases? Some of these issues are emotional and could be dealt with quickly and clearly by an arbitrator. Let us not forget what has happened in the High Court in other jurisdictions.[11]

---

9. White [1991] I.L.T. 92 at 94.
10. White [1991] I.L.T. 92 at 95.
11. 452 *Dáil Debates* Cols 322–333.

In considering the validity and appropriateness of the clause, as well as whether the plaintiff would be best served by arbitration or by court proceedings, it is always necessary to take into account the amount of loss claimed and the circumstances of the case as, naturally, in smaller cases where it is just a case of distress and disappointment and some refund on part or all of the package holiday price, then arbitration may be a better, cheaper and more efficient means of recovering compensation for and on behalf of the consumer/plaintiff.

However, in cases where there is serious personal injury it may be best to try and proceed by way of court proceedings despite the fact that personal injury damages can now be recovered by means of arbitration. This has the obvious advantage of ensuring that the most appropriate compensation is recovered and secondly, all the advantages of court procedures as in, for example, discovery and the subpoena of witnesses can be available. It is true to say that these procedures can also be availed of by way of the arbitration but only on a voluntary basis by virtue of the arbitrator or by virtue of a court application under section 20 of the Arbitration Act 1954.

CHAPTER ELEVEN

Unfair Contract Terms Regulations 1995

Directive 93/13 on Unfair Terms and Consumer Contracts 1993[1] was implemented in this jurisdiction by virtue of the European Communities (Unfair Terms in Consumer Contracts) Regulations 1995.[2] The basic rule of application of these Regulations is that they apply to all consumer contracts which are not individually negotiated as being general, standard form contracts and that in any such contract any term which is deemed to be unfair by virtue of the Regulations does not bind the consumer. This is relevant to the exercise of the courts' discretion in enforcing or not enforcing a particular term in a consumer contract by virtue of the guidelines set out in the Regulations.

The Regulations only apply to contracts between a seller of goods or a supplier of services and a consumer that have not been individually negotiated. A consumer is defined as the natural person who is acting for purposes which are outside his business by virtue of Regulations 2 and 3(1). It is open to question as to what exactly is meant by individual negotiation as to whether there should be an expressed negotiation on the term or merely some mention or discussion of the term between the supplier and the consumer. But, however this is clarified, to some extent as, virtue of Regulation 3(4), it is deemed that a term is not individually negotiated if it has been drafted in advance as the consumer has not been able to influence its substance, particularly in the context of a preformulated standard contract. The onus is on the seller or supplier to prove that the term being challenged was individually negotiated and this applies to each individual term and not just a general requirement for the contract as a whole.[3]

The basic test for unfairness is set out in Regulation 3(2) whereby a term would be regarded as unfair if contrary to the requirement of good faith, the causes are significant in balance to the parties rights and obligations under the contract to the detriment of the consumer. This takes into account the nature

---

1 OJ L95/93, 5/4/93, p. 29.
2 S.I. 27 of 1995 which came into force for all consumer contracts concluded after 31 December 1994. See Appendix 7.
3 See generally, Forde, *Commercial Law* (2nd edn, 1997) paras 5-16 *et seq.*; Chitty, *On Contracts* (27th edn, 1994) Vol. 1, Chapter 14; Murphy [1995] C.L.P. 52; Carney [1995] C.L.P. 118 and Dean [1993] M.L.R. 581.

of the goods or services for which the contract was concluded and all circumstances attending the conclusion of the contract and all other terms of the contract or of another contract of which it is dependent. Therefore, there are several elements to this basic test. Firstly, one has to consider whether the balance of obligations and duties under the contract has shifted to the detriment of the consumer. Secondly, one has to consider the nature of the goods and services involved and the circumstances under which the contract was concluded. Thirdly, one has to take into account four basic factors with regard to ascertaining the unfairness of the contract. These four factors are set out as follows.

1. The strength of the bargaining position of the parties.

2. Where the consumer had an inducement to agree to the term.

3. Whether the goods or services were sold or supplied to the special order of the consumer.

4. The extent to which the seller or the supplier has dealt fairly and equitably with the consumer, whose legitimate interests he has to take into account.

Based on all these factors, the court then has to exercise its discretion as to whether the term is unfair or not. This basic test is supported by the examples given in Schedule 3 of the Regulations which lists a variety of terms which are presumed to be unfair, such as exclusion clauses, terms allowing unilateral alteration by the seller and also exclusive arbitration clauses.

With regard to the purpose and objective of the Regulations as set out in the Directive, and approved in the preamble to Directive 93/13, it was emphasised that the consumer protection objective not only facilitated greater freedom of movement in terms of buying goods across the EU and facilitating the establishment of the internal market, but also allowed that the purchase of goods and services should be protected against the abuse of a seller or a supplier, in particular against one side of the standard contracts and the unfair exclusion of essential rights and contracts. Therefore, it allowed the consumer to have equal protection under oral, written and standard form contracts. It was emphasised that, with regard to the criteria for determining unfairness, the Directive was minimal and that the list of factors to be included for that adjudication were of indicative value only so the scope of these terms may be the subject of application of more restrictive requirements by the Member States in their national law.

With regard to unfairness, there is an important qualification in Regulation 4 as to when a term may be considered unfair or not. It provides that a term shall not, of itself, be considered to be unfair by relation to the definition of the main subject matter of the contract or to the adequacy of the price and remuneration, as against the goods and services supplied, insofar as these terms are in plain, intelligible language. This means that unfairness can not of itself be determined by reference to the price and quality of the goods as whether they are more dear or expensive, as long as they by themselves are terms which do not confuse in plain or intelligible language. With regard to the terms which may be considered unfair it is important to note that the terms outlined in the Directive, and hence in Schedule 3 of the Regulations, are an indicative and non-exhaustive list of the terms as per Regulation 3(7).

The scope of the Regulations is limited by virtue of Schedule 1, which outlines a series of contracts which are not the subject of the Regulations relating to such areas as employment, succession rights, family law, company law and any terms which reflect mandatory, statutory or regulated provisions of Ireland or by virtue of membership of the Community. The terms alleged to be unfair by virtue of the Schedule include for example:

- terms (a) and (b) covering exclusion clauses;

- term (c) concerning penalty clauses for cancellation or the consumer not concluding the contract;

- terms (d) (e), (f), (g), (j) and (l) regarding unilateral cancellation by the supplier with no compensation to the consumer or a penalty paid by the consumer.

It also extends to other general provisions of terms, which will probably have the most likely impact in the package holiday area, namely:

- (i) whereby terms which irrevocably bind the consumer to terms and with which he had no real opportunity of becoming equated before the conclusion of the contract, and

- (q) terms which are excluding or hindering in the consumer's right to take legal action or exercise any other legal remedy, particularly by requiring the consumer to take disputes exclusively to arbitration not covered by legal provisions, unduly restricting the evidence available to him or imposing on him a burden of proof which, according to the applicable law, should lie with another part of the contract.

Therefore, the general provision in term (i) affects all general standard booking conditions with which the consumer could not have any input or be aware of the detail or content thereof and secondly, with regard to any arbitration clause which unduly restricts the consumer's remedies and the way he may prove his case.

The impact on ordinary arbitration clauses which are standard to the Tour Operators' Scheme, remains to be seen. But it could be said that the requirements under term (q) relate only to arbitration not covered by legal provisions. This, on the face it, means arbitration not covered by law but all arbitration in Ireland is automatically covered by the Arbitration Acts 1954 to 1980 unless otherwise specified and since this is the case ordinarily with the Tour Operators' Scheme, would not seem to apply. Further, it can be said that unless the arbitrator unduly restricts the evidence available to him (for example, foreign evidence, witnesses, expert reports etc.) or alters the burden of proof, it could not be considered unfair. It should be borne in mind that by virtue of the 1995 Act the burden of proof, under section 20 of the Act, for failure of performance is essentially reversed and for the tour organiser anyway and not on the consumer. By applying the Act, it would prevent such a clause being unfair with regard to this particular provision under the Unfair Terms Regulations.

There are two further requirements which were imposed by virtue of the Regulations. Firstly, that written contracts must be drafted in plain intelligible language by sellers or suppliers by virtue of Regulation 4. However it seems that there is no particular specific form laid out in the Regulations for failure to do so. It could be the case that where appropriate, an ambiguous term could be disregarded. However, so long as the language is clear, a term will not, of itself, be deemed unfair by virtue of the sum agreed to be payable for the goods of services or the definition the subject matter of the contract. Finally, the Regulations, by virtue of Regulation 5(2), imposes a strict rule of interpretation as to the meaning of terms of contracts where there is doubt about the meaning of a term, the interpretation which is the most favourable to the consumer shall prevail.

The list of examples set out in Schedule 3 to the Regulations, includes the basic exclusion clauses which either exclude or limit the consumers rights and remedies against non-performance of the contract. It is possible that this could be interpreted as also covering clauses which fix limited sums of compensation for certain failures under the contract and, in a package holiday context, this could include sums for significant pre-departure changes or alterations to essential terms of the contract. The Regulations also include instances where consumers are required to pay overly high compensation when they opt out of a contract, such as in cancellation charges which, if they do not reflect the true loss to the package holiday provider, could arguably be considered unfair.

Another example that could have an impact in this area is to bind a consumer to terms with which he had no real opportunity to become acquainted before the conclusion of the contract. For example, if this would occur in last-minute bookings by telephone where the main provisions of the contract were not recited in full and in advance of the contract being made by way of the telephone call. Further, the Regulations include terms which permit the supplier to charge the consumer where the latter decided not to include or perform the contract, without providing for the consumer to receive compensation of an equivalent amount from the supplier where the latter is the party cancelling the contract. This is relevant, again, with relation to cancellation charges, if there are large cancellation charges imposed on the consumer for cancelling his holiday. Yet if the operator or package holiday provider was in the same position and he was the one cancelling, there would be a minimal or nominal amount of compensation on a scale payable to the consumer which did not reflect the true cost to the consumer.

The other important example is in relation to arbitration clauses whereby the liability or the rules of evidence are limited by virtue of the scheme or clause in question and this could be used as an argument to get round an arbitration clause in a package holiday contract, even though it was in conformance with the basic Chartered Institute Arbitration Rules and the general standard conditions applicable to the arbitration clauses in the industry.

CONCLUSION

Therefore, the Unfair Contract Terms Regulations 1995 provide the basis for an argument in trying to avoid certain onerous provisions imposed on the consumer by the general standard conditions of the package holiday provider above and beyond the rights and obligations granted in favour of the consumer in the 1995 Act. It remains to be seen what impact these will have in general terms or in the more specific context of the package holiday industry. There are still a lot of unresolved questions with the 1995 Act and its consequences, which will only be clarified by means of specific judicial determinations on the issues raised.

This again would only be a product of both consumer awareness and awareness of their advisers, as to the best way to benefit the consumer in the context of both the 1995 Act and the Unfair Contract Terms Regulations. It must be remembered that the effect of a term being deemed to be unfair by virtue of the Regulations is that it will be void under Regulation 5(1), but the contract itself will continue to bind the parties, if it is capable of continuing in existence without the unfair term by virtue of Regulation 5(2). Therefore, it is only a defence against a specific term imposed on behalf of the consumer and does not provide that a contract as a whole or any other obligations the consumer may have under the contract which is not the subject of the specific term in question will be void.

APPENDIX ONE

TRANSPORT (TOUR OPERATORS AND TRAVEL AGENTS) ACT, 1982

TRANSPORT (TOUR OPERATORS AND TRAVEL AGENTS) ACT, 1982

ARRANGEMENT OF SECTIONS

PART 1

PRELIMINARY AND GENERAL

PART II

LICENCES

PART III

THE BOND

PART IV

TRAVELLERS' PROTECTION BOND

PART V

MISCELLANEOUS

20. Offences and penalties.
21. Provisions in relation to offences.
22. Indictment of bodies corporate.
23. Provisions as to proceedings in court or in liquidation.
24. Payments to Fund and Bond not part of tour operator's or travel agent's assets.
25. Orders and regulations.

ACTS REFERRED TO

Criminal Procedure Act, 1967	1967, No. 12
Public Offices Fees Act, 1879	1879, c. 58
Petty Sessions (Ireland) Act, 1851	1851, c. 93

TRANSPORT (TOUR OPERATORS AND TRAVEL AGENTS) ACT, 1982
Number 3 of 1982

AN ACT TO PROVIDE FOR THE REGULATION OF THE TRAVEL TRADE AND FOR THE PROTECTION OF CUSTOMERS OF TOUR OPERATORS AND TRAVEL AGENTS, FOR THOSE PURPOSES TO ENABLE THE MINISTER FOR TRANSPORT TO ISSUE LICENCES TO TOUR OPERATORS AND TRAVEL AGENTS, AND TO REQUIRE TOUR OPERATORS AND TRAVEL AGENTS TO ENTER INTO AND MAINTAIN BONDS, TO PROVIDE FOR THE ESTABLISHMENT OF A FUND TO BE KNOWN AS THE TRAVELLERS' PROTECTION FUND AND FOR TUE PAYMENT OF CONTRIBUTIONS BY TOUR OPERATORS TOWARDS THE RESOURCES OF THAT FUND: AND TO PROVIDE FOR OTHER MATTERS CONNECTED WITH THE FOREGOING. [30th March, 1982]

BE IT ENACTED BY THE OIREACHTAS AS FOLLOWS:

PART 1

PRELIMINARY AND GENERAL

1.—(1) This Act may be cited as the Transport (Tour Operators and Travel Agents) Act, 1982.

(2) This Act shall come into operation on such day or days as may be fixed therefore by order or orders of the Minister, either generally or by reference to a particular purpose or provision or mode of transport and different days may be so fixed for different purposes and different provisions of this Act.

Short title and commencement.

2.—(1) In this Act

Interpretation.

"the Bond" has the meaning specified in section 13 of this Act;

"carrier" means a person whose principal business is the provision of transport by land, sea or air on aircraft, vessels or other modes of transport owned and operated by such person;

"the Fund" means the Travellers' Protection Fund established pursuant to section 15 of this Act;

"the Minister" means the Minister for Transport;

"overseas travel contract" means a contract for the carriage of a party to the contract (with or without any other person) by air, sea or land transport to a place outside Ireland, whether the provision of the carriage is the sole subject matter of the contract or is associated with the provision thereunder, of any accommodation, facilities or services;

"tour operator" means a person other than a carrier who arranges for the purpose of selling or offering for sale to the public accommodation for travel by air, sea or land transport to destinations outside Ireland, or who holds himself out by advertising or otherwise as one who may make available such accommodation, either solely or in association with other accommodation, facilities or services;

"travel agent" means a person other than a carrier who, as agent, sells or offers to sell to, or purchases or offers to. purchase on behalf of, the public accommodation on air. sea or land transport to destinations outside Ireland or who holds himself out by advertising or otherwise as one who may make available such accommodation, either solely or in association with other accommodation, facilities or services.

(2) For the purpose of this Act, a person shall be deemed to be a customer of a tour operator or travel agent if he has made any payment, either directly or indirectly, to the tour operator or travel agent, under or with the intention of entering into an overseas travel contract.

(3) For the purposes of this Act, a loss or liability incurred by a customer of a tour operator or travel agent is a loss or liability incurred in connection with an overseas travel contract if it results from the inability or failure of the tour operator or travel agent to meet his financial or contractual obligations in relation to the overseas travel contract.

(4) For the purposes of this Act "the inability or failure of a tour operator or travel agent to meet his financial or contractual obligations" means that, in relation to that tour operator or travel agent, one or more of the following events has occurred–

    (*a*) a petition is granted by a court for the compulsory winding up of the business of the tour operator or travel agent,

    (*b*) the tour operator or travel agent by reason of being unable to fulfil his financial obligations seeks a voluntary winding up of his business or has convened a meeting of his creditors for the purpose of considering a settlement of his liabilities to such creditors,

    (*c*) a receiver is appointed over the assets of the tour operator or travel agent,

    (*d*) the tour operator or travel agent has failed to discharge his debts or is unable to discharge his debts or has ceased to carry on business by reason of his inability to discharge his debts,

    (*e*) the tour operator or travel agent has committed an act of bankruptcy,

    (*f*) the Minister has reasonable grounds for believing that, having regard to all the circumstances, the tour operator or travel agent is unable to, or has failed to, carry out his obligations to his customers in relation to an overseas travel contract.

Expenses.   **3.**—Any expenses incurred by the Minister in the administration of this Act shall, to such extent as may be sanctioned by the Minister for Finance, be paid out of moneys provided by the Oireachtas.

PART II

LICENCES

Restriction on carrying on business as tour operator.   **4.**—A person shall not carry on business as a tour operator or hold himself out, by advertisement or otherwise, as carrying on such business unless he is the holder of a licence under this Act authorising the carrying on of such business.

Restriction on carrying on business as a travel agent.   **5.**—A person shall not carry on business as a travel agent or hold himself out, by advertisement or otherwise, as carrying on such business unless he is the holder of a licence under this Act authorising the carrying on of such business.

Licences.   **6.**—(1) The Minister shall grant a licence to carry on business as a tour operator or as a travel agent to a person if he is satisfied that such person complies with the requirements of this Act.

(2) The Minister shall refuse a licence to carry on business as a tour operator or as a travel agent if he is not satisfied that such person complies with the requirements of this Act.

(3) Without prejudice to the generality of subsection (2) of this section, the Minister shall refuse a licence under this Act to a person if he is not satisfied that –

    (*a*) the financial, business and organisational resources of such person and any financial arrangements made or to be made by him are adequate for discharging his actual and potential obligations in respect of the activities (if any) in which he is engaged or in which he proposes to engage if the licence is granted, or

    (*b*) having regard to the past activities of such person or of any person employed by him or, if such person is a body corporate, having regard to the past activities of any director, secretary, shareholder, officer or servant of the body corporate, such person is a fit and proper person to carry on business as a tour operator or travel agent, as the case may be.

(4) A licence granted under this Act may contain such terms and conditions as the Minister may think appropriate and specifies in the licence.

(5) A licence granted under this Act shall remain in force for such period as the Minister thinks fit and specifies in the licence.

7.—The Minister may by regulations made under this section specify –

    (*a*) the conditions that shall be complied with before a licence is granted under this Act,

    (*b*) the manner in which applications for the grant of a licence under this Act shall be made,

    (*c*) the nature and extent of the information required to be furnished by an applicant for the grant of a licence under this Act,

    (*d*) the form in which an application for a licence under this Act shall be made,

    (*e*) the form of licence to be granted under this Act,

    (*f*) the manner in which members of the public shall be made aware that a tour operator or travel agent is the holder of a licence granted under this Act,

    (*g*) the books, accounts and other records required to be maintained by the holder of a licence granted under this Act,

    (*h*) the place where any books, accounts or other records required to be maintained pursuant to this Act shall be kept.

Power to make regulations in relation to licences.

8.—(1) Where the holder of a licence is in breach of, or fails, neglects or refuses to comply with any term or condition of a licence under this Act, the Minister may –

    (*a*) revoke the licence, or

    (*b*) vary any term or condition of the licence.

(2) Notwithstanding the generality of subsection (1) of this section, the Minister may revoke, or vary the terms and conditions of, a licence granted under this Act if he is no longer satisfied that–

    (*a*) the financial, business and organisational resources of the holder of the licence or any financial arrangements made by him are adequate for discharging his actual and potential obligations in respect of the business for which he has been granted a licence, or

    (*b*) having regard to the manner in which the holder of the licence is carrying on his business, he is a fit and proper person to carry on business as a tour operator or travel agent.

Revocation and varying of terms and conditions of licences.

9.—(1) Whenever the Minister proposes to revoke, other than pursuant to section 10 of this Act, or to vary the terms and conditions of, a licence granted under this Act, he shall notify the holder of the licence of his proposal and of the reasons for such proposal and shall, if any representations are made in writing by such holder within seven days, consider the representations.

(2) Whenever the Minister refuses to grant a licence or decides, having considered any representations that may have been made by the holder of a licence, to revoke the licence or to vary any term or condition of the licence, he shall notify the applicant for, or as the case

may be, the holder of, the licence of the refusal or decision and such applicant or such holder may within seven days appeal to the High Court against such refusal or such decision.

(3) On the hearing of an appeal under this section in relation to a refusal to grant a licence under this Act or in relation to a decision of the Minister to revoke, or vary the terms and conditions of, a licence granted under this Act, the High Court may either confirm the refusal or decision or may allow the appeal and, where an appeal is allowed, the Minister shall grant the licence or shall not revoke, or vary the terms and conditions of the licence as the case may be.

(4) A decision of the High Court on an appeal under this section shall be final save that, by leave of that Court, an appeal from the decision shall lie to the Supreme Court on a specified question of law.

(5) An appeal shall not lie in any case where the Minister refuses to grant a licence to an applicant who does not comply with the provisions of section 13 of this Act or in any case where the Minister revokes a licence pursuant to section 10 of this Act.

(6) Where, after the commencement of Part III of this Act, a person appeals against a decision of the Minister to revoke or vary any term or condition of a licence or appeals against a refusal of the Minister to grant a licence, such person shall not, pending the determination of the appeal, carry on business as a tour operator or travel agent unless he complies with the provisions of section 13 of this Act.

Revocation of licence in certain circumstances.

10.—Where, owing to the failure or inability of a tour operator or travel agent to meet his financial or contractual obligations, any payment is or falls to be made pursuant to the Bond or from the Fund to a customer, the Minister shall forthwith revoke any licence granted under this Act.

Power of entry and inspection.

11.—A person authorised by the Minister may at any time enter into any premises in which the Minister has reason to believe that a inspection person is carrying on business as a tour operator or travel agent and there inspect and examine books, accounts or records required to be maintained pursuant to this Act.

Fees.

12.—(1) The Minister may, by regulations, made with the consent of the Minister for Finance, specify the scale of fees payable in respect of applications for licences under this Act.

(2) The Minister may make such charges as he considers appropriate in relation to any matter connected with a licence under this Act and the amount of any such charge shall be determined by the Minister, after consultation with the Minister for Finance, and shall be specified in regulations made under subsection (1) of this section.

(3) All fees and charges payable under this Act shall be paid into, or disposed of for the benefit of, the Exchequer in accordance with the directions of the Minister for Finance.

(4) The Public Offices Fees Act, 1879, shall not apply in respect of fees payable pursuant to this Act.

PART III

THE BOND

The Bond.

13.—(1) A tour operator or travel agent shall, before a licence is granted to him under this Act, furnish evidence acceptable to the Minister that the tour operator or travel agent, as the case may be, has entered into an arrangement satisfactory to the Minister for the protection of persons who, during the period of validity of the licence, enter into contracts with him relating to overseas travel.

(2) The arrangement referred to in subsection (1) of this section is in this Act referred to as "the Bond".

(3) The Bond shall provide that, in the event of the inability or failure of the tour operator or travel agent concerned to meet his financial or contractual obligations in relation to overseas travel contracts, a sum of money will become available to the Minister, or to any person nominated or approved of by the Minister, as trustee, to be applied for the benefit of any customer of the tour operator or travel agent concerned who has incurred loss or liability because of such inability or failure to meet financial or contractual obligations.

(4) The sum of money referred to in subsection (3) of this section may be applied for all or any of the following purposes–

(*a*) to provide travel facilities for any customer of the tour operator or travel agent concerned who is outside Ireland and who is unable to make the return journey provided for in the overseas travel contract by reason of the inability or failure of the tour operator or travel agent concerned to fulfil his financial or contractual obligations in relation to such overseas travel contract;

(*b*) to reimburse a customer of a tour operator or travel agent for any reasonable expenses necessarily incurred by such customer by reason of the inability or failure of the tour operator or travel agent to meet his financial or contractual obligations in relation to an overseas travel contract;

(*c*) to refund, as far as possible, to a customer of a tour operator or travel agent any payments made by him to the tour operator or travel agent in respect of an overseas travel contract which could not be completed by reason of the inability or failure of the tour operator or travel agent to meet his financial or contractual obligations in relation to such overseas travel contract;

(*d*) to defray any reasonable expenses incurred by the Minister, or provide for any payments by the Minister, on behalf of a customer of a tour operator or travel agent in respect of an overseas travel contract which could not be completed by reason of the inability or failure of the tour operator or travel agent to meet his financial or contractual obligations in relation to such overseas travel contract.

(5) The Minister or, as the case may be, the person nominated or approved of by the Minister, as trustee, shall keep all proper and usual accounts, including an income and expenditure account and a balance sheet, of all moneys received by him on foot of a bond and of all disbursements made by him from any such moneys.

(6) As soon as may be after the end of each year, accounts kept in pursuance of this section shall be submitted to the Comptroller and Auditor General for audit and, immediately after the audit, a copy of the income and expenditure account and of the balance sheet and a copy of the report of the Comptroller and Auditor General on the accounts shall be laid before each House of the Oireachtas.

(7) Without prejudice to any existing right of a customer of a tour operator or travel agent to recover damages in relation to the standard of accommodation or service provided pursuant to an overseas travel contract, nothing in this section shall be construed as enabling such customer to recover any damages out of any sum of money made available under the Bond.

14.—The Minister may, by regulations, provide that – Requirements in

(*a*) arrangements in relation to the Bond shall be entered into only with persons of relation to a class or classes specified in the regulations, and the Bond.

(*b*) the Bond shall be for such minimum sum and valid for such minimum period as may be specified in the regulations.

PART IV

TRAVELLERS' PROTECTION BOND

Travellers' Protection Fund.

15.—(1) The Minister shall establish a fund to be known as the Travellers' Protection Fund (in this Act referred to as "the Fund") from which payments may be made in accordance with the provisions of section 18 of this Act in respect of losses or liabilities incurred by customers of tour operators or travel agents who held a licence under this Act or whose licence has been revoked and the revocation is the subject of an appeal to the court, in consequence of the inability or failure of the tour operators or travel agents to meet their financial or contractual obligations in respect of overseas travel contracts.

(2) The collection, retention and disbursement of the resources of the Fund shall be a function of the Minister.

(3) The Minister may by regulations made under this section nominate any person specified in the regulations to carry out any or all of the functions conferred on the Minister by this section.

Contributions to Fund.

16.—(1) A tour operator shall make contributions to the Fund of such amounts and at such times on such basis as may be specified in regulations made by the Minister, with the consent of the Minister for Finance.

(2) Regulations made by the Minister under this section may –
(*a*) provide that contributions for the Fund may be paid to the Minister or to such other person as may be specified in the regulations;
(*b*) provide that different contributions may be made by different classes of tour operators having regard to the scale of business of the tour operator and may specify the manner for determining the amounts of different contributions;
(*c*) specify the time and manner in which payments of sums due in respect of contributions to the Fund may be made.

Resources of the Fund.

17.—(1) The resources of the Fund shall be maintained and administered by the Minister or, as the case may be, by a person nominated by him pursuant to section 15 of this Act.

(2) The costs of administration of the Fund shall be defrayed from the resources of the Fund.

(3) The Minister or, as the case may be, the person nominated by him pursuant to section 15 of this Act, shall keep all proper and usual accounts of all moneys paid into the Fund and of all disbursements from the Fund including an income and expenditure account and a balance sheet.

(4) As soon as may be after the end of each year, accounts kept in pursuance of this section shall be submitted to the Comptroller and Auditor General for audit and, immediately after the audit, a copy of the income and expenditure account and of the balance sheet and a copy of the report of the Comptroller and Auditor General on the accounts shall be laid before each House of the Oireachtas.

Disbursements from Funds.

18.—(1) Payments may be made from the Fund for all or any of from the following purposes–
(*a*) to provide travel facilities for any customer of a tour operator or travel agent who is outside Ireland and who is unable to make the return journey provided for in an overseas travel contract by reason of the inability or failure of the tour operator or travel agent concerned to fulfil his financial or contractual obligations in relation to such overseas travel contract;
(*b*) to reimburse a customer of a tour operator or travel agent for any reasonable expenses necessarily incurred by such customer by reason of the inability or failure of the tour operator or travel agent to meet his financial or contractual obligations in relation to an overseas travel contract;
(*c*) to refund, as far as possible, to a customer of a tour operator or travel agent any

payments made by him to the tour operator or travel agent in respect of an overseas travel contract which could not be completed by reason of the inability or failure of the tour operator or travel agent to meet his financial or contractual obligations in relation to such overseas travel contract;

(*d*) to defray any reasonable expenses incurred by the Minister, or provide for any payments by the Minister, on behalf of a customer of a tour operator or travel agent in respect of an overseas travel contract which could not be completed by reason of the inability or failure of the tour operator or travel agent to meet his financial or contractual obligations in relation to such overseas travel contract.

(2) Payments may not be made from the Fund to a person in respect of any loss or liability incurred in connection with an overseas travel contract unless the tour operator or travel agent concerned held, at the time such person entered into the contract, a licence under this Act, or unless the licence of such operator or travel agent was, at that time, revoked and the revocation is the subject of an appeal to the court.

(3) Where money is payable on foot of the Bond to, or for the benefit of, a customer of a tour operator or travel agent for the purpose of compensating such customer for losses or liabilities incurred by him in connection with an overseas travel contract

(*a*) a payment shall not be made out of the Fund until all moneys payable under the Bond have been paid to, or for the benefit of, such person, and

(*b*) a payment shall not be made out of the Fund to any person in respect of losses or liabilities incurred by him in any case where such person has already been reimbursed in full from moneys payable pursuant to the Bond.

(4) If any event occurs which may affect or delay payments pursuant to the Bond, the Minister or any person nominated by him pursuant to this Act, at his discretion, may make payments from the Fund to or for the benefit of any customer of a tour operator or travel agent who may be affected and any amount so paid shall be repaid to the Fund as soon as may be after any funds payable pursuant to the Bond have been realised.

(5) Without prejudice to any existing right of a customer of a tour operator or travel agent to recover damages in relation to the standard of accommodation or service provided pursuant to an overseas travel contract, nothing in this section shall be construed as enabling such customer to recover any such damages from the Fund.

(6) Regulations made by the Minister under this section may–

(*a*) provide for the determination of the amounts of payments from the Fund,

(*b*) provide for the terms on which and the manner in which any payments from the Fund may be made in any particular case or classes of case,

(*c*) specify the manner in which payments are to be made in any case where the amount of the Fund and any sums due pursuant to the Bond of a tour operator or travel agent are insufficient to satisfy the claims of all persons concerned, and, in particular, may specify that in any such case payments shall be made in proportion to the amount established to be due in respect of each claim.

19.—(1) Moneys of the Fund shall be maintained in a current account to be managed and controlled by the Minister or in an investment account to be managed and controlled by the Minister for Finance.

Investment of money of fund

(2) Sums payable into the Fund shall be paid into the current account thereof and sums payable out of the Fund shall be paid out of that account.

(3) Moneys standing to the credit of the current account and not required to meet current expenditure shall be transferred to the investment account of the Fund.

(4) Whenever the moneys in the current account of the Fund are insufficient to meet the liabilities of that account, there shall be transferred to that account from the investment account of the Fund such sums as may be necessary for the purpose of discharging those liabilities.

(5) Subject to subsection (4) of this section, moneys standing to the credit of the investment account of the Fund shall be invested by the Minister for Finance, and income

arising from any such investment shall be paid into that account.

(6) An investment pursuant to subsection (5) of this section may be in any securities in which trustees are for the time being by law empowered to invest trust funds or in any of the stocks, funds and securities as are for the time being authorised by law as, investments for Post Office Savings Bank funds.

PART V

MISCELLANEOUS

Offences and Penalties.

20.—(1) Any person who carries on business, or holds himself out as carrying on business, as a tour operator in contravention of section 4 of this Act, or as a travel agent in contravention of section 5 of this Act, shall be guilty of an offence and shall be liable, on conviction on indictment, to a fine not exceeding £100,000 or, at the discretion of the court, to imprisonment for a term not exceeding 5 years, or to both the fine and the imprisonment.

(2) Any person who obstructs or impedes a person authorised by the Minister in the exercise of the powers conferred on him by section 11 of this Act, shall be guilty of an offence and shall be liable on conviction on indictment to a fine not exceeding £10,000 or, at the discretion of the court, to imprisonment for a term not exceeding 2 years or, to both such fine and imprisonment.

(3) Any person who, for the purpose of obtaining for himself or for any other person, a licence under this Act, makes a statement which he knows to be false, or who recklessly makes a statement which is false in a material particular shall be guilty of an offence and shall be liable on conviction on indictment to a fine not exceeding £5,000 or, at the discretion of the court, to imprisonment for a term not exceeding 2 years, or to both the fine and the imprisonment.

(4) A Justice of the District Court shall have jurisdiction to try summarily an offence under this section if–

(a) that Justice is of opinion that the facts proved or alleged against a defendant charged with such an offence constitute a minor offence fit to be tried summarily,

(b) the Director of Public Prosecutions consents, and

(c) the defendant (on being informed by the Justice of his right to be tried by a jury) does not object to being tried summarily,

and, upon conviction under this subsection, the said defendant shall be liable to a fine not exceeding £500 or, at the discretion of the court, to imprisonment for a term not exceeding 12 months, or to both the fine and the imprisonment.

(5) Section 13 of the Criminal Procedure Act, 1967, shall apply in relation to an offence under this section as if, in lieu of the penalties specified in subsection (3) of the said section 13, there were specified therein the penalty provided for in this section, and the reference in subsection (2) (a) of the said section 13 to the penalties provided for in the said subsection (3) shall be, construed and have effect accordingly.

Provisions in relation to offences.

21.—(1) Summary proceedings in respect of an offence under this Act may be brought and prosecuted by the Minister.

(2) Notwithstanding section 10 (4) of the Petty Sessions (Ireland) Act, 1851, summary proceedings for an offence under this Act may be instituted–

(a) in every case, within two years from the date of the offence, and

(b) if at the expiry of that period, the person to be charged is outside the State, within six months of the date on which he enters the State.

(3) Where an offence under this Act is committed by a body corporate and the offence is proved to have been committed with the consent or connivance of, or to be attributable to

any neglect on the part of, any director, manager, secretary or other similar officer of the body or any person who was purporting to act in any such capacity, he, as well as the body, shall be guilty of the offence and shall be liable to be proceeded against and punished accordingly.

22.—(1) A body corporate may be sent forward for trial on indictment for an offence under section 20 of this Act with or without recognisances.

(2) On arraignment before the Circuit Court, the body corporate may enter in writing by its representative a plea of guilty or not guilty and, if it does not appear by a representative appointed by it for the purpose, or, though it does so appear, fails to enter any plea, the court shall order a plea of not guilty to be entered and the trial shall proceed as though the body corporate had duly entered that plea.

Indictment of bodies corporate.

23.—In determining, in proceedings in any court, or in any liquidation, a claim by a person in respect of an overseas travel contract against a tour operator or travel agent, the extent, if any, to which such person may have benefited pursuant to the provisions of this Act shall be taken into account by the court or, as the case may be, by the liquidator.

Provisions as to proceedings in cout or in litigation.

24.—Neither payments made to the Fund pursuant to section 15 of this Act by a tour operator nor any moneys payable on foot of the Bond entered into by such tour operator or by a travel agent pursuant to section 13 of this Act shall be reckoned to be part of the assets of such tour operator or travel agent and none of such moneys shall be used to discharge any liability of the tour operator or travel agent otherwise than in accordance with this Act.

Payments to Fune and Bond not part of tour operator's or travel agent's assets.

25.—(1) Any order or regulation made by the Minister under this Act may contain such incidental or consequential provisions as appear to the Minister to be necessary or expedient for the purpose of implementing the provisions of this Act.

Orders and Regulations.

(2) The Minister may make such orders or regulations as appear to him to be necessary or expedient to implement the provisions of this Act and the Minister may amend or revoke any order made under this section.

(3) Every order and regulation made by the Minister under this Act shall be laid before each House of the Oireachtas as soon as may be after it is made, and if a resolution annulling the order or regulation, as the case may be, is passed by either House within the next subsequent twenty-one days on which that House has sat after the order or regulation is laid before it, the order or regulation shall be annulled accordingly, but without prejudice to the validity of anything previously done thereunder.

APPENDIX TWO

PACKAGE HOLIDAYS AND TRAVEL TRADE ACT, 1995

PACKAGE HOLIDAYS AND TRAVEL TRADE ACT, 1995

ARRANGEMENT OF SECTIONS

PART I

PRELIMINARY AND GENERAL

PART II

REGULATION OF TRAVEL CONTRACT

PART III

SECURITY

PART IV

AMENDMENT OF TRANSPORT (TOUR OPERATORS AND TRAVEL AGENTS) ACT, 1982

SCHEDULE

COUNCIL DIRECTIVE No. 90/314/EEC

ACTS REFERRED TO

PACKAGE HOLIDAYS AND TRAVEL TRADE ACT, 1995
Number 17 *of* 1995

AN ACT TO ENABLE EFFECT TO BE GIVEN TO COUNCIL DIRECTIVE NO. 90/314/EEC OF 13 JUNE 1990 OF THE EUROPEAN COMMUNITIES ON PACKAGE TRAVEL, PACKAGE HOLIDAYS AND PACKAGE TOURS, TO AMEND THE TRANSPORT (TOUR OPERATORS AND TRAVEL AGENTS) ACT, 1982, AND TO PROVIDE FOR CONNECTED MATTERS. [17th July, 1995]

BE IT ENACTED BY THE OIREACHTAS AS FOLLOWS:

PART 1

PRELIMINARY AND GENERAL

1.—(1) This Act may be cited as the Package Holidays and Travel Trade Act, 1995.

(2) The Transport (Tour Operators and Travel Agents) Act, 1982 and this Act may be cited together as the Transport (Travel Trade) Acts, 1982 and 1995.

(3) This Act shall come into operation on such day or days as may be fixed therefor by order or orders of the Minister either generally or with reference to any particular purpose or provision and different days may be so fixed for different purposes or different provisions of this Act.

Short title, collective citation and commencement.

2.—(1) In this Act, except where the context otherwise requires –

Interpretation.

"the Act of 1982' means the Transport (Tour Operators and Travel Agents) Act, 1982;

"authorised officer" has the meaning assigned to it by *section 21*;

"consumer" –

    (a) in relation to a contract, means the person who takes or agrees to take the package ("the principal contractor");

    (b) in any other case, means, as the context requires–

        (i)   the principal contractor,

        (ii) any person on whose behalf the principal contractor agrees to purchase a package ("another beneficiary"), or

        (iii) any person to whom the principal contractor or another beneficiary transfers the package ("the transferee");

"contract" means an agreement linking the consumer to the organiser (whether dealing directly with the consumer or through a retailer);

"contravenes", in reference to any provision of this Act, includes a failure or refusal to comply with the provision;

"the Directive" means Council Directive No. 90/314/EEC of 13 June 1990[1] on package travel, package holidays and package tours the text of which in the English language is set out for convenience of reference in the *Schedule* to this Act;

"the Director" means the Director of Consumer Affairs;

---

1.   O.J. No. L 158/59 23.6.1990

"functions" includes powers and duties;

"the Minister" means the Minister for Transport, Energy and Communications;

"offer" includes an invitation to a person, whether by means of advertising or otherwise, to make an offer to buy a package;

"organiser" has the meaning assigned to it by *section 3*;

"package", subject to *subsection (2)*, means a combination of at least two of the following components pre-arranged by the organiser when sold or offered for sale at an inclusive price and when the service covers a period of more than twenty-four hours or includes overnight accommodation–

 (a) transport;

 (b) accommodation;

 (c) other tourist services, not ancillary to transport or accommodation, accounting for a significant proportion of the package;

"package provider" (or "provider") means–

 (a) in circumstances other than those described at *paragraph (b)*, the organiser, or where the retailer is also party to the contract, both the organiser and the retailer, or

 (b) in the case of a package sold or offered for sale by an organiser established outside the State through a retailer established within the State (and where the transport component of the package commences outside the State), the retailer;

"premises" includes any building, dwelling, temporary construction, vehicle, ship or aircraft;

"record" means any book, document or any other written or printed material in any form including any information stored, maintained or preserved by means of any mechanical or electronic device, whether or not stored, maintained or preserved in a legible form;

"repatriation" means the return of the consumer to the place of departure or other place agreed with the consumer;

"retailer" means the person who sells or offers for sale the package put together by the organiser.

(2) The submission of separate accounts for different components of the package shall not cause the arrangements to be other than a package for the purpose of this Act.

(3) This Act applies to packages offered for sale or sold in the State.

(4) In this Act–

 (a) a reference to a section or a Part is a reference to a section or a Part of this Act unless it is indicated that a reference to some other enactment is intended;

 (b) a reference to a subsection, paragraph or subparagraph is a reference to the subsection, paragraph or subparagraph of the provision in which the reference occurs unless it is indicated that reference to some other provision is intended.

(5) In this Act a reference to any enactment shall be construed as a reference to that enactment, as adapted or extended by or under any subsequent enactment including this Act.

(6) A word or expression that is used in this Act and is also used in the Directive has, unless the contrary intention appears, the meaning in this Act that it has in the Directive.

(7) In construing a provision of this Act, a court shall give to it a construction that will give effect to the Directive and, for this purpose a court shall have regard to the provisions of the Directive including its preamble.

Organiser.   **3.**—(1) In this Act "organiser" means a person who, otherwise than occasionally, organises packages and sells or offers them for sale to a consumer, whether directly or through a retailer.

(2) For the purposes of *subsection (1)*, a person shall not be regarded as organising packages occasionally unless that person is a member of a class specified in regulations made by the Minister under this subsection.

4.—The expenses incurred by the Minister, any other Minister of the Government or the Director in the administration of this Act (including the costs and expenses incurred in the investigation and prosecution of offences) shall, to such extent as may be sanctioned by the Minister for Finance, be paid out of moneys provided by the Oireachtas.

Expenses.

5.—(1) The Minister may, with the consent of the Minister for Finance, from time to time specify the scale of fees payable in respect of the approval of an approved body under section 23 or 24.

Fees.

(2) The Minister may make such charges in relation to any matter connected with the approval of an approved body under section 23 or 24 as are determined by the Minister, after consultation with the Minister for Finance.

(3) All fees and charges payable under this Act shall be paid into, or disposed of for the benefit of, the Exchequer in accordance with the directions of the Minister for Finance.

(4) The Public Offices Fees Act, 1879, shall not apply in respect of fees payable pursuant to this Act.

6.—(1) A person who contravenes any provision of this Act, contravention of which is deemed to be an offence, shall be liable on summary conviction to a fine not exceeding £1,500.

(2) A person who is guilty of an offence under *section 21, 22 (3)* or *26* shall be liable on summary conviction to a fine not exceeding £1,500 or, on conviction on indictment, to a fine not exceeding £50,000 or imprisonment for a term not exceeding two years or to both.

(3) Where an offence under this Act has been committed by a body corporate and is proved to have been committed with the consent or connivance of, or to have been facilitated by any neglect on the part of any director, manager, secretary or other similar officer of such body or of any person who was purporting to act in any such capacity, that officer or person, as well as such body, shall be guilty of an offence and shall be liable to be proceeded against and punished as if he were guilty of the first mentioned offence.

(4) No contract shall become enforceable or unenforceable and no right of action in civil proceedings in respect of any loss shall arise by reason only of the commission of an offence under *section 22*.

7.—(1) Summary proceedings in respect of an offence under any section of this Act may be brought and prosecuted by the Director.

Proceedings.

(2) Summary proceedings in respect of an offence under *section 21* or *26* may be brought and prosecuted by the Minister.

(3) Nothwithstanding the provisions of section 10(4) of the Petty Sessions (Ireland) Act, 1851, summary proceedings for an offence under this Act may be commenced at any time within 12 months from the date on which the offence was committed.

(4)*(a)* Where a judge of the District Court proposes to make an order for the release on bail of a defendant charged with an offence under this Act or the Act of 1982 who is ordinarily resident outside the State, the judge may (unless satisfied that all documents required by law to be served on the defendant in connection with or for the purpose of the charge or of any proceedings arising out of or connected with the charge can be duly served on the defendant in the State) direct that those documents may, in lieu of being served on the defendant, be served on a person specified in the direction who is ordinarily resident in the State.

(b) Service of a document referred to in this subsection on a person specified in the direction shall be deemed for all purposes to be served on the defendant.

(5) In the case of a person ordinarily resident, or a body corporate established, outside

the State service of documents relating to the charge may be effected by being served either on the person to be charged or on a person being a nominated agent under *section 10(1)(i)* or *14(1)(h)(ii)*.

(6) A body corporate may be sent forward for trial on indictment for an offence under *section 21, 22 (3)* or *26* with or without recognisances.

(7) Where a person is convicted of an offence under this Act, the court shall, unless it is satisfied that there are special and substantial reasons for not so doing, order the person to pay to the Minister or the Director, as the case may be, the costs and expenses, measured by the court, incurred by the Minister or the Director, as the case may be, in relation to the investigation, detection and prosecution of the offence.

(8) The provisions of section 382 of the Companies Act, 1963, shall extend to every body corporate (whether or not a company within the meaning of that Act) charged on indictment with an offence under *section 21, 22(3)* or *26*.

Particular Functions of Director.

8.—The Director may–

    (a) request persons engaging in or proposing to engage in such practices, business or activities as are, or are likely to be, contrary to the obligations imposed on them by any provision of this Act to refrain from such practices, business or activities;

    (b) institute proceedings in the High Court for orders requiring persons engaging or proposing to engage in any practices, business or activities as are, or are likely to be, contrary to the obligations imposed on them by any provision of this Act to discontinue or refrain from such practices, business or activities.

Laying of regulations befors Houses of Oireachtas.

9.—Every regulation made under this Act shall be laid before each House of the Oireachtas as soon as may be after it is made and, if a resolution annulling the regulation is passed by either such House within the next 21 days on which that House has sat after the regulation is laid before it, the regulation shall be annulled accordingly but without prejudice to the validity of anything previously done thereunder.

PART II

REGULATION OF TRAVEL CONTRACT

Brochure content.

10.—(1) An organiser shall not make available a brochure to a possible consumer unless it indicates in a legible, comprehensible and accurate manner the price and adequate information about the following matters –

    (a) the destination and the means, characteristics and categories of transport used;

    (b) the type of accommodation, its location, category or degree of comfort and its main features and, where accommodation is to be provided in a Member State, its approval or where applicable, tourist classification under the laws of that Member State;

    (c) the meal plan;

    (d) the itinerary;

    (e) general information about passport and visa requirements which apply to purchase of the package and health formalities required for the journey and the stay;

    (f) either the monetary amount or the percentage of the price which is to be paid on account and the timetable for payment of the balance;

    (g) whether a minimum number of persons is required for the package to take place and, if so, the latest time for informing the consumer in the event of cancellation;

    (h) any tax or compulsory charge;

    (i) in the case of packages offered by an organiser who has no place of business in the State, a nominated agent with an address within the State who will accept

service on behalf of and represent the organiser in any proceedings (including criminal proceedings) in respect of or arising out of or connected with any contract or brought pursuant to or in connection with any provision of this Act;

(j) in the event of insolvency of the organiser, the arrangements for security for money paid over and (where applicable) for the repatriation of the consumer.

(2) A retailer shall not supply a brochure knowing or having reasonable cause to believe that it does not comply with the requirements of *subsection (1)*.

(3) An organiser who contravenes *subsection (1)* and a retailer who contravenes *subsection (2)* shall be guilty of an offence.

(4) Subject to *subsections (5)* and *(6)*, where a consumer enters into a contract on the basis of information which is set out in a brochure, the particulars in the brochure (whether or not they are required by this Act to be included in the brochure) shall constitute warranties (whether express or implied as the case may be) as to the matters to which they relate.

(5) *Subsection (4)* shall not apply in respect of particulars where–
  (a) the brochure contains a clear and legible statement that changes may be made in the particulars contained in it before a contract is concluded, and
  (b) changes in those particulars so contained are clearly communicated to and accepted by the other party before a contract is concluded.

(6) *Subsection (4)* shall not apply in respect of particulars when the consumer and the organiser (whether directly or through a retailer) agree on or after the date on which the contract is made that those particulars should not form part of the contract.

11.—(1) An organiser or a retailer shall not supply to a consumer a brochure or other descriptive matter concerning a package, the price of a package or any conditions applying to a contract in respect of a package which contains any false or misleading information. *Liability for misleading.*

(2) In any proceedings against a retailer under this section it shall be a defence to show that the retailer did not know and had no reason to suspect that the brochure or other descriptive matter concerned contained information which was false or misleading.

(3) An organiser who provides a brochure or other descriptive matter concerning a package to a consumer (whether directly or through a retailer) shall be liable to compensate the consumer for any damage caused to the consumer as a direct consequence of and attributable to the consumer's reliance on information which is false or misleading–
  (a) contained in the brochure or other descriptive matter; or
  (b) given by the organiser in respect of the brochure or other descriptive matter.

(4) A retailer shall be liable to compensate the consumer for any damage caused to the consumer as a direct consequence of and attributable to the consumer's reliance on information which is false or misleading–
  (a) contained in any brochure or descriptive matter supplied by the retailer, or
  (b) given by the retailer in respect of the brochure or other descriptive matter.

12.—(1) Before a contract is made, the organiser (whether directly or through a retailer) shall provide the intending consumer with the following information in writing or in some other appropriate form – *Information to be provided before the conclusion of contract.*
  (a) general information about passport and visa requirements which apply to purchase of the package, including information about the length of time it is likely to take to obtain the appropriate passports and visas;
  (b) information about health formalities required by national administrations for the journey and the stay;
  (c) where the consumer is required as a term of the contract to take out insurance to cover the cost of cancellation by the consumer or the cost of assistance, including repatriation, in the event of accident or illness, the minimum level of insurance cover stipulated by the organiser but so that nothing in this Act authorises an organiser to make it compulsory for the intending consumer to purchase any specified insurance policy;

(d) in the event of insolvency, the arrangements for security for the money paid over and (where applicable) for the repatriation of the consumer.

(2)*(a)* An organiser who contravenes *subsection (1)* shall be guilty of an offence unless the contravention is shown to be due to the failure of the retailer to pass on to the intending consumer the information supplied to the retailer by the organiser.

(b) A retailer who fails to provide the intending consumer with the information shall be guilty of an offence.

(3) The obligations of *subsection (1)* may be fulfilled by referring the intending consumer to such information contained in a brochure supplied to the intending consumer and which complies with *sections 10* and *11(1)* and to which no relevant alterations have been made since the brochure was supplied.

(4) Where the consumer is not required as a term of the contract to take out insurance to cover the cost of cancellation by the consumer or the cost of assistance, including repatriation, in the event of accident or illness, the organiser shall, where such is available to him, provide the intending consumer with information about the optional conclusion of an insurance policy to cover those risks.

Information to be provided before start of package.

13.—(1) The organiser shall in good time before the package is due to start (whether before or after the contract has been made) provide the consumer (whether directly or through a retailer) with the information specified in *subsection (2)* in writing or in some other appropriate form.

(2) The information referred to in *subsection (1)* is–

(a) where the package includes a transport component, the times and places of intermediate stops and transport connections and details of the place to be occupied by the traveller, including, cabin or berth on ship, sleeper compartment on train;

(b) the name, address and telephone number–

  (i)   of the representative of the organiser in the locality where the consumer is to stay, or

  (ii) if there is no such representative, of an agency in that locality to provide assistance to a consumer in difficulty,

  or, if there is no such representative or agency, a telephone number or other information which will enable the consumer to contact the organiser and the retailer, or either of them, during the course of the package;

(c) in the case of a journey or stay outside the State by a minor, information enabling direct contact to be made with the minor or with the person responsible at the minor's place of stay.

(3)*(a)* An organiser who contravenes *subsection (1)* shall be guilty of an offence unless the contravention is due to the failure of the retailer to pass on to the consumer or intending consumer the information supplied to the retailer by the organiser.

(b) A retailer who fails to provide the consumer or intending consumer with the information shall be guilty of an offence.

(4) The obligations of *subsection (1)* may be fulfilled by–

(a) referring the consumer or intending consumer to such information contained in a brochure supplied to the consumer or intending consumer which complies with *section 10* and to which no relevant alterations have been made since the brochure was supplied, or

(b) supplying the consumer with such information under the terms of the contract in writing or some other form as is comprehensible and accessible to the consumer provided that such information is supplied in good time before the start of the package.

Essential terms of contract.

14.—(1) The organiser (whether dealing directly with the consumer or through a retailer) shall ensure that, depending on the nature of the package being purchased, the contract contains at least the following elements if relevant to the particular package–

(*a*) the travel destination or destinations and, where periods of stay are involved, the relevant periods, with dates;

(*b*) the means, characteristics and categories of transport to be used and the dates, times and points of departure and return;

(*c*) where the package includes accommodation, its location, its tourist category (if any) or degree of comfort, its main features and, where the accommodation is to be provided in a Member State, its compliance with the laws of that Member State;

(*d*) the meal plan;

(*e*) whether a minimum number of persons is required for the package to take place and, if so, the latest time for informing the consumer in the event of cancellation;

(*f*) the itinerary;

(*g*) visits, excursions or other services which are included in the total price agreed for the package;

(*h*) (i) the name and address of the organiser, the retailer and, where appropriate, the insurer;

(ii) in the case of packages sold by an organiser (whether dealing directly with the consumer or through a retailer) who has no place of business in the State, a nominated agent with an address within the State who will accept service on behalf of and represent the organiser in any proceedings (including criminal proceedings) in respect of or arising out of or connected with any contract or brought pursuant to or in connection with any provision of this Act;

(*i*) the price of the package, if price revisions may be made in accordance with the terms which may be included in a contract, an indication of the possibility of such price revisions, and an indication of any dues, taxes or fees chargeable for certain services (such as landing, embarkation or disembarkation fees at ports and airports and tourist taxes) where such costs are not included in the package;

(*j*) the payment schedule and method of payment;

(*k*) special requirements which the consumer has communicated to the organiser or retailer when making the booking and which both have accepted;

(*l*) the periods within which the consumer must make any complaint about the failure to perform or the inadequate performance of the contract provided that such periods shall not be less than twenty eight days from the date of completion of the package.

(2) Without prejudice to the liability of the organiser under *subsection (1)*, it shall be an express term in every contract that the consumer shall communicate at the earliest opportunity, in writing or any other appropriate form, to the supplier of the services concerned, and to the organiser or local representative, if there is one, any failure which the consumer perceives at the place where the services concerned are supplied.

(3) The words "any other appropriate form" in *subsection (2)* include oral communication, provided written details of the complaint are confirmed to the organiser or the local representative if the consumer fails to obtain a satisfactory response to the complaint.

(4) In cases of complaint the organiser or local representative shall make prompt efforts to find appropriate solutions.

15.—(1) The organiser (whether dealing directly with the consumer or through a retailer) shall ensure that– *(Form of contract.)*

(*a*) all the terms of the contract are set out in writing or in such other form as is comprehensible and accessible to the intending consumer and are communicated to the intending consumer before the contract is made;

(*b*) a written copy of these terms is supplied to the consumer.

(2) *Subsection (1)(a)* shall not apply in the case of a proposal by an intending consumer

made to the organiser or the retailer not more than fourteen days before the date of departure under the proposed contract.

(3) An organiser (whether dealing directly with the consumer or through a retailer) who contravenes *subsection (1)(b)* shall be guilty of an offence unless the contravention is due to the failure of the retailer to provide the consumer with a written copy of the terms of the contract supplied to the retailer by the organiser.

(4) A retailer who fails to provide the consumer with a written copy of the terms of a contract supplied to the retailer by the organiser shall be guilty of an offence.

Transfer of booking.
16.—(1) In every contract there shall be an implied term that where the consumer is prevented from proceeding with the package, the consumer may transfer the booking to a person who satisfies all the conditions required to be satisfied by a person who takes the package, provided that the consumer gives reasonable notice to the organiser or to the retailer acting on the instructions of the organiser of the consumer's intention to transfer the booking before the specified departure date.

(2) Where a transfer is made in accordance with the implied term set out in *subsection (1)*, the transferor and the transferee shall be jointly and severally liable to the organiser or the retailer acting on the instructions of the organiser for payment of the price of the package (or, if part of the price has been paid, for payment of the balance) and for any additional fair and reasonable costs incurred by the organiser as a result of the transfer.

Contract price revision.
17.—(1) A term in a contract to the effect that the prices laid down in the contract may be revised shall be void unless the contract provides for the possibility of upward or downward revision and satisfies the conditions of *subsection (2)*.

(2) The conditions mentioned in *subsection (1)* are–

    (a) that the manner in which the price revision, if made, will be calculated, is described precisely in the term, and

    (b) that the circumstances in which the price may be revised shall be described in the term and shall be such as to provide that price revisions may be made only to allow for variations in–

        (i) transport costs, including the cost of fuel,

        (ii) dues, taxes or fees chargeable for services such as landing taxes or embarkation or disembarkation fees at ports and airports, or

        (iii) the exchange rates which apply to the particular package.

(3) Notwithstanding any terms of the contract no price increase may be made later than a date specified in the contract which shall not be less than twenty days before the specified departure date.

Alteration of cancellation by organiser.
18.—(1) In every contract the following terms are implied –

    (a) that, subject to *section 17*, where the organiser is compelled before departure to alter significantly an essential term of the contract, such as the price, the consumer will be notified as soon as possible in order to enable the consumer to take appropriate decisions and in particular to withdraw from the contract without penalty or to accept a variation to the contract specifying the alterations made and their impact on the price; and

    (b) that the consumer will inform the organiser or the retailer (as appropriate, in the light of the organiser's instructions) of the decision as soon as possible.

(2) (a) The terms set out in *paragraphs (b)* and *(c)* shall be implied in every contract and shall apply where the consumer withdraws from the contract pursuant to the term in it implied by virtue of *subsection (1)(a)* or where the organiser, for any reason other than the fault of the consumer, cancels the package before the date when it is due to start.

    (b) The consumer is entitled –

        (i) to take a replacement package of equivalent or superior quality if the organiser (whether directly or through a retailer) is able to offer such a replacement; or

(ii) to take a replacement package of lower quality if the organiser is able to offer such a replacement and to recover from the organiser the difference in price between that of the package purchased and the replacement package; or

(iii) to have repaid as soon as possible all the moneys paid under the contract.

(c) The consumer is entitled, without prejudice to *paragraph (b)*, to be compensated by the organiser for non-performance of the contract except where –

(i) the package is cancelled because the number of persons who agree to take it is less than the minimum number required and the consumer is informed of the cancellation, in writing, within the period prescribed in the contract, or

(ii) the package is cancelled by *force majeure*, that is to say the package is cancelled by reason of unusual and unforeseeable circumstances beyond the control of the organiser, the retailer or other supplier of services, the consequences of which could not have been avoided even if all due care had been exercised.

(d) Overbooking shall not be regarded as a circumstance falling within *paragraph (c)(ii)*.

19.—(1) The terms set out in *subsections (2)* and *(3)* shall be implied in every contract and shall apply where, after departure, a significant proportion of the services contracted for is not provided, or the organiser becomes aware that a significant proportion of the services cannot be provided. [*Significant failure of performance after start of package.*]

(2) The organiser shall make suitable alternative arrangements, at no extra cost to the consumer, for the continuation of the package and shall compensate the consumer for any difference between the services to be supplied under the contract and those actually supplied.

(3) If it is impossible to make arrangements as described in *subsection (2)*, or these are not accepted by the consumer on reasonable grounds, the organiser shall, where homeward transport arrangements are a term of the contract, provide the consumer at no extra cost with equivalent transport back to the place of departure or to another place to which the consumer has agreed and shall compensate the consumer for the proportion of services not supplied.

20.—(1) The organiser shall be liable to the consumer for the proper performance of the obligations under the contract, irrespective of whether such obligations are to be performed by the organiser, the retailer, or other suppliers of services but this shall not affect any remedy or right of action which the organiser may have against the retailer or those other suppliers of services. [*Extent and financial limits of liability.*]

(2) The organiser shall be liable to the consumer for any damage caused by the failure to perform the contract or the improper performance of the contract unless the failure or the improper performance is due neither to any fault of the organiser or the retailer nor to that of another supplier of services, because –

(a) the failures which occur in the performance of the contract are attributable to the consumer,

(b) such failures are attributable to a third party unconnected with the provision of the services contracted for, and are unforeseeable or unavoidable, or

(c) such failures are due to –

(i) *force majeure*, that is to say, unusual and unforeseeable circumstances beyond the control of the organiser, the retailer or other supplier of services, the consequences of which could not have been avoided even if all due care had been exercised, or

(ii) an event which the organiser, the retailer or the supplier of services, even with all due care, could not foresee or forestall.

(3) In the case of damage arising from the non-performance or improper performance of the services involved in the package, other than –

(*a*) death or personal injury, or

(*b*) damage caused to the consumer by the wilful misconduct or gross negligence of the organiser,

the contract may, save as provided in *subsection (5)*, include a term limiting, in accordance with *subsection (4)*, the amount of compensation payable to the consumer.

(4) Where compensation limits are a term of the contract under *subsection (3)*, the organiser may not limit liability to less than –

(*a*) in the case of an adult, an amount equal to double the inclusive price of the package to the adult concerned,

(*b*) in the case of a minor, an amount equal to the inclusive price of the package to the minor concerned.

(5) In the case of damage arising from the non-performance or improper performance of the services involved in the package, the contract may provide for compensation to be limited in accordance with any international conventions in force governing such services in the place where they are performed or are due to be performed.

(6) Without prejudice to *subsections (3), (4)* and *(5)*, liability under *subsections (1)* and *(2)* cannot be excluded by any contractual term.

(7) In the circumstances described in *paragraphs (b)* and *(c)* of *subsection (2)*, it shall be an implied term of the contract that the organiser, or the retailer acting on the instructions of the organiser, as the case may be, will give prompt assistance to a consumer in difficulty.

(8) The provisions of this section are without prejudice to the provisions of the Hotel Proprietors Act, 1963.

Authorised officers.

21.—(1) In this section "authorised officer" means –

(*a*) a person appointed and authorised in writing by the Director to exercise, for the purpose of this Act, the functions conferred by this section,

(*b*) a person appointed and authorised in writing by the Minister to exercise for the purpose of the Act of 1982, the functions conferred by this section.

(2) Every authorised officer shall be furnished with a warrant of appointment and, when exercising any function conferred by this section shall, if requested to do so by a person affected, produce the warrant or a copy thereof to that person.

(3) An appointment as an authorised officer shall cease –

(*a*) in the case of an appointment made by the Minister, when the Minister revokes the appointment;

(*b*) in the case of an appointment made by the Director, when the Director revokes the appointment;

(*c*) where it is for a fixed period, upon the expiry of that period; or

(*d*) where the person appointed is an officer of the Minister, the Director or the Minister for Enterprise and Employment, upon ceasing to be such an officer.

(4) An authorised officer may, for the purpose of obtaining any information which may be required in relation to the matter under investigation in order to enable the Minister to exercise functions under the Act of 1982, or the Director to exercise functions under this Act, on production of his authorisation, if so required –

(*a*) at all reasonable times enter any premises, at which there are reasonable grounds to believe that any trade or business or any activity in connection with a trade or business is or has been carried on, or that records in relation to such trade, business or activities are kept, and search and inspect the premises and any records on the premises;

(*b*) secure for later inspection any premises or any part of a premises in which such records are kept or there are reasonable grounds for believing that such records are kept;

(*c*) require any person who carries on such trade, business or activity or any person employed in connection therewith to produce such records and in the case of information in a non-legible form to reproduce it in a legible form or to give to the officer such information as the officer may reasonably require in relation to any entries in such records;

(d) inspect and take copies of or extracts from any such records (including in the case of information in a non-legible form a copy of or extract from such information in a permanent legible form);

(e) remove and retain the said records for such period as may be reasonable for further examination, subject to a warrant being issued for that purpose by the District Court;

(f) require any such person to give to the officer any information which the officer may reasonably require in regard to the trade, business or activity or in regard to the persons carrying on such trade, business or activity (including, in particular, in the case of an incorporated body of persons, information in regard to the membership thereof and of its committee of management or other controlling authority) or employed in connection therewith;

(g) require any such person to give to the officer any other information which the officer may reasonably require in regard to such trade, business or activity;

(h) require any person by or on whose behalf data equipment is or has been used or any person having charge of, or otherwise concerned with the operation of, the data equipment or any associated apparatus or material, to afford the officer all reasonable assistance in relation thereto;

(i) summon, at any reasonable time, any other person employed in connection with the trade, business or activity to give to the officer any information which the officer may reasonably require in regard to such activity and to produce to the officer any records which are in that person's power and control.

(5) An authorised officer shall not, other than with the consent of the occupier, enter a private dwelling unless the officer has obtained a warrant from the District Court authorising such entry.

(6) Where an authorised officer, in the exercise of any power under this section, is prevented from entering any premises that officer or the person by whom the officer was appointed may apply to the District Court for a warrant authorising such entry.

(7) An authorised officer, where the officer considers it necessary, may be accompanied by a member of the Garda Síochána when performing any powers conferred on an authorised officer by this Act.

(8) A person who obstructs or interferes with an authorised officer in the exercise of functions under this Act or gives to an authorised officer information which is false or misleading shall be guilty of an offence.

(9) A person who refuses to comply with any request or requirement of an authorised officer in the exercise of functions under this Act shall be guilty of an offence.

PART III

SECURITY

22.—(1) In relation to a package to which this Act applies, a package provider shall have sufficient evidence of security for the refund of money paid over and for the repatriation of the consumer in the event of insolvency.

(2) A package provider shall be deemed to have satisfied the requirements of *subsection (1)* –

(a) by making any one or more of the arrangements as described in *sections 23* to *25* in relation to the package, or

(b) if the package is one in respect of which the provider is required to hold a licence under the Act of 1982, and is covered by arrangements entered into for

Security requirements in the event of insolvency.

the purposes of that Act.

(3) A package provider, other than a package provider who holds a licence under the Act of 1982 in respect of the package in question and has made the necessary arrangements for the purposes of that Act, who fails to –

(*a*) make one of the arrangements described in *subsection (2),* or

(*b*) ensure that such arrangements are in force,

shall be guilty of an offence.

(4) For the purposes of this Part, a contract shall be deemed to have been fully performed if the package, or, as the case may be, the part of the package has been completed irrespective of whether the obligations under the contract have been properly performed for the purposes of *section 20.*

Bonding where and approved body has a reserve fund or insurance.

23.—(1) This section relates to a bond entered into by an authorised institution under which the institution pays to an approved body of which the package provider is a member such sum as may reasonably be expected–

(*a*) to enable all moneys paid over by consumers under or in contemplation of contracts for packages which have not been fully performed to be repaid,

(*b*) to enable consumers to be repatriated, where appropriate, and

(*c*) to defray any reasonable expenses necessarily incurred by the approved body,

in the event of the insolvency of the package provider.

(2) A body may not be approved for the purposes of this section unless –

(*a*) it has a reserve fund or insurance cover with an institution authorised in respect of such business in a Member State of an amount in each case which is designed in the event of the insolvency of a member to enable all monies paid over to that member of the body by consumers under or in contemplation of contracts for packages which have not been fully performed to be repaid to those consumers and to provide for the repatriation, where appropriate, of consumers; and

(*b*) where it has a reserve fund it agrees that the fund will be held by persons and in a manner approved by the Minister.

(3) The Minister may by regulations provide that the bond may be for such minimum sum and valid for such maximum period as may be specified in the regulations.

(4) (*a*) In this section "approved body" means a body which is for the time being approved by the Minister (in consultation with the Minister for Tourism and Trade where arrangements cover a package which is to take place exclusively within the State) for the purposes of this section and no such approval shall be given unless the conditions mentioned in *subsection (2)* are satisfied in relation to it.

(*b*) The Minister may by regulations specify additional conditions that shall be complied with and other appropriate matters relating to the grant of approval to a body which applies to the Minister to be an approved body.

(5) Before a bond is given pursuant to *subsection (1),* the package provider shall inform an approved body of which the provider is a member of the minimum sum proposed for the purposes of that subsection and it shall be the duty of the approved body to consider whether such sum is sufficient for the purpose mentioned in that subsection and, if it does not consider that this is the case, it shall be the duty of the approved body to inform the package provider of the sum which, in the opinion of the approved body, is sufficient for that purpose.

(6) It shall be the duty of an approved body to ensure that there are adequate arrangements for the repatriation of the consumer in the event of the insolvency of a package provider who is a member of that approved body.

(7) In this section "authorised institution" means a person authorised under the law of a Member State to carry on the business of entering into bonds of the kind required by this section.

24.—(1) This section relates to a bond entered into by an authorised institution under which the institution agrees, in the event of the insolvency of the package provider, to pay to an approved body which does not have a reserve fund or insurance as set out in *section 23(2)* of which the package provider is a member such sum as may reasonably be expected to –

Bonding where an approval body does not have a reserve fund or insurance.

(a) enable all moneys paid over by consumers under or in contemplation of contracts for packages which have not been fully performed to be repaid,

(b) enable consumers to be repatriated, where appropriate, and

(c) defray any expenses necessarily incurred by the approved body.

(2) The Minister may by regulations provide that the bond may be for such minimum sum and valid for such maximum period as may be specified in the regulations.

(3) Before a bond is given pursuant to *subsection (1),* the package provider shall inform an approved body of which the provider is a member of the minimum sum proposed for the purposes of that subsection and it shall be the duty of the approved body to consider whether such sum is sufficient for the purpose mentioned in that subsection and, if it does not consider that this is the case, it shall be the duty of the approved body to inform the package provider of the sum which, in the opinion of the approved body, is sufficient for that purpose.

(4) It shall be the duty of an approved body to ensure that there are adequate arrangements for the repatriation of the consumer in the event of the insolvency of a package provider who is a member of that approved body.

(5) The Minister may by regulations specify conditions that shall be complied with and other appropriate matters relating to the grant of approval to a body which applies to the Minister to be an approved body.

(6) In this section –

"approved body" means a body which is for the time being approved by the Minister (in consultation with the Minister for Tourism and Trade where arrangements cover a package which is to take place exclusively within the State) for the purpose of this section;

"authorised institution" has the meaning given to that expression by *section 23(7).*

25.—(1) The package provider shall have insurance under one or more appropriate policies with an insurer authorised in respect of such business in a Member State under which the insurer agrees to indemnify consumers (who shall be insured persons under the policy), against –

(a) the loss of all money paid over by them under or in contemplation of contracts for relevant packages, and

(b) where applicable to the package concerned, the cost of repatriation of consumers based on administrative arrangements established by the insurer to enable repatriation of such consumers,

in the event of insolvency of the package provider.

(2) The package provider shall ensure that it is a term of every contract with a consumer that the consumer acquires the benefit of a policy of a kind mentioned in *subsection (1)* in the event of the insolvency of the package provider.

(3) In this section "appropriate policy" means one which does not contain a condition which provides (in whatever terms) that no liability shall arise under the policy, or that any liability so arising shall cease –

(a) in the event of some specified thing being done or omitted to be done after the happening of the event giving rise to a claim under the policy,

(b) in the event of the failure of the policy holder to make payments to the insurer in connection with that policy or with other policies, or

(c) unless the policy holder keeps specified records or provides the insurer with information therefrom.

PART IV

AMENDMENT OF TRANSPORT (TOUR OPERATORS AND TRAVEL AGENTS) ACT, 1982

Functions of authorised persons.

26.—(1) The functions set out in *subsections (4)* and *(5)* of *section 21*, shall be exercisable, for the purposes of the Act of 1982, by a person authorised by the Minister under section 11 of that Act.

(2) A person who –

(a) obstructs or interferes with a person authorised by the Minister under the Act of 1982 in the exercise of functions under that Act shall be guilty of an offence under this Act,

(b) refuses to comply with any request or requirement of a person so authorised in the exercise of functions under that Act shall be guilty of an offence under this Act.

27.—Section 2(1) of the Act of 1982 is hereby amended by –

(a) the substitution for the definitions of "carrier", "Minister", "overseas travel contract", "tour operator" and "travel agent" of the following definitions:

"carrier" means a person (other than a package provider where the package includes transport commencing in the State to destinations outside the State or Northern Ireland) whose principal business is the provision of transport by land, sea or air on aircraft, vessels or other modes of transport owned and operated by such person;

"the Minister" means the Minister for Transport, Energy and Communications;

"overseas travel contract" means a contract for the carriage of a party to the contract (with or without any other person) by air, sea or land transport commencing in the State to a place outside the State or Northern Ireland, whether the provision of the carriage is the sole subject matter of the contract or is associated with the provision thereunder of any accommodation, facility or service;

"tour operator" means a person other than a carrier who arranges for the purpose of selling or offering for sale to any person accommodation for travel by air, sea or land transport commencing in the State to destinations outside the State or Northern Ireland or who holds himself out by advertising or otherwise as one who may make available such accommodation, either solely or in association with other accommodation, facilities or other services;

"travel agent" means a person other than a carrier who as agent sells or offers to sell to, or purchases or offers to purchase on behalf of, any person, accommodation on air, sea or land transport commencing in the State to destinations outside the State or Northern Ireland or who holds himself out by advertising or otherwise as one who may make available such accommodation, either solely or in association with other accommodation, facilities or services;",

(b) the insertion of the following definitions:

"package" and "package provider" have the meanings assigned to them by the *Package Holidays and Travel Trade Act, 1995*;".

Amendment of section 2 of the Act of 1982.

28.—Section 6 of the Act of 1982 is hereby amended by the substitution for subsection (5) of the following:

"(5) A licence granted under this Act shall, unless earlier surrendered or revoked, remain in force for such period as the Minister thinks fit and specifies in the licence."

29.—Section 8 of the Act of 1982 is hereby amended by the substitution for subsection (2) of the following:

"(2) The Minister may also revoke, or vary the terms and conditions of, a licence granted under this Act if he is no longer satisfied that–

(*a*) the financial, business and organisational resources of the holder of the licence or any financial arrangements made by him are adequate for discharging his actual and potential obligations in respect of the business for which he has been granted a licence, or

(*b*) having regard to–

    (i) the past activities of the holder of the licence or of any person employed by him or, if such licence holder is a body corporate, having regard to the past activities of any director, secretary, shareholder, officer or servant of the body corporate, or

    (ii) the manner in which the holder of the licence is carrying on his business, he is a fit and proper person to carry on business as a tour operator or travel agent, as the case may be.".

Amendment of section 8 of the Act of 1982.

30.—Section 13(4) of the Act of 1982 is hereby amended by the substitution for paragraph (*d*) of the following paragraph:

"(*d*) to defray any reasonable expenses incurred by the Minister or, as the case may be, the person nominated or approved of by the Minister as trustee, or provide for any payments to the Minister or trustee on behalf of a customer of a tour operator or travel agent in respect of an overseas travel contract which could not be completed by reason of the inability or failure of the tour operator or travel agent to meet his financial or contractual obligations in relation to such overseas travel contract.".

Amendment of section 24(4)(d) of the Act of 1982.

31.—(1) Section 18(1) of the Act of 1982 is hereby amended by the insertion of the following paragraph:

"(*e*) to defray any reasonable expenses related to the recovery of monies due under subsection (7) where the Minister is satisfied that in undertaking such expenses there would be a substantial interest in protecting the fund.".

(2) Section 18 of the Act of 1982 is hereby amended by the insertion of the following subsection:

"(7) Where payments have been made from the fund under subsection (1), because the Bond is insufficient, the fund shall be an unsecured creditor of the tour operator or travel agent concerned, in respect of such payments.".

Amendment of section 18 of the Act of 1982.

32.—Section 20 of the Act of 1982 is hereby amended by:

(*a*) the substitution in subsection (2) of "£50,000" for "£10,000",

(*b*) the substitution in subsection (4) of "£1,500" for "£500",

(*c*) the insertion of the following subsection –

"(6) Where a person is convicted of an offence under this section the court shall, unless it is satisfied that there are special and substantial reasons for not so doing, order that person to pay to the Minister the costs and expenses, measured by the Court, incurred by the Minister in relation to the investigation, detection and prosecution of the offence.".

Amendment of section 20 of the Act of 1982.

33.—Section 22 of the Act of 1982 is hereby amended by the substitution for subsection (2) of the following:

"(2) The provisions of section 382 of the Companies Act, 1963 shall extend to every body corporate (whether or not a company within the meaning of the Act) charged on indictment with an offence under section 20 of this Act.".

Amendment of section 22(2) of the Act of 1982.

34.—The High Court may, on the application of the Minister, make orders requiring persons engaging or proposing to engage in any practices, business or activities as are, or

Powers of Court under the Act of 1982.

are likely to be, contrary to the obligations imposed on them by any provision of the Act of 1982 to discontinue or refrain from such practices, business or activities.

SCHEDULE

COUNCIL DIRECTIVE

of 13 June 1990

on package travel, package holidays and package tours

(90/314/EEC)

THE COUNCIL OF THE EUROPEAN COMMUNITIES,

Having regard to the Treaty establishing the European Economic Community, and in particular Article 100a thereof,

Having regard to the proposal from the Commission,[1]

In cooperation with the European Parliament,[2]

Having regard to the opinion of the Economic and Social Committee,[3]

Whereas one of the main objectives of the Community is to complete the internal market, of which the tourist sector is an essential part;

Whereas the national laws of Member States concerning package travel, package holidays and package tours, hereinafter referred to as 'packages', show many disparities and national practices in this field are markedly different, which gives rise to obstacles to the freedom to provide services in respect of packages and distortions of competition amongst operators established in different Member States;

Whereas the establishment of common rules on packages will contribute to the elimination of these obstacles and thereby to the achievement of a common market in services, thus enabling operators established in one Member State to offer their services in other Member States and Community consumers to benefit from comparable conditions when buying a package in any Member State;

Whereas paragraph 36 *(b)* of the Annex to the Council resolution of 19 May 1981 on a second programme of the European Economic Community for a consumer protection and information policy[4] invites the Commission to study, *inter alia*, tourism and, if appropriate, to put forward suitable proposals, with due regard for their significance for consumer protection and the effects of differences in Member States' legislation on the proper functioning of the common market;

---

1.   O.J. No. C 96, 12.4.1988, p.5.
2.   O.J. No. C 69, 20.3.1989, p.102 and OJ. No. C 149, 18.6.1990.
3.   O.J. No. C 102, 24.4.1989, p.27.
4.   O.J. No. C 165, 23.6.1981, p.24.

Whereas in the resolution on a Community policy on tourism on 10 April 1984[5] the Council welcomed the Commission's initiative in drawing attention to the importance of tourism and took note of the Commission's initial guidelines for a Community policy on tourism;

Whereas the Commission communication to the Council entitled 'A New Impetus for Consumer Protection Policy', which was approved by resolution of the Council on 6 May 1986,[6] lists in paragraph 37, among the measures proposed by the Commission, the harmonization of legislation on packages;

Whereas tourism plays an increasingly important role in the economies of the Member States; whereas the package system is a fundamental part of tourism; whereas the package travel industry in Member States would be stimulated to greater growth and productivity if at least a minimum of common rules were adopted in order to give it a Community dimension; whereas this would not only produce benefits for Community citizens buying packages organized on the basis of those rules, but would attract tourists from outside the Community seeking the advantages of guaranteed standards in packages;

Whereas disparities in the rules protecting consumers in different Member States are a disincentive to consumers in one Member State from buying packages in another Member State;

Whereas this disincentive is particularly effective in deterring consumers from buying packages outside their own Member State, and more effective than it would be in relation to the acquisition of other services, having regard to the special nature of the services supplied in a package which generally involve the expenditure of substantial amounts of money in advance and the supply of the services in a State other than that in which the consumer is resident;

Whereas the consumer should have the benefit of the protection introduced by this Directive irrespective of whether he is a direct contracting party, a transferee or a member of a group on whose behalf another person has concluded a contract in respect of a package;

Whereas the organizer of the package and/or the retailer of it should be tinder obligation to ensure that in descriptive matter relating to packages which they respectively organize and sell, the information which is given is not misleading and brochures made available to consumers contain information which is comprehensible and accurate;

Whereas the consumer needs to have a record of the terms of contract applicable to the package; whereas this can conveniently be achieved by requiring that all the terms of the contract be stated in writing of such other documentary form as shall be comprehensible and accessible to him, and that he be given a copy thereof;

Whereas the consumer should be at liberty in certain circumstances to transfer to a willing third person a booking made by him for a package;

Whereas the price established under the contract should not in principle be subject to revision except where the possibility of upward or downward revision is expressly provided for in the contract; whereas that possibility should nonetheless be subject to certain conditions;

Whereas the consumer should in certain circumstances be free to withdraw before departure from a package travel contract;

---

5. O.J. No. C 115, 30.4.1984, p.l.
6. O.J. No. C 118, 7.3.1986, p.28.

Whereas there should be a clear definition of the rights available to the consumer in circumstances where the organizer of the package cancels it before the agreed date of departure;

Whereas if, after the consumer has departed, there occurs a significant failure of performance of the services for which he has contracted or the organizer perceives that he will be unable to procure a significant part of the services to be provided; the organizer should have certain obligations towards the consumer;

Whereas the organizer and/or retailer party to the contract should be liable to the consumer for the proper performance of the obligations arising from the contract; whereas, moreover, the organizer and/or retailer should be liable for the damage resulting for the consumer from failure to perform or improper performance of the contract unless the defects in the performance of the contract are attributable neither to any fault of theirs nor to that of another supplier of services;

Whereas in cases where the organizer and/or retailer is liable for failure to perform or improper performance of the services involved in the package, such liability should be limited in accordance with the international conventions governing such services, in particular the Warsaw Convention of 1929 in International Carriage by Air, the Berne Convention of 1961 on Carriage by Rail, the Athens Convention of 1974 on Carriage by Sea and the Paris Convention of 1962 on the Liability of Hotel-keepers; whereas, moreover, with regard to damage other than personal injury, it should be possible for liability also to be limited under the package contract provided, however, that such limits are not unreasonable;

Whereas certain arrangements should be made for the information of consumers and the handling of complaints;

Whereas both the consumer and the package travel industry would benefit if organizers and/or retailers were placed under an obligation to provide sufficient evidence of security in the event of insolvency;

Whereas Member States should be at liberty to adopt, or retain, more stringent provisions relating to package travel for the purpose of protecting the consumer,

HAS ADOPTED THIS DIRECTIVE:

Article 1

The purpose of this Directive is to approximate the laws, regulations and administrative provisions of the Member States relating to packages sold or offered for sale in the territory of the Community.

Article 2

For the purposes of this Directive:

1. 'package' means the pre-arranged combination of not fewer than two of the following when sold or offered for sale at an inclusive price and when the service covers a period of more than twenty-four hours or includes overnight accommodation:
   (a) transport;
   (b) accommodation;
   (c) other tourist services not ancillary to transport or accommodation and accounting for a significant proportion of the package.

The separate billing of various components of the same package shall not absolve the organizer or retailer from the obligations under this Directive;

2. 'organizer' means the person who, other than occasionally, organizes packages and sells or offers them for sale, whether directly or through a retailer;

3. 'retailer' means the person who sells or offers for sale the package put together by the organizer;

4. 'consumer' means the person who takes or agrees to take the package ('the principal contractor'), or any person on whose behalf the principal contractor agrees to purchase the package (the other beneficiaries') or any person to whom the principal contractor or any of the other beneficiaries transfers the package ('the transferee');

5. 'contract' means the agreement linking the consumer to the organizer and/or the retailer.

Article 3

1. Any descriptive matter concerning a package and supplied by the organizer or the retailer to the consumer, the price of the package and any other conditions applying to the contract must not contain any misleading information.

2. When a brochure is made available to the consumer, it shall indicate in a legible, comprehensible and accurate manner both the price and adequate information concerning:
  (*a*) the destination and the means, characteristics and categories of transport used;
  (*b*) the type of accommodation, its location, category or degree of comfort and its main features, its approval and tourist classification under the rules of the host Member State concerned;
  (*c*) the meal plan;
  (*d*) the itinerary;
  (*e*) general information on passport and visa requirements for nationals of the Member State or States concerned and health formalities required for the journey and the stay;
  (*f*) either the monetary amount or the percentage of the price which is to be paid on account, and the time-table for payment of the balance;
  (*g*) whether a minimum number of persons is required for the package to take place and, if so, the deadline for informing the consumer in the event of cancellation.

The particulars contained in the brochure are binding on the organizer or retailer, unless:
  – changes in such particulars have been clearly communicated to the consumer before conclusion of the contract, in which case the brochure shall expressly state so,
  – changes are made later following an agreement between the parties to the contract.

Article 4

1. (*a*) The organizer and/or the retailer shall provide the consumer, in writing or any other appropriate form, before the contract is concluded, with general information on passport and visa requirements applicable to nationals of the Member State or States concerned and in particular on the periods for obtaining them, as well as with information on the health formalities required for the journey and the stay;

(b) The organizer and/or retailer shall also provide the consumer, in writing or any other appropriate form, with the following information in good time before the start of the journey:

(i)   the times and places of intermediate stops, and transport connections as well as details of the place to be occupied by the traveller, e.g. cabin or berth on ship, sleeper compartment on train;

(ii) the name, address and telephone number of the organizer's and/or retailer's local representative or, failing that, of local agencies on whose assistance a consumer in difficulty could call.

Where no such representatives or agencies exist, the consumer must in any case be provided with an emergency telephone number or any other information that will enable him to contract the organizer and/or the retailer;

(iii) in the case of journeys or stays abroad by minors, information enabling direct contact to be established with the child or the person responsible at the child's place of stay;

(iv) information on the optional conclusion of an insurance policy to cover the cost of cancellation by the consumer or the cost of assistance, including repatriation, in the event of accident or illness.

2. Member States shall ensure that in relation to the contract the following principles apply:

(a) depending on the particular package, the contract shall contain at least the elements listed in the Annex;

(b) all the terms of the contract are set out in writing or such other form as is comprehensible and accessible to the consumer and must be communicated to him before the conclusion of the contract; the consumer is given a copy of these terms;

(c) the provision under (b) shall not preclude the belated conclusion of last-minute reservations or contracts.

3. Where the consumer is prevented from proceeding with the package, he may transfer his booking, having first given the organizer or the retailer reasonable notice of his intention before departure, to a person who satisfies all the conditions applicable to the package. The transferor of the package and the transferee shall be jointly and severally liable to the organizer or retailer party to the contract for payment of the balance due and for any additional costs arising from such transfer.

4. (a) The prices laid down in the contract shall not be subject to revision unless the contract expressly provides for the possibility of upward or downward revision and states precisely how the revised price is to be calculated, and solely to allow for variations in:

– transportation costs, including the cost of fuel,
– dues, taxes or fees chargeable for certain services, such as landing taxes or embarkation or disembarkation fees at ports and airports,
– the exchange rates applied to the particular package.

(b) During the twenty days prior to the departure date stipulated, the price stated in the contract shall not be increased.

5. If the organizer finds that before the departure he is constrained to alter significantly any of the essential terms, such as the price, he shall notify the consumer as quickly as possible in order to enable him to take appropriate decisions and in particular:

– either to withdraw from the contract without penalty,
– or to accept a rider to the contract specifying the alterations made and their impact on the price.

The consumer shall inform the organizer or the retailer of his decision as soon as possible.

6. If the consumer withdraws from the contract pursuant to paragraph 5, or if, for whatever cause, other than the fault of the consumer, the organizer cancels the package before the agreed date of departure, the consumer shall be entitled:

(a) either to take a substitute package of equivalent or higher quality where the organizer and/or retailer is able to offer him such a substitute. If the replacement package offered is of lower quality, the organizer shall refund the difference in price to the consumer;

(b) or to be repaid as soon as possible all sums paid by him under the contract.

In such a case, he shall be entitled, if appropriate, to be compensated by either the organizer or the retailer, whichever the relevant Member State's law requires, for non-performance of the contract, except where:

(i) cancellation is on the grounds that the number of persons enrolled for the package is less than the minimum number required and the consumer is informed of the cancellation, in writing, within the period indicated in the package description; or

(ii) cancellation, excluding overbooking, is for reasons of *force majeure*, i.e. unusual and unforeseeable circumstances beyond the control of the party by whom it is pleaded, the consequences of which could not have been avoided even if all due care had been exercised.

7. Where, after departure, a significant proportion of the services contracted for is not provided or the organizer perceives that he will be unable to procure a significant proportion of the services to be provided, the organizer shall make suitable alternative arrangements, at no extra cost to the consumer, for the continuation of the package, and where appropriate compensate the consumer for the difference between the services offered and those supplied.

If it is impossible to make such arrangements or these are not accepted by the consumer for good reasons, the organizer shall, where appropriate, provide the consumer, at no extra cost, with equivalent transport back to the place of departure, or to another return point to which the consumer has agreed and shall, where appropriate, compensate the consumer.

Article 5

1. Member States shall take the necessary steps to ensure that the organizer and/or retailer party to the contract is liable to the consumer for the proper performance of the obligations arising from the contract, irrespective of whether such obligations are to be performed by that organizer and/or retailer or by other suppliers of services without prejudice to the right of the organizer and/or retailer to pursue those other suppliers of services.

2. With regard to the damage resulting for the consumer from the failure to perform or the improper performance of the contract, Member States shall take the necessary steps to ensure that the organizer and/or retailer is/are liable unless such failure to perform or improper performance is attributable neither to any fault of theirs nor to that of another supplier of services, because:

- the failures which occur in the performance of the contract are attributable to the consumer,
- such failures are attributable to a third party unconnected with the provision of the services contracted for, and are unforeseeable or unavoidable,
- such failures are due to a case of *force majeure* such as that defined in Article 4 (6), second subparagraph (ii), or to an event which the organizer and/or retailer or the supplier of services, even with all due care, could not foresee or forestall.

In the cases referred to in the second and third indents, the organizer and/or retailer party to the contract shall be required to give prompt assistance to a consumer in difficulty.

In the matter of damages arising from the non-performance or improper performance of the services involved in the package, the Member States may allow compensation to be limited in accordance with the international conventions governing such services.

In the matter of damage other than personal injury resulting from the non-performance or improper performance of the services involved in the package, the Member States may allow compensation to be limited under the contract. Such limitation shall not be unreasonable.

3. Without prejudice to the fourth subparagraph of paragraph 2, there may be no exclusion by means of a contractual clause from the provisions of paragraphs 1 and 2.

4. The consumer must communicate any failure in the performance of a contract which he perceives on the spot to the supplier of the services concerned and to the organizer and/ or retailer in writing or any other appropriate form at the earliest opportunity.

This obligation must be stated clearly and explicitly in the contract.

Article 6

In cases of complaint, the organizer and/or retailer or his local representative, if there is one, must make prompt efforts to find appropriate solutions.

Article 7

The organizer and/or retailer party to the contract shall provide sufficient evidence of security for the refund of money paid over and for the repatriation of the consumer in the event of insolvency.

Article 8

Member States may adopt or return more stringent provisions in the field covered by this Directive to protect the consumer.

Article 9

1. Member States shall bring into force the measures necessary to comply with this Directive before 31 December 1992. They shall forthwith inform the Commission thereof.

2. Member States shall communicate to the Commission the texts of the main provisions of national law which they adopt in the field governed by this Directive. The Commission shall inform the other Member States thereof.

Article 10

This Directive is addressed to the Member States.

Done at Luxembourg, 13 June 1990.

For the Council
The President
D. J. O'MALLEY

ANNEX

Elements to be included in the contract if relevant to the particular package;

  (a) the travel destination(s) and, where periods of stay are involved, the relevant periods, with dates;
  (b) the means, characteristics and categories of transport to be used, the dates, times and points of departure and return;
  (c) where the package includes accommodation, its location, its tourist category or degree of comfort, its main features, its compliance with the rules of the host Member State concerned and the meal plan;
  (d) whether a minimum number of persons is required for the package to take place and, if so, the deadline for informing the consumer in the event of cancellation;
  (e) the itinerary;
  (f) visits, excursions or other services which are included in the total price agreed for the package;
  (g) the name and address of the organizer, the retailer and, where appropriate, the insurer;
  (h) the price of the package, an indication of the possibility of price revisions under Article 4 (4) and an indication of any dues, taxes or fees chargeable for certain services (landing, embarkation or disembarkation fees at ports and airports, tourist taxes) where such costs are not included in the package;
  (i) the payment schedule and method of payment;
  (j) special requirements which the consumer has communicated to the organizer or retailer when making the booking, and which both have accepted;
  (k) periods within which the consumer must make any complaint concerning failure to perform or improper performance of the contract.

APPENDIX THREE

PACKAGE HOLIDAYS AND TRAVEL TRADE ACT, 1995
(COMMENCEMENT) ORDER, 1995
S.I. No. 235 of 1995

PACKAGE HOLIDAYS AND TRAVEL TRADE ACT, 1995 (COMMENCEMENT) ORDER, 1995
S.I. No. 235 of 1995

I, MICHAEL LOWRY, Minister for Transport, Energy and Communications, in exercise of the powers conferred on me by section 1 of the Package Holidays and Travel Trade Act, 1995 (No. 17 of 1995) hereby order as follows:

1. This Order may be cited as the Package Holidays and Travel Trade Act, 1995 (Commencement) Order, 1995.

2. The 1st day of September, 1995, is hereby fixed as the day on which section 5 of the Act, shall come into operation.

3. The 1st day of October, 1995, is hereby fixed as the day on which all other sections of the Act, 1995, shall come into operation.

GIVEN under the Official Seal of the Minister for Transport, Energy and Communications, this 1st day of September, 1995.

JOHN LUMSDEN, A person authorised to authenticate the Seal of the Minister for Transport, Energy and Communications.

EXPLANATORY NOTE

(This note is not part of the Instrument and does not purport to be a legal interpretation.)

The effect of this order is to fix the dates on which the various sections of the Package Holidays and Travel Trade Act, 1995 shall come into operation.

Notice of the making of this Statutory Instrument was published in "Iris Oifigiúil" of 12th September, 1995.

APPENDIX FOUR

APPROVED BODIES (FEES) REGULATIONS, 1995
S.I. No. 236 of 1995

APPROVED BODIES (FEES) REGULATIONS, 1995
S.I. No. 236 of 1995

I, MICHAEL LOWRY, Minister for Transport, Energy and Communications in exercise of the powers conferred on me by Section 5 of the Package Holidays and Travel Trade Act, 1995 (No. 17 of 1995) and after consultation with the Minister for Finance, hereby make the following Regulations:

1. These Regulations may be cited as Approved Bodies (Fees) Regulations, 1995.

2. These Regulations shall come into operation on the 1st day of September, 1995.

3. The amount of the fee payable on application to be an approved body for the purpose of section 23 or 24 of the Package Holidays and Travel Trade Act, 1995, shall be £250.

4. Fees payable under these Regulations shall be non-refundable.

5. The maximum period for which a body may be approved for the purpose of these regulations shall be two years.

GIVEN under the Official Seal of the Minister for Finance, this 1st day of September, 1995.

PHILIP FURLONG, A person authorised to authenticate the Seal of the Minister for Finance.

GIVEN under the Official Seal of the Minister for Transport, Energy and Communications, this 1st day of September, 1995.

JOHN LUMSDEN, A person authorised to authenticate the Seal of the Minister for Transport, Energy and Communications.

EXPLANATORY NOTE.

(This note is not part of the Instrument and does not purport to be a legal interpretation.)

The effect of these regulations is to set an application fee for bodies which are applying to be approved bodies for the purpose of sections 23 and 24 of the Package Holidays and Travel Trade Act, 1995 and to set the maximum period for which such approval may be granted.

Notice of the making of this Statutory Instrument was published in "Iris Oifigiúil" of 12th September, 1995.

APPENDIX FIVE

PACKAGE HOLIDAYS AND TRAVEL TRADE ACT, 1995 (OCCASIONAL ORGANISERS) REGULATIONS, 1995 S.I. No. 271 of 1995

PACKAGE HOLIDAYS AND TRAVEL TRADE ACT, 1995 (OCCASIONAL ORGANISERS) REGULATIONS, 1995
S.I. No. 271 of 1995

I, MICHAEL LOWRY, Minister for Transport, Energy and Communications, in exercise of powers conferred on me by section 3 of the Package Holidays and Travel Trade Act, 1995 (No. 17 of 1995) hereby make the following Regulations.

1. These Regulations may be cited as the Package Holidays and Travel Trade Act, 1995 (Occasional Organisers) Regulations, 1995.

2. The following classes of person are hereby specified as classes whose members may, subject to Regulation 3, be regarded as operating packages occasionally–

(a) a professional, medical, scientific, cultural or trade association or society which organises a package, either directly or through an organising committee established for that purpose, during a conference, convention, meeting or seminar held in pursuance of aims and objectives of any such body,

(b) a firm which organises a package for its employees,

(c) a community, social, sporting or voluntary organisation which organises a package as part of the general objectives of that organisation, including a club or association operating within a firm,

(d) a school or educational institution which organises a package for its teachers and students,

(e) a religious or denominational group which organises a package involving a pilgrimage for members of that group, and

(f) a package organised by a charitable or benevolent institution in pursuance of its objectives.

3. Where a package is one in respect of which a licence is required under the Transport (Tour Operators and Travel Agents) Act, 1982 or is one that is covered by arrangements which have been entered into for the purposes of that Act, a person shall not be regarded as organising any such package occasionally.

GIVEN under my Official Seal, this 29th day of September, 1995.

MICHAEL LOWRY, Minister for Transport, Energy and Communications.

EXPLANATORY NOTE

(This note is not part of the Instrument and does not purport to be a legal interpretation.)

The effect of these Regulations is to specify the classes of persons who may be regarded as organising packages occasionally for the purpose of section 3 of the Act.

Notice of the making of this Statutory Instrument was published in "Iris Oifigiúil" of 24th October, 1995.

APPENDIX SIX

PACKAGE HOLIDAYS AND TRAVEL TRADE ACT, 1995 (BONDS) REGULATIONS, 1995
S.I. No. 270 of 1995

PACKAGE HOLIDAYS AND TRAVEL TRADE ACT, 1995
(BONDS) REGULATIONS, 1995
S.I. No. 270 of 1995

I, MICHAEL LOWRY, Minister for Transport, Energy and Communications, in exercise of the powers conferred on me by sections 23 and 24 of the Package Holidays and Travel Trade Act, 1995 (No. 17 of 1995), hereby make the following Regulations:

1. These Regulations may be cited as the Package Holidays and Travel Trade Act, 1995 (Bonds) Regulations. 1995.

2. These Regulations shall come into operation on the 1st day of October, 1995.

3. In these Regulations–

"the Act" means the Package Holidays and Travel Trade Act, 1995,

"bond" means a bond under section 23 or 24 of the Act, as the context admits.

4. These Regulations apply to packages to which the Act relates, with the exception of–
    (*a*) packages in respect of which the provider is required to hold a licence under the Transport (Tour Operators and Travel Agents) Act, 1982, and
    (*b*) packages in respect of which the provider has complied with section 25 of the Act.

5. A bond shall–
    (i)   in the case of a person who is a member of an approved body which has a reserve fund or insurance cover, as specified in section 23 of the Act, be for a sum of 10% of the projected turnover in the period of the validity of the bond in respect of packages to which these Regulations apply;
    (ii) in the case of a person who is a member of an approved body which does not have a reserve fund or insurance cover as specified in section 23 (2) of the Act, be for a sum of 15% of the projected turnover in the period of the validity of the bond in respect of packages to which these Regulations apply.

6. The maximum period for which a bond may be maintained is one year and the date of expiry or revocation shall be without prejudice to any liability which may be incurred under the bond in respect of any obligations to customers arising out of contracts in respect of packages to which these Regulations apply, entered into during the period of validity of the bond or of a previous bond which expired immediately prior to the period to which the current bond applies.

7. Any demand under a bond by an approved body shall be made in writing not later than six months after the date on which the bond ceases to have effect, but on being satisfied that the package provider has discharged all obligations to consumers under the contracts to which the bond relates the approved body may, at its discretion, release the provider of the bond and any guarantor thereof from their obligations under the bond and any guarantee relating thereto at any earlier date within the period of six months.

8. Where a new bond which comes into effect before or from the date on which the current bond ceases to have effect, is provided, or procured, by a package provider, the previous bond shall cease to be effective from the commencement of the new bond, and any

losses or liabilities incurred by customers of the package provider as a result of the inability or failure of the package provider to meet financial or contractual obligations to such customers in respect of packages covered by these Regulations, shall fall to be discharged from moneys payable under the new bond.

9. A bond may comprise all or any one or more of the following–
    (*a*) a sum deposited in a bank or financial institution in the State in the sole name of the approved body of which the package provider is a member;
    (*b*) a guarantee with a bank or insurance company;
    (*c*) a guarantee of such other type as may be acceptable to the approved body of which the package provider is a member;
    (*d*) an arrangement or scheme entered into on a collective basis by package providers or any group of package providers for the protection of consumers, provided that in the event of the inability or failure of any member of such collectible groups to meet obligations to consumers in relation to packages covered by these Regulations, the amount of money payable to the approved body from such collective arrangements would be at the same level as that specified in Regulation 5 in respect of a particular package provider.

10. In the case of a bond of the type specified in Regulation 9(*a*), or where it has been necessary for an approved body to apply such a bond for the purposes specified in the Act, the amount of the bond or any residual balance thereof, as the case might be, shall be returned to the provider of the bond with such interest as may have accrued thereon, provided that all obligations to consumers of the package provider concerned who, during the period of validity of the bond or of a previous bond which expired immediately prior to the period to which the current bond relates, entered into contracts in respect of packages to which these Regulations apply with such package provider have been fully discharged.

11. A bond of the type specified in Regulations 9(*b*)–
    (*a*) shall be secured only with–
        (i) insurance companies authorised to carry out suretyship business (Class 15) in accordance with the European Communities (Non Life Insurance) Framework Regulations, 1994 (S.I. No. 395 of 1994), or
        (ii) banks duly licensed under the Central Bank Act, 1971 (No. 24 of 1971).
    (*b*) shall be in the form and contain the terms and conditions set out in the First Schedule to these Regulations where the bond is secured with an insurance company pursuant to paragraph (*a*) (i) of this Regulation or the Second Schedule thereto where the bond is secured with a bank pursuant to paragraph (*a*) (ii) of this Regulation, and
    (*c*) shall be lodged with the approved body of which the package provider is a member.

FIRST SCHEDULE

PACKAGE HOLIDAY AND TRAVEL TRADE ACT, 1995

Terms of Bond to be Secured by a Package Provider with an Insurance Company

I/We (name of Insurance Company) _____

_____

_____

hereafter referred to as the Surety, having our registered office at _____

at the behest of (_____

of _____) ____

(being a package provider under the above Act) hereby undertake and acknowledge our-

selves bound to pay to _____

(an approved body for the purposes of the Act), such sum as that approved body may

demand, but not exceeding IR£ (_____

_____ Irish pounds)

to be applied in accordance with the provisions of sections 23 and 24 of the Act for the
purposes of therein provided.

This bond shall come into effect on the _____ day of _____, 19 ____, and shall
cease to have effect after the _____ day of _____, 19 ___, but without prejudice to
any liability which may be incurred under this bond in respect of obligations to consumers
arising under contracts for packages to which the Package Holidays and Travel Trade Act,
1995 (Bonds) Regulations, 1995 apply entered into during the period of validity of the
bond, or a previous bond which expired immediately prior to the commencement of the
period to which this bond relates, PROVIDED THAT any demand on us hereunder by the
approved body shall be made in writing not later than six months after the date after which
this bond ceases to have effect.

Notwithstanding the generality of the foregoing, where a new bond which comes into
effect before or from the date after which this bond ceases to have effect is provided or
procured by the package provider, the liability of the Surety under this bond shall cease on
the commencement of such new bond.

IT IS AGREED that this money shall become payable upon demand in writing from
the approved body in one or more of the following events–
    (*a*) a petition is granted by a court for the compulsory winding up of the business of
        the package provider;
    (*b*) the package provider by reason of being unable to fulfil financial obligations
        seeks a voluntary winding up of the business or has convened a meeting of
        creditors for the purpose of considering a settlement of liabilities to such
        creditors;
    (*c*) a receiver is appointed over the assets of the package provider;
    (*d*) the package provider has failed to discharge debts or is unable to discharge
        debts or has ceased to carry on business by reason of an inability to discharge
        debts;
    (*e*) the package provider has committed an act of bankruptcy;
    (*f*) the approved body has reasonable grounds for believing that, having regard to
        all the circumstances, the package provider is unable to, or has failed to, carry

out obligations to customers in relation to a contract for a package to which the Package Holidays and Travel Trade Act, 1995 (Bonds) Regulations, 1995 apply.

IT IS FURTHER AGREED that, in circumstances outlined at paragraph (*f*), the approved body will, before calling for payment under the bond, notify the package provider in writing by delivering the notice to the package provider's principal place of business, of its proposal to call the bond and the reasons for such proposal and shall afford the package provider all reasonable opportunity to make representations to the approved body.

IT IS A CONDITION of this bond that the approved body will repay to the Surety such part of the sum advanced as shall not be expended for the benefit of the customers of the package provider.

Monies payable under this bond shall be applied for all or any of the following purposes–
   (*a*) to enable all monies paid over by consumers under or in comtemplation of con-
           tracts for packages which have not been fully performed to be repaid,
   (*b*) to enable customers to be repatriated, where appropriate, and
   (*c*) to defray any expenses necessarily incurred by the approved body.

Without prejudice to any existing right of a customer of the package provider to recover damages in relation to the standard of accommodation or service provided pursuant to a contract in respect of particular package, nothing in this instrument shall be construed as enabling such customer to recover any damages out of any sum of money made available under this bond.

Signed FOR AND ON BEHALF OF _____

_____

_____

this _____ day of _____ 19 _____.

SECOND SCHEDULE

PACKAGE HOLIDAY AND TRAVEL TRADE ACT, 1995

Terms of Bond to be Provided by a Package Provider and Guaranteed by a Bank

Part I (to he completed by the package provider)

I/We _____ of _____
(being a package provider under the above Act), hereby undertake and acknowledge my-
self/ourselves bound as a package provider to pay to _____
(an approved body for the purpose of the Act), such sum as it may demand, but not exceeding IR£ _____
(_____ Irish pounds)
to be applied in accordance with the provisions of section 23 and 24 of the above Act and for the purposes therein provided.

This bond shall come into effect on the _____ day of _____, 19_____, and shall cease to have effect after the _____ day of _____, 19____, but without prejudice to any liability which may be incurred under this bond in respect of obligations to consumers arising under contracts for packages to which the Package Holidays and Travel Trade Act, 1995 (Bonds) Regulations, 1995 apply entered into during the period of validity of the bond, or a previous bond which expired immediately prior to the commencement of the period to which this bond relates PROVIDED THAT any demand on us hereunder by the approved body shall be made in writing not later than six months after the date which this bond ceases to have effect.

Notwithstanding the foregoing, where a new bond which comes into effect before or from the date on which this bond ceases to have effect is provided, or procured, by me/us, my/our liability under this bond shall cease on the commencement of such new bond.

IT IS AGREED that this money shall become payable upon demand in writing from the approved body in one or more of the following events–
    (*a*) a petition is granted by a court for the compulsory winding up of the business of the package provider;
    (*b*) the package provider by reason of being unable to fulfil financial obligations seeks a voluntary winding up of the business or has convened a meeting of creditors for the purposes of considering a settlement of liabilities to such creditors;
    (*c*) a receiver is appointed over the assets of the package provider;
    (*d*) the package provider has failed to discharge debts or is unable to discharge debts or has ceased to carry on business by reason of an inability to discharge debts;
    (*e*) the package provider has committed an act of bankruptcy;
    (*f*) the approved body has reasonable grounds for believing that, having regard to all the circumstances, the package provider is unable to, or has failed to, carry out obligations to customers in relation to a contract for a package to which the Package Holidays and Travel Trade Act, 1995 (Bonds) Regulations, 1995 apply.

Moneys payable under this bond shall be applied for all or any of the following purposes–
    (*a*) to enable all moneys paid over by a consumer under or in contemplation of contracts for packages which have not been fully performed to be repaid,
    (*b*) to enable customers to be repatriated, where appropriate, and
    (*c*) to defray any expenses necessarily incurred by the approved body.

Without prejudice to any existing right of a customer of a package provider to recover damages in relation to the standard of accommodation or service provided pursuant to a contract in respect of a particular package, nothing in this instrument shall be construed as enabling such customer to recover any damages out of any sum of money made available under this bond.

Signed FOR AND ON BEHALF OF _____

_____

_____

this _____ day of _____ 19_____.

Part II Guaranteed by Bank

We _____ (name of Bank),

having our registered office at _____

hereafter referred to as "the Guarantor", hereby guarantee the due payment of the sum

specified in Part 1 above i.e. IR£ _____

_____ Irish pounds) upon demand in writing from

(an approved body for the purpose of the Act).

IT IS A CONDITION of this Guarantee that the approved body will repay to us as the Guarantor such part of the sum paid by us to the approved body and shall not be expended in accordance with Part I above.

IT IS AGREED THAT in circumstances outlined in paragraph (f) of Part I above, the approved body will, before calling on the Guarantor for payment under the bond, notify the package provider in writing by delivering the notice to the package provider's principal place of business, of its proposal to call the bond and the reasons for such proposal and shall afford the package provider all reasonable opportunity to make representations to the approved body.

This Guarantee shall come into effect on the _____day of _____, 19____, and shall cease to have effect after the day of _____, 19 ____, but without prejudice to any liability incurred in respect of any obligations of the package provider to the approved body arising out of contracts for packages to which the Package Holiday and Travel Trade Act, 1995 (Bonds) Regulations, 1995 apply and which are entered into during the period of validity of the Guarantee, or a previous guarantee which expired immediately prior to the commencement of the period to which this Guarantee relates PROVIDED THAT any demand on us hereunder by the approved body shall be made in writing not later than six months after the date on which this Guarantee ceases to have effect.

Notwithstanding the foregoing, where a new bond which comes into effect before or from the date after which this Guarantee ceases to have effect, is provided, or procured, by the package provider, our liability under this Guarantee shall cease from the date of commencement of such new bond.

Signed FOR AND ON BEHALF OF _____

_____

_____

this _____ day of _____ 19____.

GIVEN under my Official Seal, this 29th day of September, 1995.

MICHAEL LOWRY,
Minister for Transport, Energy and Communications.

EXPLANATORY NOTE

(This note is not part of the Instrument and does not purport to be a legal interpretation.)

The effect of these Regulations is to introduce a system of bonding for members of approved bodies as provided for in Part III of the Package Holidays and Travel Trade Act, 1995 (No. 17 of 1995).

APPENDIX SEVEN

EUROPEAN COMMUNITIES (UNFAIR TERMS IN CONSUMER CONTRACTS) REGULATIONS, 1995
S.I. No. 27 of 1995

EUROPEAN COMMUNITIES (UNFAIR TERMS IN CONSUMER CONTRACTS) REGULATIONS, 1995
S.I. No. 27 of 1995

I, RICHARD BRUTON, Minister for Enterprise and Employment, in exercise of the powers conferred on me by section 3 of the European Communities Act, 1972 (No. 27 of 1972), and for the purpose of giving effect to Council Directive No. 93113/EEC of 5 April 1993 on unfair terms in consumer contracts[a] hereby make the following Regulations:

1. (1) These Regulations may be cited as the European Communities (Unfair Terms in Consumer Contracts) Regulations, 1995.
(2) These Regulations shall apply to all contracts concluded after 31st December, 1994.

2. In these Regulations–

"authorised officer" means a person appointed under Regulation 10 of these Regulations;

"business" includes a trade or profession and the activities of any government department or local or public authority;

"consumer" means a natural person who is acting for purposes which are outside his business;

"the Council Directive" means Council Directive No. 93/13/EEC, of 5 April 1993 on unfair terms in consumer contracts;

"the Director" means the Director of Consumer Affairs;

"the Minister" means the Minister for Enterprise and Employment;

"seller" means a person who, acting for purposes related to his business, sells goods;

"supplier" means a person who, acting for purposes related to his business, supplies services;

"unfair term" shall be construed in accordance with the provisions of the Council Directive and these Regulations.

3. (1) Subject to the provisions of Schedule 1, these Regulations apply to any term in a contract concluded between a seller of goods or supplier of services and a consumer which has not been individually negotiated.
(2) For the purpose of these Regulations a contractual term shall be regarded as unfair if, contrary to the requirement of good faith, it causes a significant imbalance in the parties' rights and obligations under the contract to the detriment of the consumer, taking into account the nature of the goods or services for which the contract was concluded and all circumstances attending the conclusion of the contract and all other terms of the contract or of another contract on which it is dependent.
(3) In determining whether a term satisfies the requirement of good faith, regard shall be had to the matters specified in Schedule 2 to these Regulations.
(4) A term shall always be regarded as having not been individually negotiated where it has been drafted in advance and the consumer has therefore not been able to influence its substance, particularly in the context of a pre-formulated standard contract.
(5) The fact that a specific term or any aspect of a term has been individually negotiated shall not exclude the application of this Regulation to the rest of the contract if an overall assessment of the contract indicates that it is nevertheless a contract as described in paragraph

---

[a] O.J. No. L95129, 21.4.1993

(4) of this Regulation referred to in Article 3.2 of the Council Directive as a pre-formulated standard contract.

(6) It shall be for any seller or supplier who claims that a term was individually negotiated to show that it was.

(7) An indicative and non-exhaustive list of the terms which may be regarded as unfair, pursuant to Article 3.3 of the Council Directive, is set out in the Annex to the Directive and in Schedule 3 to these Regulations.

4. A term shall not of itself be considered to be unfair by relation to the definition of the main subject matter of the contract or to the adequacy of the price and remuneration, as against the goods and services supplied, in so far as these terms are in plain, intelligible language.

5. (1) In the case of contracts where all or certain terms offered to the consumer are in writing, the seller or supplier shall ensure that terms are drafted in plain, intelligible language.

(2) Where there is a doubt about the meaning of a term, the interpretation most favourable to the consumer shall prevail.

6. (1) An unfair term in a contract concluded with a consumer by a seller or supplier shall not be binding on the consumer.

(2) The contract shall continue to bind the parties, if it is capable of continuing in existence without the unfair term.

7. These Regulations shall apply notwithstanding any contract term which applies or purports to apply the law of a country other than a Member State and would thereby deprive a consumer of protection under the Council Directive.

8. (1) The Director may apply to the High Court for, and may, at the discretion of the Court, be granted, an order prohibiting the use or, as may be appropriate, the continued use of any term in contracts concluded by sellers or suppliers adjudged by the Court to be an unfair term.

(2) The Director shall cause to be published notice of intention to apply to the High Court for an order under paragraph (1) of this Regulation in *Iris Oifigiúil* and at least two national newspapers and in such further or other manner as the Court may direct.

(3) Every person claiming to have an interest in any such application shall be entitled to appear before and be heard by the Court on the hearing of he application.

(4) On any such application it shall not be necessary for the Director or any such person to prove–

    (*a*) actual loss or damage, or

    (*b*) recklessness or negligence on the part of the seller or supplier.

(5) In the exercise of its jurisdiction under paragraph (1) of this Regulation the Court shall take account of all the interests involved and in particular the public interest.

(6) Paragraph (1) of this Regulation is without prejudice to the right of a consumer to rely on the provisions of these Regulations in any case before a court of competent jurisdiction.

9. In determining whether or not the terms of a contract are unfair account shall be taken of all its features and in particular of any information it contains concerning the matters set out in the Annex to the Council Directive and in Schedule 3 to these Regulations.

10. (1) The Minister or the Director may appoint in writing any person being a whole-time officer of the Minister to be an authorised officer for the purposes of these Regulations.

(2) The Minister or the Director may appoint in writing any person to be an authorised officer for a fixed period for the purposes of all or any of the provisions of these Regulations.

(3) Every authorised officer shall be furnished with a warrant of appointment as an

authorised officer stating that the officer is acting under these Regulations and, when exercising any power conferred by paragraph (4) of this Regulation, if requested to do so, produce the said warrant.

(4) An authorised officer may, for the purpose of obtaining information which may enable the Director to discharge functions under these Regulations, on production of the warrant of appointment, if so required-

 (*a*) at all reasonable times enter premises at which any business or any activity in connection with a business is carried on and inspect the premises and any goods on the premises and, on paying or making tender of payment therefor, take any of the goods,

 (*b*) require any person who carries on such business or activity and any person employed in connection therewith to produce to the authorised officer any books, documents or records relating to such business or activity which are in that person's power or control and to give the officer information in regard to any entries in any books, documents and records,

 (*c*) inspect and take copies from such books, documents and records.

 (*d*) require any such person to give to the authorised officer any information the officer may require in regard to the persons carrying on such business or activity (including, in particular, in the case of an unincorporated body of persons, information in regard to the membership thereof and of its committee of management or other controlling authority) or employed in connection therewith,

 (*e*) require any such person to give to the officer any other information which the officer may reasonably require in regard to such business or activity.

(5) A person who obstructs or impedes an authorised officer in the exercise of a power under this Regulation, or does not comply with a requirement under this Regulation shall be guilty of an offence.

(6) A person guilty of an offence under this Regulation shall be liable on summary conviction to a fine not exceeding £1,500.

(7) An offence under this Regulation may be prosecuted by the Director.

SCHEDULE 1

Contracts and Particular Terms Excluded from the Scope of these Regulations

The provisions of these Regulations do not apply to-

 (*a*) any contracts of employment;

 (*b*) any contract relating to succession rights;

 (*c*) any contract relating to rights under family law;

 (*d*) any contract relating to the incorporation and organisation of companies or partnerships;

 (*e*) any terms which reflect-

  (i) mandatory, statutory or regulatory provisions of Ireland, or

  (ii) the provisions or principles of international conventions to which the Member States or the Community are party.

SCHEDULE 2

Guidelines for Application of the Test of Good Faith

In making an assessment of good faith, particular regard shall be had to

— the strength of the bargaining positions of the parties,

— whether the consumer had an inducement to agree to the term,

— whether the goods or services were sold or supplied to the special order of the consumer, and

— the extent to which the seller or supplier has dealt fairly and equitably with the consumer whose legitimate interests he has to take into account.

SCHEDULE 3

Unfair Terms in Consumer Contracts

1. Terms which have the object or effect of:
    (a) excluding or limiting the legal liability of a seller or supplier in the event of the death of a consumer or personal injury to the latter resulting from an act or omission of that seller or supplier;
    (b) inappropriately excluding or limiting the legal rights of the consumer vis-à-vis the seller or supplier or another party in the event of total or partial non-performance or inadequate performance by the seller or supplier of any of the contractual obligations, including the option of offsetting a debt owed to the seller or supplier against any claim which the consumer may have against him;
    (c) making an agreement binding on the consumer whereas provision of services by the seller or supplier is subject to a condition whose realization depends on his own will alone;
    (d) permitting the seller or supplier to retain sums paid by the consumer where the latter decides not to conclude or perform the contract, without providing for the consumer to receive compensation of an equivalent amount from the seller or supplier where the latter is the party cancelling the contract;
    (e) requiring any consumer who fails to fulfil his obligation to pay a disproportionately high sum in compensation;
    (f) authorizing the seller or supplier to dissolve the contract on a discretionary basis where the same facility is not granted to the consumer, or permitting the seller or supplier to retain the sums paid for services not yet supplied by him where it is the seller or supplier himself who dissolves the contract;
    (g) enabling the seller or supplier to terminate a contract of indeterminate duration without reasonable notice except where there are serious grounds for doing so;
    (h) automatically extending a contract of fixed duration where the consumer does not indicate otherwise, when the deadline fixed for the consumer to express this desire not to extend the contract is unreasonably early;
    (i) irrevocably binding the consumer to terms with which he had no real opportunity of becoming acquainted before the conclusion of the contract;
    (j) enabling the seller or supplier to alter the terms of the contract unilaterally without a valid reason which is specified in the contract;

(*k*) enabling the seller or supplier to alter unilaterally without a valid reason any characteristics of the product or service to be provided;

(*l*) providing for the price of goods to be determined at the time of delivery or allowing a seller of goods or supplier of services to increase their price without in both cases giving the consumer the corresponding right to cancel the contract if the final price is too high in relation to the price agreed when the contract was concluded;

(*m*) giving the seller or supplier the right to determine whether the goods or services supplied are in conformity with the contract, or giving him the exclusive right to interpret any term of the contract;

(*n*) limiting the seller's or supplier's obligation to respect commitments undertaken by his agents or making his commitments subject to compliance with a particular formality;

(*o*) obliging the consumer to fulfil all his obligations where the seller or supplier does not perform his;

(*p*) giving the seller or supplier the possibility of transferring his rights and obligations under the contract, where this may serve to reduce the guarantees for the consumer, without the latter's agreement;

(*q*) excluding or hindering the consumer's right to take legal action or exercise any other legal remedy, particularly by requiring the consumer to take disputes exclusively to arbitration not covered by legal provisions, unduly restricting the evidence available to him or imposing on him a burden of proof which, according to the applicable law, should lie with another party to the contract.

2. Scope of subparagraphs (*g*), (*j*) and (*l*)

(*a*) Subparagraph (*g*) is without hindrance to terms by which a supplier of financial services reserves the right to terminate unilaterally a contract of indeterminate duration without notice where there is a valid reason, provided that the supplier is required to inform the other contracting party or parties thereof immediately.

(*b*) Subparagraph (*j*) is without hindrance to terms under which a supplier of financial services reserves the right to alter the rate of interest payable by the consumer or due to the latter, or the amount of other charges for financial services without notice where there is a valid reason, provided that the supplier is required to inform the other contracting party or parties thereof at the earliest opportunity and that the latter are free to dissolve the contract immediately.

Subparagraph (*j*) is also without hindrance to terms under which a seller or supplier reserves the right to alter unilaterally the conditions of a contract of indeterminate duration, provided that he is required to inform the consumer with reasonable notice and that the consumer is free to dissolve the contract.

(*c*) Subparagraphs (*g*), (*j*) and (*l*) do not apply to;

— transactions in transferable securities, financial instruments and other products or services where the price is linked to fluctuations in a stock exchange quotation or index or a financial market rate that the seller or supplier does not control;

— contracts for the purchase or sate of foreign currency, traveller's cheques or international money orders denominated in foreign currency;

(*d*) Subparagraph (*l*) is without hindrance to price-indexation clauses, where lawful, provided that the method by which prices vary is explicitly described.

GIVEN under my Official Seal, this lst day of February, 1995
RICHARD BRUTON, Minister for Enterprise and Employment.

EXPLANATORY NOTE

(This note is not part of the Instrument and does not purport to be a legal interpretation.)

These Regulations have been made to give effect to Council Directive No. 93/13/EEC on unfair terms in consumer contracts.

Notice of the making of this Statutory Instrument was published in "Iris Oifigiúil" of 7th February, 1995.

Index